DISCARD

CONTEMPORARY POLITICAL THEORY

THE EDITORS

Anthony de Crespigny is Associate Professor of Political Science and Chairman of the Political Science Department of Case Western Reserve University. He received his B.A. from the University of Oxford, his M.A. from the University of St. Andrews, and his Ph.D. from the University of London. A frequent contributor of articles and reviews to scholarly journals, Professor de Crespigny has also taught at the University of Witwatersrand, the University of Natal, and Monash University of Australia.

Alan Wertheimer is Assistant Professor of Political Science at the University of Vermont. He received his A.B. from New York University and his Ph.D. from Case Western Reserve University.

CONTEMPORARY

POLITICAL THEORY

Edited by

Anthony de Crespigny

Alan Wertheimer

Atherton Press · *New York 1970*

Contemporary Political Theory
Edited by Anthony de Crespigny and Alan Wertheimer

Copyright © 1970 by Atherton Press, Inc.

Address all inquiries to:
Atherton Press, Inc.
70 Fifth Avenue
New York 10011

Library of Congress Catalog Card Number 72–80907

FIRST EDITION

Manufactured in the United States of America

Designed by Andrea Clark

Contents

The Contributors

STUART M. BROWN
> *College of Arts and Sciences, Dean*
> *Cornell University*

C. W. CASSINELLI
> *Department of Political Science*
> *University of Washington*

JOHN CHARVET
> *Department of Political Science*
> *The London School of Economics*

ANTHONY DE CRESPIGNY
> *Department of Political Science*
> *Case Western Reserve University*

GERALD C. MaCCALLUM, JR.
> *Department of Philosophy*
> *The University of Wisconsin*

MARGARET MACDONALD
> *late of University of London*

P. H. PARTRIDGE
> *Department of Philosophy*
> *Australian National University*

R. S. PETERS
> *Institute of Education*
> *University of London*

D. D. RAPHAEL
> *Department of Politics and Sociology*
> *The University of Glasgow*

JOHN RAWLS
> *Department of Philosophy*
> *Harvard University*

JOHN H. SCHAAR
> *Department of Political Science*
> *University of California, Berkeley*

K. J. SCOTT
late of Victoria University College, Wellington

MICHAEL WALZER
Department of Government
Harvard University

RICHARD A. WASSERSTROM
School of Law and Department of Philosophy
University of California, Los Angeles

CONTEMPORARY POLITICAL THEORY

Introduction

WHETHER he has lived among philosophers or political scientists, the position of the political theorist has in recent decades been a difficult one. On the one hand, he has had to face the criticisms of those who claim that the proper object of philosophy is clarification, and in particular that it is not the job of the philosopher to prescribe or recommend. On the other hand, his subject has been criticized by those whose conception of the social sciences as value-free leads them to argue that political scientists should confine themselves to the study and explanation of facts.

In this general introduction we want to consider briefly some of the more important criticisms of political philosophy and to say something about the nature and possibilities of the subject. It is tempting to ignore such criticisms and simply write positively about the value of political philosophy. Unfortunately, these criticisms are still influential and must, for this reason, be examined. But although it is necessary to defend political philosophy, it should not be thought that we feel at all defensive about it. On the contrary, it is our belief that this subject has seldom been more important and more relevant than it is at the present time.

The great political philosophers of the past were engaged in a number of different kinds of activity. They investigated or speculated about matters of fact and framed generalizations about social and political phenomena. They also sought to clarify and sometimes to criticize the words and phrases commonly used in political discussion. Furthermore, they expressed views about the ends that governments should pursue and how governments should be organized to secure those ends. These views were usually connected with philosophical or psychological theories.

Critics of the main works of traditional political philosophy have observed, among other things, (1) that they contain a host of statements about matters of fact that can be shown to be false or inadequate or wholly speculative, (2) that their authors frequently commit the fallacy of deriving prescriptive conclusions from factual premises, (3) that these works reflect a false conception of the philosopher's task, (4) that they have impeded the progress of political science,

1

(5) that they abound in vague statements and ask improper questions, (6) that they are largely irrelevant since they were written long ago and in circumstances very different from our own, and (7) that the prescriptive theories advanced in them are the determined product of objective historical factors.

Let us look at these criticisms. It is undeniable that the empirical inquiries of the traditional political philosophers tend to be unimpressive when judged in the light of contemporary knowledge and by contemporary standards of scientific investigation. Their writings are full of speculative assertions about matters of fact—assertions about human nature, about how men would behave in hypothetical circumstances, about the origins of private property and the state, about the connection between the extension of liberty and the promotion of other goods, and so on. Of particular importance in the construction of their prescriptive theories were their conceptions of human nature, for their doctrines about how society should be constituted and how men should live were developed in intimate connection with their beliefs about human wants, needs, and purposes. As different desires and needs were distinguished as essential, different forms of society were prescribed.

It has been objected that this form of argument is of doubtful validity, since it has become increasingly difficult in the last hundred years to believe that there is such a thing as human nature, fixed, finished, and ascertainable.

Can the ground-plan of men's nature ever be known, and therefore the fitting forms of its expression prescribed? Suppose that one has been gradually convinced that there is no universally valid statement to be made about human nature, except the negative statement that it is essentially unfinished, uncertain, left open for indefinite development in many diverging directions; that the range of human needs, and their order of priority, cannot be anticipated and circumscribed, except in physical and biological terms; that we can never know in advance what men's minds and temperaments may become as a result of their continuing experiments on themselves; and that the only limit to experiment is set by the unanticipated desires and needs which appear in particular men at some particular time. Then no deduction of the proper order of society is possible: political philosophy...must begin again from new premisses.[1]

This is a large question which cannot be discussed adequately here. Nevertheless, there do appear to be certain basic needs and wants, other than bodily ones, which all or most men share. Such human needs and wants, together with other contingent facts about human nature and the world in which men live, provide a basis for understanding the point of having certain rules and institutions and for making recommendations about human relationships and forms of social organization. Thus H. L. A. Hart bases what he calls the "minimum content of natural law" on five truisms (not necessary truths) about human beings and their natural environment: human vulnerability, approximate equality, limited altruism, limited resources, and limited understanding and will. Assuming that in general men desire to live, Hart shows that there is a rational connection between these truisms and the content of certain moral and legal rules.[2] This approach is very illuminating, and could presumably be taken much further, though at a cost of mounting risk as increasingly questionable desires or needs are assumed.

The prescriptive theories of traditional political philosophers are often said to involve a logical fallacy because political recommendations are derived from premises which consist solely of necessary propositions, or propositions of fact. If, for instance, they are derived from psychological principles or from metaphysical doctrines, they involve an illicit transition from "is" to "ought." But it may be countered that there is nothing necessarily illicit about inferring prescriptive conclusions from psychological premises. This procedure would be logically fallacious only if the prescriptions were moral prescriptions in the strict sense of the term. Morality, however, has no monopoly over the word "ought." Moreover, metaphysical doctrines may have a logical relevance for political doctrines even though the latter cannot be deduced from the former.

In his excellent book on Hobbes, J. W. N. Watkins points out that although, in his interpretation, Hobbes derived his political prescriptions from psychological premises, he did not commit a logical fallacy because his prescriptions are not *moral* prescriptions—they are, in Kant's sense, hypothetical imperatives enjoining actions as practically necessary means to the end of self-preservation. Watkins writes: "A theory which claims to describe the chief end which men do in fact pursue need not confine itself thereafter to describing their more or less inefficient pursuit of it: it may go on to prescribe the best way to attain that end."[3] And the same author has argued convincingly elsewhere that while political recommendations cannot be derived from factual metaphysical premises alone, "a political doctrine may stand in a peculiarly dependent relation to a metaphysical doctrine, so that the latter may be said to 'endorse' or 'sanction' the former."[4] One of Watkins' examples is the relation between Plato's theory of the just state and his theory of ideas.

It has been argued that much of what political philosophers have done in the past is not really philosophy at all, for the business of philosophy is clarification or analysis. According to this conception, philosophy is what is called a second-order activity, which is an impressive way of saying that it is concerned only with how we talk about the world. It is not the job of the philosopher to describe or explain the world, nor is it his job to prescribe or recommend. His task is to clarify or analyze the concepts, arguments, assumptions, and methods of the substantive, first-order disciplines. Moreover, his task is often conceived as that of showing that many of the traditional problems of philosophy are spurious, that they arise from a failure to understand the logic of our language. Thus it has been claimed that the central question of traditional political philosophy—why ought a subject to obey his ruler?— is an improper one. But we shall come to this later.

It may, of course, be accepted that it is not the job of the political philosopher as such to engage in empirical inquiry. He has done this in the past, and in the process has exposed himself to a good deal of contemporary ridicule, but this was largely because the social sciences had not yet developed. It may also be agreed that clarification is a very important part of his work. (That this is our view will be evident from the character of this collection of essays.) But we differ from those who claim that clarification is the sole purpose of political philosophy. Its object is also to help us decide what ends political activity should pursue and how it should go about pursuing them. We must stress that this does not mean that those employed by universities to teach political philosophy should regard it as a necessary part of their function to introduce captive audiences to their own political convictions. It is merely to say that the systematic evaluation of political ends is an essential part of political philosophy.

We have not so far considered why it is not regarded as the business of philosophy to prescribe or recommend. The doctrine of "neutrality" may be a derivative of the view that all genuine, true-or-false statements must be either empirical or analytic. Value judgments, we are told, fall into neither of these categories since they do not inform us about the world nor are they true by virtue of logic and the meanings of their terms. Therefore, they are literally meaningless. Their function, it is often said, is to express emotions or to direct the behavior of others. They are unarguable, arbitrary, and impervious to criticism.

The doctrine that all genuine statements must be analytic or empirical has been intensively criticized. While this is not the place to enter into the complexities of the dispute, we shall risk another reference to Hart. "It is a truth," he observes, "of some importance that for the adequate description not only of law but of many other social institutions, a place must be reserved, besides definitions and ordinary statements of fact, for a third category of statements: those the truth of which is contingent on human beings and the world they live in retaining the salient

characteristics which they have" (our italics).[5] While these characteristics persist, there are certain rules of conduct which must be embodied
in any social organization which is to be viable.

But in criticizing the view that it is not the business of philosophy
to make recommendations, it is not sufficient to attack the thesis that
all value judgments are meaningless, for many philosophers who hold
a "clarificatory" conception of their subject would not wish to maintain
this thesis. A more important argument for neutrality appears to be
that it is impossible by purely *philosophical* reasoning to establish or
demolish an evaluative position. If such a position is supported by
reasons, it may be possible to show by clarification alone that these
reasons do not in any way entail that position. And this may well have
the effect of inducing its proponent to abandon it. But he would not
be *logically* committed to doing this since one can hold true convictions
for bad reasons.[6]

It may be agreed that one cannot justify a value position by philosophical means alone. But the conclusion to be drawn is not that philosophy
should avoid evaluation; it is rather that those who engage in it will
need to be more than philosophers if their work is to be of any great
interest. In particular, they will have to possess some considerable
acquaintance with the relevant findings of psychology and the social
sciences. While purely deductive argument may be pertinent to the
defense of a value position, it is more likely to need to be defended by
reference to empirical evidence. This brings us back to the hoary
fact-value problem which was touched on earlier. The philosophical
belief in the complete logical gulf between descriptive statements and
statements of value has contributed to the doctrine of neutrality in
both philosophy and political science. This belief, however, need not
be accepted. We may quite properly support a value position by relating
it in an intelligible way to human needs, wants, and purposes. Indeed,
there can be no other way of justifying values since they have no
independent existence of their own.

Political philosophers have been accused not only of doing what it
is not their business as philosophers to do but also of impeding the
development of political science. They have allowed their values to
influence their factual findings; they have failed to distinguish between
explanation and advocacy; they have defined terms in ways that suit
the requirements of their prescriptive theories; and so on. In short, their
writings have stood in the way of a dispassionate study of the facts.
Since the task of political science is to get at and account for the facts,
it is neutral and should be wholly divorced from political philosophy
conceived as reasoned argument about the purposes of government.

It is agreed, of course, that the findings of political science may be very important in helping us promote the values we wish to promote. It is claimed, however, that these findings cannot help us to decide what those values should be.

It may be true that prescriptive political philosophy has at times hindered the progress of political science. Nevertheless, it is a misconception of the relation between empirical findings in politics and normative positions to suppose that the two can be completely separated. It has been pointed out by David Easton and others that a value-free political science is an impossibility, since values inevitably influence the work of political scientists however strenuously they strive for objectivity. They influence such things as their selection of problems for empirical investigation, their choice of frameworks of explanations, the vocabulary they use, and the way in which they perceive social reality. The terms in which they see the social world will reflect their interests and past experience. There is no neutral, objective way of seeing it. (This does not mean, of course, that political scientists should not do their utmost to avoid bias.)

Values affect the findings of political science. The converse is also true. It has been convincingly argued by Charles Taylor that the theoretical findings of political science give support to or undermine particular sets of values and, therefore, that there is "a convergence between science and normative theory in the field of politics."[7] Among the examples which he cites are the incompatibility between Aristotle's insight in political science and the prescriptive theory of Plato's *Republic*, and the way in which S. M. Lipset's value position in *Political Man* flows out of his analysis of the fundamental role of class in politics. Taylor explicitly attacks the view that questions of value are independent of questions of fact, arguing instead that "a given framework of explanation in political science tends to support an associated value position, secretes its own norms for the assessment of polities and policies."[8] The upshot of his argument is that insofar as political science cannot do without an explanatory framework, it cannot stop producing normative theory.

A common objection to the main works of traditional political philosophy is that their authors make vague assertions and address themselves to the solution of spurious problems. Typical examples of the former defect are statements like "The purpose of the State is to promote fulfillment of personality," "Human beings ought to be bound only by laws of their own making," and "We should always treat men as ends in themselves and never merely as means." It is argued that such statements are so vague that no specific conclusions can be inferred from them, or that almost anything can. Without precise criteria, how are we to know whether a state is promoting "fulfillment of personality"? What *is* this desirable condition? And how can practical conclusions be derived from the precept that we should always treat human beings as ends?

The second line of criticism is more radical since it seeks to demonstrate the spuriousness of what are taken to be the central questions of classical political philosophy. These are said to include: "What is the purpose of the state?" "Why ought a subject to obey his ruler?" "What is the proper relation between the state and the individual?" "Where ought we to draw the line between the claims of liberty and equality?" "Is liberty a good thing?" "What is the true nature of justice?" It is objected that such questions are too general to be answerable or else betray a mistaken essentialism. Instead of concerning themselves with specific and sensible questions like "Why should I support *this* government?" political theorists have asked senseless general questions like "Why should I support *any* government?" They have also supposed that words have essential meanings, so that it makes sense to ask such questions as "What *is* liberty?" or "What is the true nature of the state?" Such questions, however, are senseless because there are no essential meanings to be discovered. Words simply have uses.

It must be conceded that the old political theorists were often vague and that they raised many spurious problems. By failing to understand the workings of language they were misled into raising problems which are in principle insoluble. And analytical philosophers perform a salutary service when they expose the linguistic misconceptions from which such problems arose. It is equally clear, however, that the old theorists were not as vague as their more extreme critics claim and that they did tackle genuine and important problems. To support this statement sufficiently here is impossible, but we shall comment on two of the above examples. It is surely the case that Kant's principle that we should always treat human beings as ends *is* of some practical use. It would surely rule out the institution of slavery as well as much of the legislation which has been enacted in South Africa over the past twenty years. And it is surely not generally the case that political theorists have sought to justify obedience to *any* government. Hobbes and Locke did not advocate obedience to *any* government, but respectively to governments which do not menace our lives and those which protect our natural rights. Contract theories can never assign unlimited authority to the state. If the ultimate purpose of the contract is not fulfilled, political obligation may always lapse.

It is often argued that, insofar as their purpose was to justify or condemn, the principal works of traditional political philosophy are no longer relevant. Although Rousseau regarded the *Contrat social* as "un livre pour tous les temps," the traditional political theorists, it is said, were mainly concerned with the practical politics of their day. Consequently, their writings are now of only antiquarian interest as stale polemics from a no longer relevant context. The issues which inspired the old prescriptive theories are dead. Moreover, these critics may add, there is little interest nowadays in prescriptive discussion of any kind. In America and Britain as well as in other liberal-democratic societies there now prevails a general consensus which includes not only institutions and procedures but also broad objectives of policy. Ideological politics have in these societies been largely replaced by the politics of bargaining and adjustment. Hence it is a matter of small surprise that in the Anglo-Saxon democracies the prescriptive discussion of general political issues evokes slight enthusiasm.

If it were true that the major political theorists of the past were primarily concerned with the politics of their day, their writings would indeed hold little interest for us. But though they usually wished to influence political affairs, these theorists were not primarily publicists. Their theories are best understood as philosophies of man, as theories about what men are and how they are situated in the world. They are of perennial interest because they deal with intellectual problems which preserve a marked degree of continuity and similarity from age to age and from culture to culture, though this fact is often concealed by changes in the language used to express them. They are the product of historical conditions, but they are also of more universal application. They are of enduring relevance because while man and his condition in the world change, they also remain the same.

It is plainly absurd to argue that in America today an ideological consensus has left no opening for prescriptive political theory. There are profound conflicts and frustrations in our society, and serious disagreements about the ultimate objectives of public policy. Events in recent years have raised a number of important theoretical issues such as the problem of political obligation in a constitutional democracy, the justification of civil violence, and the value and proper limits of participation. But even if, *per impossible,* our society were pervaded by a universal harmony, there would still be a need for prescriptive theory. There would still be a need for people to examine critically the received standards of value in actual political use. Inadequate scales of value are not rendered less inadequate by being generalized.

It remains to take a brief look at one further criticism of traditional political theory. It has been argued by the "sociologists of knowledge" that all human thinking, political thinking included, can be shown to be socially determined. What is believed to be true in a particular society at a given time can be shown to be the determined product of objective historical factors at work in that society. Marx, for example, treated prescriptive political theories as reflections of prevailing socioeconomic conditions and of the positions of their authors under these conditions. While political theorists might speak in universal terms, their doctrines were merely rationalizations of the interests of some class or group. They were a form of "ideology" or "false consciousness." Marx conceded that these doctrines were important because they were influential, but insisted that they were nevertheless the determined product of particular economic and social conditions, that they did not provide real knowledge.

This line of argument has been attacked in various ways. It has been pointed out that if all knowledge is relative to its historical context, then so is the knowledge that this statement is itself true. It has also been remarked that the causal roots of our beliefs are logically irrelevant to their validity, whatever criteria of value and truth are selected. And aside from these standard logical points, there is the fact that the political beliefs of persons who are similarly situated, in terms of their social or economic or cultural milieu, are often radically opposed. While it would be foolish to underestimate the "ideological" component in political theories, it would be equally foolish to exaggerate it. It is of course true that even by their greatest exertions men can achieve only a limited degree of detachment from the linguistic conventions and social institutions of their own societies. For this reason, theories about man and his situation, and the prescriptive theories developed in connection with them, can never be final.

So much for what appear to be the principal criticisms of traditional political philosophy. We have considered them at some length in order to introduce students to the controversy over the nature and possibilities of political philosophy which has been carried on largely in academic journals, particularly since 1953. The year 1953 is mentioned because it saw the publication of the late T. D. Weldon's *The Vocabulary of Politics*[9] and of Alfred Cobban's article "The Decline of Political Theory."[10] Much of the subsequent writing has been done under the impact of Weldon's radical critique of the conventional content of political philosophy.

Something more should perhaps be said about the value of political philosophy and about the sorts of problems which require philosophical attention. Mention may be made of John Plamenatz's important argument that in all "sophisticated" societies there is a *need* for a coherent practical philosophy, whether or not it is possible to derive universal principles from beliefs about man or the world or God.[11] Plamenatz argues that while men in primitive societies may be able to get along without a systematic practical philosophy, this is not true of the "sophisticated" man.

> He lives in a changing society, and he is socially mobile in that society. . . . He lives in a society where men strive deliberately to change their institutions. If he is not to feel lost in society, he needs to be able to take his bearings in it, which involves more than understanding what society is like and how it is changing. It also involves having a coherent set of values and knowing how to use them to estimate what is happening; it involves having a practical philosophy, which cannot, in the modern world, be adequate unless it is also a social and political philosophy.[12]

We must be careful not to misunderstand Plamenatz's argument. He does not argue that all men feel the need for a coherent practical philosophy, or that those who do, feel it equally. What he does say is that men who are self-conscious and critical have a need to "place" themselves in the world, to *make* themselves at home in the world, to come to terms with themselves and their environment. This need is much more urgent today than it used to be because societies change much more rapidly and people are much more socially mobile within them. And this need is satisfied neither by science nor by analytical philosophy. It can be satisfied only by a practical philosophy the purpose of which is to help us decide how we shall live and what we shall be.

We come finally to a point which has been emphasized by David Braybrooke, G. C. Field, and A. D. Lindsay, among others. This is that an important task of the political philosopher is to examine the assumptions, standards, or ideals which are actually operative in political life, whether in justifying or condemning particular policies or systems. What is needed, according to Braybrooke, is an *inventory* of the standards of value which are in actual political use and then a careful explanation of their logical characteristics. Such an inventory, if properly conducted, will reveal that many of our received standards are much less useful than they might be. "A standard that discriminates between the policy alternatives that we are likely to confront is more useful than the same standard, left in a state of such ambiguity that discriminations are impossible, or possible only between alternatives that will not in practice be presented."[13] But Braybrooke warns that the investigation and elucidation of evaluative standards will not yield valuable results unless philosophers pay careful attention to the actual process of political choice. "Standards will determine policies only insofar as they actually function in the system of choice; and they can be, so far as they are effective, only as subtle as the procedures of choice allow."[14]

It is important to stress that a primary task of the political theorist is to consider and understand the "operative ideals" of a society. While they act on such ideals, men in general are only vaguely aware of them, and it is a central function of political theory to make men understand what their purposes actually are and the assumptions on which they actually act. This has been a seriously neglected field of inquiry. Philosophers who turn their attention to problems of politics often appear to assume that a detailed knowledge of the political process is unnecessary. The result is that their writings are apt to be academic in the worst sense.

Notes

1. Stuart Hampshire, *Encounter* (January 1957), p. 35.
2. H. L. A. Hart, *The Concept of Law* (Oxford: Clarendon Press, 1961), pp. 189–195.
3. J. W. N. Watkins, *Hobbes's System of Ideas* (London: Hutchinson University Library, 1965), p. 88.
4. J. W. N. Watkins, "Epistemology and Politics," *Proceedings of the Aristotelian Society*, 58 (1957–1958), 81.
5. Hart, *Concept of Law*, p. 195.
6. See Richard Wollheim, "Philosophie analytique et pensée politique," *Revue française de science politique*, XI (1961).
7. Charles Taylor, "Neutrality in Political Science," in Peter Laslett and W. G. Runciman, eds., *Philosophy, Politics and Society*, Third Series (Oxford: Basil Blackwell, 1967), p. 27.
8. *Ibid*, p. 48.
9. Harmondsworth: Penguin Books, 1953.
10. *Political Science Quarterly*, LXVIII (September 1953).
11. John Plamenatz, "The Use of Political Theory," *Political Studies*, 8 (1960), 27.
12. *Ibid*, p. 25.
13. David Braybrooke, "The Expanding Universe of Political Philosophy," *Review of Metaphysics*, 11 (1957–1958), 654–655.
14. *Ibid.*, p. 656.

POWER

Money has always been a key concept of economics. As a concept (although obviously not only as a concept), money has several advantages. Money is easily defined, has the same meaning in most cultures, is easily quantified, and can be transferred from one field to another. One hundred dollars can be used to purchase either food or clothes. Consequently, economists have been able to use the concept of money in developing sophisticated theories and models. Political scientists have not been so fortunate. It has been said that politics is nothing but the use of power, and many approaches to the study of politics have placed great emphasis on power as a key concept. Unlike money, however, power is not so easily defined, quantified, or transferred.

The difficulty in making power a useful analytic tool has led political scientists to other approaches, such as "systems analysis." Yet power remains an important concept and element of politics. The debate over the proper methods of studying "community power structures" is essentially a debate over the concept of power. One concept of power seems to produce an "elitist" view of the community while a different one leads to a "pluralist" view. Philosophers as well as political scientists, have attempted to come to grips with this elusive concept. Professors P. H. Partridge and Anthony de Crespigny have attempted to use a philosophical analysis to develop an analytically useful concept of power.

Partridge and de Crespigny agree on several major points. First, both suggest that power must be defined in morally neutral terms, stripped of any moral or emotional connotations. Power has long been considered an "evil," but this view must be avoided at all costs if the concept is to be useful. Second, the analyses and distinctions they offer are intended to be useful for certain purposes. Since the empirical problems under investigation may differ from case to case, the scholar may want to employ other distinctions. Neither author contends that his analysis is adequate for all purposes. Third, both articles discuss power at the interpersonal level. The reader will note that most of the examples are drawn from relations between two persons. Nothing in either article prohibits use of the analysis at the group or institutional level, but distinctions that are applicable at one level may not be at another. Fourth, the relation between power and liberty is an important theme in both articles. Partridge says that his analysis was developed with that problem in mind, and de Crespigny makes several suggestions regarding the compatibility of liberty and various forms of power. Fifth, both articles focus on qualitative distinctions between power and

15

related concepts or between various forms of power. Both authors feel that the identification of power is a prerequisite to its measurement and quantification. Sixth, "intention" and "conflict" are important criteria in both articles. While the authors differ in their treatment of these problems, both feel that they are central to an adequate analysis of power.

Partridge suggests that power can best be understood in terms of a continuum between influence and domination. A crucial distinction between the two poles of power is the presence or absence of conflict. When A dominates B, the latter subordinates his wishes to those of A. Their wishes conflict. When A influences B, the latter may not subordinate his wishes to those of A. In fact, one manifestation of A's influence over B is that their wishes coincide. As one moves along the continuum from influence to domination, sanctions (inducements or penalties) are brought into play. Partridge does not sharply distinguish inducements from penalties. Both are found along the same continuum. Domination, unlike influence, requires that A has intentions regarding B's behavior. But a great writer may *influence* other writers without intending to do so. Since influence is a form of power, Partridge is arguing that some uses of power do not require any intention on the part of the power wielder. De Crespigny disagrees. He feels that influence is not necessarily a manifestation of power, in that whereas all uses of power require A's intention, this is not the case with influence. De Crespigny introduces a distinction between "particular intentions" and "general intentions" which allows him to argue that all uses of power require intention, although an exercise of power need not be conscious or deliberate.

While de Crespigny's article contains few major disagreements with Partridge, it goes further in developing distinctions among seven modes of power. Two points should be noted, although de Crespigny does not address himself specifically to them. One, the forms he distinguishes are not comprehensive. He does not argue that these are the only forms that power may take. Second, the use of one form of power does not preclude the simultaneous use of another. The forms are often used in combination, although certain combinations may be logically impossible.

De Crespigny's treatment of "coercive power" is similar to Partridge's treatment of domination. Coercive power results from A's ability to make things unpleasant for B by applying force, sanctions, or threats. De Crespigny argues that an exercise of power presupposes that the subject acts voluntarily, i.e., that his behavior is "subject to choice." Therefore, the physical coercion of B is not an exercise of power over him. If A had B physically removed from a room, he would not be exercising power since B would not be behaving voluntarily. De

Crespigny then distinguishes coercive power from "inducive power," pointing out that while the former involves "negative" sanctions, the latter involves "positive" sanctions or rewards. A may induce B to do X by promising him a gift. Although the distinction between coercion and inducement is first drawn in terms of the type of sanctions, de Crespigny finds other crucial distinctions between them. Unlike coercive power, inducive power implies the absence of social conflict. B is not compelled to subordinate his wishes to those of A, so there is no social conflict. Second, inducive power is typically compatible with B's liberty, since he is not compelled to do anything.

Against his wishes, a worker is asked to work overtime. He feels that if he does not comply, he will be fired. He agrees to do the work. The worker also wishes to take a fifteen-minute coffee break, but fears that his boss will not approve, so he abstains. In both cases, de Crespigny would argue that the boss has exercised "reactional power." This mode of power is particularly difficult to analyze since it depends on the perceptions of the relevant parties. The boss may not have fired the worker if the latter refused to work overtime. The boss may have been perfectly willing to let him take a coffee break. Would we say that the boss exercised power? A leader refrains from endorsing socialized medicine for fear of the electorate's reactions. As observers of politics, how can we ascertain what the leader has refrained from doing? De Crespigny has developed this mode of power at the analytical level, and it is clear that it is a significant form. But the empirical study of reactional power presents difficult, if not insurmountable, problems for the political scientist.

Neither author argues that power should be restored as the central concept of political science, but both feel that the concept, while elusive, is not entirely vague and amorphous. It can be made analytically useful for philosophical and empirical work. Some have suggested that political scientists discard the concept of power from their bag of tools. It seems that this suggestion, if not mistaken, is at least quite premature.

1

Some Notes
on the Concept of Power

P. H. Partridge

POWER is one of the many terms of popular wisdom and discourse that
philosophers, historians, and social theorists have also always found
indispensable. Until very recently, I think, they have habitually let the
word fall in their confident periods without any uncomfortable pricking
of the intellectual conscience. This, of course, is no longer true. Power
is now a subject of specialized study; there are some even who would
make it the "field" of a separate science—I refer especially to those
political scientists who have proposed that their subject should be
defined as the study of "power" or "influence" or "control," a suggestion which, if there is anything at all in the argument I advance in
these "Notes," would certainly present the political scientist with a
job and a half. Power has been subjected to minute and detailed
conceptual analysis as in the work of Lasswell and Kaplan; it has
attracted the attention of the quantifiers; and it is the subject of an
ever-increasing flood of empirical studies of actual power structures.
It is no longer a common coin of the linguistic realm; at least, every
effort is being made to give it the dignity of a scientific concept.

It is permissible to ask: With what success? One might even let fall
the subversive hint that the conclusion most clearly intimated by
much of the recent work is that power is a concept or phenomenon too
amorphous, sprawling, or chameleon-like ever to be amenable to
exact identification, to say nothing of anything that deserves to be
called "measurement." Perhaps the sociologists and political scientists

From *Political Studies*, XI (1963), 107–125.

would do better to search for a set of more manageable concepts to replace it with, or perhaps it is after all indispensable; but, if this is so, we must reconcile ourselves to the thought that where we are concerned with power, we must be satisfied to live with vagueness, indeterminateness, and generality. I do not propose to consider *this* question in these "Notes": it is too hard for me. But we can be sure at least of this, that we have not approached any nearer the point where we can expect either precision or uniformity in the employment of the concept.

Talcott Parsons, in a review article attacking Wright Mills's *The Power Elite,* rejects many of Mills's empirical conclusions about the distribution of power in the U.S.A. He gives as one of his reasons that Mills works with a defective concept of the nature of power. Parsons goes on to remark that "unfortunately the concept of power is not a settled one in the social sciences, either in political science or in sociology,"[1] no one who has read the recent literature of the subject could disagree with him. The same uncertainty attaches to other closely related concepts. Thus, in the *Encyclopedia of the Social Sciences,* Michels defines "authority" as "the capacity, innate or acquired, for exercising ascendency over a group," but Bierstedt,[2] an American sociologist who has written a good deal on these matters, says that this is wrong in every one of its terms: authority is not a capacity, it is not innate, and it is not a matter of exercising ascendency. He argues that what Michels has done is to confuse authority with something quite different, viz. "competence." We need not illustrate further; in the writing about power (as about freedom) there is no end to the disputes about definition and usage. And these are not merely disputes about usage; as I have briefly hinted by referring to the differences between Wright Mills and Parsons, they are sometimes connected with the different conclusions that different writers reach in their studies of the exercise and distribution of power in actual societies.

It is not hard to see why these differences should persist. We have a series of terms which are obviously very closely related, such terms as freedom, power, influence, coercion, constraint, force, compulsion, authority, leadership, prestige, and so on. In ordinary language, each of these words has an indeterminate use: they are pretty loosely used to stand now for one relationship, now for another. Most of them are open-ended terms: as regards each one of them we know that at a certain point we would at last draw the line and refuse to employ it, but usually we are not able to say at all exactly where we would draw the line. In other words, in almost every case, the situations to which we apply the terms form a continuum (as we shall see in more detail later on in the case of "power") and we do not precisely know at what point on the continuum our use of the term would stop. Thus, there are many situations to which we would not hesitate to apply the description "coercion," but suppose that one man controls the actions of another by offering him bribes which his psychological constitution makes it virtually impossible for him to resist (for instance, plying him with alcohol): is this a denial or impairment of the latter's freedom? (Political moralists have often written as if "bribing the electorate" were an illegitimate way of exercising power.) Again, since we are referring to situations which form a continuum, pairs or groups of the terms with which we are concerned overlap at the edges. Yet again, though we are dealing here with series of different situations or relationships between persons which shade into one another, for the purposes of ordinary life we are not concerned to identify and distinguish the quite different sorts of interpersonal relationships to all of which we may apply such words as "freedom," "power," "influence," or "constraint." One of the purposes of this paper is to point to a few of the different interpersonal relations all of which are frequently described as being examples of the exercise of "power."

These, then, are some of the reasons why it is not surprising that there should be no agreement about usage, or even a very high degree of consistency in the writing of a single writer. And, of course, it goes without saying that there is no set of definitions or usages which should prevail over all others for all purposes. In these "Notes" I am proposing certain ways of viewing the concept of power, but I do not recommend my usages (and my ways of distinguishing "power" from other very closely connected concepts) as being equally valid for all theoretical purposes. As a matter of fact, I have come at the subject of power in this way mainly because it has seemed to me to be useful in illuminating certain questions about freedom. Other writers, with different theoretical purposes in mind, will no doubt continue to propose other usages and other classifications. Thus, as will become apparent later, the classifications and discriminations I point to do not at all coincide with Weber's famous distinction between forms of authority, viz. charismatic, traditional, and bureaucratic authority: the distinctions I am especially concerned to illustrate and to insist upon can be found within each of Weber's three types of authority. It is not that I am offering an alternative analysis: the distinctions he is pointing to may quite well be real and extremely important, but he is concerned with different problems.

But there is one point on which it is important to be clear. However we may decide to employ the terms that are available from ordinary language, we must deal faithfully with the facts. In speaking of power, freedom, coercion, and the like, we are concerned with relations between persons and groups of persons, and different types of relations differ subtly from one another, although, as I have mentioned, some shade into others. Whatever system of nomenclature we may find it convenient to adopt, we must ensure that we do not do violence to the qualitative differences between the different sorts of relationships we are really referring to, and especially that we do not treat as being identical relationships which differ from each other in subtle but important ways.

Before I come to my subject there is one more explanation I must make. Political scientists and sociologists are primarily concerned, of course, not with individuals nor with simple groups of two or three persons but with highly organized communities; they are mainly concerned, therefore, with power in its most highly organized and institutionalized forms. In these "Notes" I shall refer only incidentally to the organized and institutionalized manifestations of power; my examples will be almost always of relations between two persons. I have two reasons for concentrating attention on these extremely simple or "primitive" forms of interpersonal relationships: first, it is easier with these simple relationships to bring out the *qualitative* differences I want to emphasize; second, I would argue that these relationships are in a sense fundamental (that is, they are the very relations which we find, most bewilderingly and intricately intertwined, within the complex institutionalized relationships of great groups and highly organized communities). I do not want to deny that institutionalization brings with it additional important elements and complexities, but I would want to maintain that the "primitive" relationships are also present, and further, and most important, that we cannot understand or judge the more complex structures unless we can identify the simpler forms of relations that are involved therein and determine some of their relevant qualitative features.

I

I shall begin with a proposal and work from it. I propose to take "power" as being the most inclusive term, and, within this wider concept, I shall distinguish two poles, the pole of "influence" and the pole of "domination." These will mark the ends of the scale. I shall suggest how we might arrange a number of situations all involving the exercise of power in order along the scale, and I shall also want to mark somewhere on the scale a point that I take to be of especial importance—the point at which a *conflict situation* between the person exercising power and the person over whom it is exercised begins to manifest itself.

First, as regards "power." Russell says that "power is the production of intended effects."[3] According to this definition, A has power over B when A can produce certain effects that he intends to produce in B's behavior. It will be convenient to accept this formulation to begin with; however, later on I shall point out that it brushes aside certain complications that it is very necessary to take into account. The complications mainly concern the notion of power as the *production* of effects and the requirement that the effects are *intended* effects. However, postponing those matters for the time being, it will be noted that Russell's definition of power is in some respects a very wide one: we could be said to have power over inanimate material like wood or iron because we have the power to produce certain intended effects on those materials. When we use the word in reference to the relations between human beings, we certainly give it a rather narrower reference: thus, the surgeon has power over my body in that he can produce intended effects upon it, but we should not say that this is an example of his power over *me*. As a concept employed in the discussion of interpersonal relations and social affairs, we give "power" a more restricted range. I shall not try to state exactly what the restriction is: it is sufficient for my purposes to say that A has power over B when A can affect B's acts or behavior in ways intended by A.

At one end of the continuum of relationships involving the exercise of power we may place "influence." A teacher may have influence over a pupil or a parent over a child; a painter like Cézanne may influence a generation of painters; or a great thinker everyone who subsequently writes about a subject. It will already be apparent that some of these examples raise questions about intended and unintended effects, but we may postpone these: let us assume that the effects are intended effects. At the extreme end of the scale I wish to place the type of situation in which it can be said that A affects the behavior of B in intended ways, *without its being true that B is required to subordinate his own wishes, inclinations, beliefs, interests, etc., to those of A.* These will be cases in which a conflict situation does not appear at all. Now, it may well be that this is an "ideal" case, never in fact realized, because it may be argued that, wherever influence exists, there is some element of conflict present, some degree of subordination of one man's desires or interests to those of another. This, also, is a matter that will have to be considered more fully later. Nevertheless, it is sufficiently obvious that we can readily distinguish situations which approximate to that which I have defined from those at the other end of the scale which I have arbitrarily called "domination." This, of course, is the type of situation in which A directs or controls the behavior of B and where A's wishes prevail over those of B: B acts as he does only because he is compelled so to act by A, and would not do so but for A's ability to make him act in ways that he does not want to act. There is manifestly a conflict situation. As an example of the pole of "influence," we may take the example of a scientist who takes a young man into his laboratory, communicates to him his own passion for scientific research, some of his own qualities of mind and character, passes on his own skills, and, perhaps by the exercise of the influence that he has, enables the student to become the independent scientist that he wanted to become. Or perhaps it is only gradually that the pupil comes to feel the spell of the master: what initially had elements of conflict or resistance in it may be changed as the situation develops. At the other end of the scale, the gunman's intimidation of his victim manifestly involves a conflict situation.

Now, it is equally obvious that if we begin with the Rutherford-pupil type of relationship, we can slightly vary the conditions and produce a series of relationships which lie along a continuum, getting nearer and nearer to the pole of "domination" or pure coercion. In the Rutherford-pupil relation we can introduce a slight element of domination: teachers are not unknown who, in order to bind disciples to themselves, use certain advantages they enjoy in order to restrain the natural inclinations or bent of their pupils; again (and we must not forget that power is generated by the beliefs, feelings, and attitudes of *both* parties to the relationship), pupils are not unknown who yield to the supposed wishes of teachers because of sanctions that they suppose teachers to possess—for instance, the disposal of good jobs. It is unnecessary to multiply examples: it will be evident that, as one goes down the scale, different types of relationships involving the presence of power shade into one another. Of course, this geometrical mode of representation is a very crude expository device; as a matter of fact, as we look more closely at a number of these very complex situations, it is perhaps not so much a matter of one sort of situation being followed by, and shading into, another, but rather of the presence in varying degrees of many different psychological and other components. For this reason, the notion of a continuum may after all be rather misleading, but I can think of no simpler method of exposition.

As you move down the scale, sanctions (inducements and penalties to induce compliance with the wishes of one party) begin to appear, but at first in such subtle ways that it is very difficult to determine whether sanctions are operating at all. The difficulty is not only that of the observer; it is often impossible for the actor or patient to know whether his action is affected by consideration of real or possible sanctions, or whether, in conforming to the wishes of another, he is acting "on his own initiative." Later, of course, sanctions become more obvious and assume increasing severity. Again as we examine types of situations arranged along the scale in relation to the absence and presence of a conflict situation, we observe differences concerning the "bases" or "sources" of the influence or domination that A enjoys over B, and also as regards the "mechanisms" by means of which power is exercised. It is not always easy to distinguish "bases" and "mechanisms." Thus, the influence of a Rutherford over his pupil may flow in part from his known standing in his science and the authority he enjoys by virtue of his achievement (and these, I suppose, would be examples of what many writers now call "bases" of power); but also in part from felt superior qualities of mind or imagination, and these may perhaps be regarded as mechanisms by means of which influence is exerted. Moving further down the scale, we know that many rulers have managed to dominate subjects not by employing manifest sanctions (either penalties or inducements) but by subtle and hidden means of manipulation — causing the subjects to want what the ruler wants them to want and think what he wants them to think. This is an example of the "shading into" of which I have spoken and of the extraordinary difficulty often in recognizing the kind of power situations we are dealing with: it is often impossible to say with any confidence whether we are observing a situation in which B "freely" subordinates himself to an imposed discipline or accepts the authority of a leader or whether his compliance has been secured by means of manipulation by A. Yet, tricky, subtle, and arguable as such distinctions often are, they are the distinctions we are compelled to try to make if we want to describe the structure of power within a social group, the qualitative features of the power relationships that are present, and their significance for the freedom of members of the group.

In ordinary talk, and in much of the writing of political scientists and sociologists, assertions about power, its distribution, its consequences, etc., are often very confidently made; one of the objects of the points I have been making is to suggest that this confidence is usually unjustified. Even in a simple relation between two persons, it is frequently extremely difficult to identify the kind of relationship it is, the motives, the psychological mechanisms, and so on, of the parties in the relation; this difficulty is, of course, very much greater when we are dealing with complex groups and institutions. The position is clearer when the patient in a power relation is aware of a conflict situation and when overt sanctions are present. In our ordinary talk about power, I imagine that we usually apply the term to situations of this kind, and this is also the practice of many political scientists. I shall return to this point also at a later stage. This does not seem to be a very convenient restriction of the application of the term "power," and, as we shall see, it can lead to misleading results in the empirical study of social groups and communities. In the political relationships of actual societies, relations of the "influence" type and those of the "domination" type are frequently so much intertwined, are causally so closely interconnected, that it is not very sensible to make an analysis of a political structure which leaves on one side the relationships which I have called "influence." For example, in the analysis of many examples of political "leadership," it would be impossible not to bring into the reckoning relations both of "influence" and "domination," and the manner in which they interact with one another.

II

Let me now return to Russell's "Power is the production of intended effects." If we confine our attention to situations down toward the "domination" end of our scale, we shall emphasize *intended* effects: the power of the gunman is certainly his production of intended effects — for instance, the handing over of the contents of the till. But if we look at relations of influence, the position is more difficult: the influence A has on B is sometimes intended, sometimes unintended; furthermore, A may be either conscious or unconscious of the influence he has upon B, and similarly B may be conscious or unconscious of the fact that he is being influenced. Toward the end of these "Notes" I want to suggest some reasons why a realistic or adequate study of political or social power cannot afford to discount unintended effects. On the other hand, it is easy to see why the majority of social scientists agree with Russell in connecting power with intended effects only. In the first place, intended effects are much easier to deal with empirically: we can observe A expressing a wish or demand or a policy; we can observe B's disagreement or reluctance; and we can observe B's final compliance with A's demand. In the case of unintended effects, it is often more difficult to establish the fact that there has been influence at all, and not merely a coincidence of decisions. Moreover, the concept of unintended influence is a tricky one to deal with; clearly, it would be impossible to claim that A is influencing B whenever he produces

unintended effects on B. Mr. Menzies produces unintended effects on
The Sydney Morning Herald: we should scarcely say that he is influencing *The Sydney Morning Herald.* (Actually he is, but not in the sense
that is relevant to this discussion.) Apparently, it is not simply a matter
of A producing unintended effects on B. It appears, roughly speaking,
that unintended effects are equated with being influenced when B becomes more like A—adopts his opinions or his preferences or his way
of living; the once much-discussed "embourgeoisement" of the working
class is perhaps a sociological example of influence in the form of
unintended effects, and one that supports the point already made that
a realistic account of social power can hardly afford to ignore influence
as the production of unintended effects. On the other hand, if the
unintended effect the parent has on the child is to stiffen the child's
determination to be as different from the parent as possible, such
influence would not be taken as an instance of power.

What has been said of unintended influence illustrates again the
manner in which any one of these power relationships becomes a whole
family of relationships as soon as we inspect it closely. Let us separate
out just two or three of the relationships that we may call unintended
influence. A may influence B in the sense that B repeatedly imitates A,
adopts his opinions or his style, acts as he acts, and so on. We may say
that A has power over B in the sense that he, albeit unconsciously,
decides for B, is the dominant character of the pair. At the same time,
it may be in no way to A's advantage that this should be so; there
may be no interest of A's that is furthered by this situation. On the
contrary, if B is a lieutenant from whose advice A wishes to profit, it
may be a defect in him from A's point of view. But, second, we may
have a situation which is identical with the first except for this, that
B's "reflection" of A may have the effect of supporting or strengthening
some interest of A's, of helping to secure him in some position or way
of life that he enjoys. Now, obviously, this is a very important type of
situation for the analysis of political power or the power structure of a
society: the tendency of the members of a society to imitate or take
their color from ruling groups or elite groups has often been one of the
most important factors in maintaining the political and social position
of such groups. Some of the things Marx says about the absorption of
the ideology of a ruling class give examples of this mechanism. Or,
third, if we say that Joyce exercised a great influence upon many
subsequent writers, what is the analysis of this relationship? The
influence is not only a matter of conscious or unconscious imitation:
some writers rather developed and exploited in their own way techniques
that he taught them, but, although they were original and independent

writers, Joyce's influence is apparent, and they could not have written as they did but for him. We may hesitate to class this example of unintended influence as a form of power, yet in principle it is not very different from forms of power or influence in the field of political and social action; political and social leadership can be sometimes partly a matter of unusual power of imagination and inventiveness. The chief difference seems to be this: unlike the influence exercised by a book, political leadership is a reciprocal relation persisting over a considerable period of time; and the leadership is, so to speak, being repeatedly renewed by fresh acts of inventiveness. But often it is a form of influence identical neither with the first nor with the second of the other two forms I have also pointed to.

III

Russell says "the *production* of intended effects." But, of course, sociologists and political scientists, when they speak of power, wish to include not only the actual production of effects but also a capacity to produce effects if and when the power holder should decide to produce them. This is a distinction which is implicit in most of our discussion of power in social affairs: we may make statements to the effect that "the working class does not realize the power that it possesses," or again, we may say that a strike or a war will be a test of the distribution of power. There is a distinction involved here between what might be called manifest and latent power which is of central importance for the study of power as a political and social phenomenon; however, it is connected with matters which cannot be dealt with in the compass of these "Notes." I shall touch on one aspect only.

In organized societies there is power that is institutionalized and power that is not; it follows from what I have said that power may be present in almost any relationship between two persons; it "flows" in every nook and cranny of interpersonal and social life; thus institutionalized, or socially sanctioned and defined, power is only one of many forms which power takes. The sanctioned or institutionalized power that a man has we may call his "powers," and it will usually be necessary in empirical study to distinguish his powers from his power, Sometimes the two coincide (thus, in this country, the power of the ticket inspector on the train will usually not exceed his powers); sometimes his power will fall a great deal short of his powers; sometimes it will exceed them. Men who occupy the greatest offices very often acquire power beyond what is authorized by their powers because high office frequently attracts to its holders an awe or deference which endows them with additional sources and forms of influence—this is what some sociologists call the "halo effect." This suggests that it will not do to define power as the *production* of intended effects. Suppose we are deciding whether to launch a revolt against the dictator who now rules us. We try to estimate the power he now has. The estimation of his present power is not the same as observing the effects he now produces or has produced in the past; our task is to estimate what effects he will be able to produce when we challenge him. In other words, the concept of power does not *always* refer to a process between persons that is actually in train; power is not something that is present only when the process of producing effects is actually going on (in the way that life can be said to be present only while certain chemical and other processes are occurring); the concept may *also* refer to the capacity to produce effects in the future. We say sometimes that a man has the power to do so and so even though we believe that he will never in fact act to produce the effects in question. The identification of power with the production of effects would make nonsense of much of what we habitually say about power in social affairs.

Thus, we encounter another difference of meanings which writers often fail to notice. When I was discussing the scale from "influence" to "domination," I had in mind interactions or transactions actually occurring between persons; it would have been meaningless to speak of such things as voluntary acceptance of discipline, manipulation, sanctions, a conflict situation, etc., if that were not so. Similarly, it would be meaningless to speak (as we have done) about qualitative differences between different sorts of power relation unless we are thinking of power as an interaction, a process actually in train. If, however, the power we are referring to is the present power to produce effects in the future, *part* of what we are talking about must be a man's control over the means sufficient to produce the effects—as when we say that "wealth is power." In recent writing the distinction is sometimes made between power itself and the "power base" (whatever it is in virtue of which a man can exercise power),[4] but it now appears that, so far as one of the most common and important conceptions of power is concerned, the "power base" is itself part of the power we attribute to the power holder.

But only part. If we say that A has great power (that is, power to produce effects in the future) we refer not only to his wealth, intelligence, skill, physical strength, or whatever the "bases" may be. Power, in any of its senses, is always a structure of relations; we can only attribute power to a man with reference to other persons; and, in fact, in most of the statements we make about the possession of power, the other persons are not specified. But obviously our estimate of A's power must refer not simply to the "bases" that A controls, but also to attributes and "bases" of B and C and D. A has as much power as he has partly because B, C, and D desire money as much as they do, or are as credulous or as physically timid as they are.

Summing up this part of the discussion, we may conclude that attributions of power always (or almost always) involve future reference. Assertions about the power that an individual or a group possesses are assertions about *both* an existing structure or system of processes and also about future effects. Influence, and other concepts of power, refer to continuing structures; they refer to systems of causally related actions which are constantly repeated; and they are often used in a way that involves a projection into the future. So far as this is so, the empirical analyses of social power structures which are undertaken by sociologists and political scientists are not purely contemporary or purely descriptive exercises; they will include rather complicated predictions about the future, assumptions which it will be very difficult to make explicit about effects that will follow if certain decisions are made or certain other events occur.

IV

Let us now glance briefly at another complication. What are the future events we have in mind when, at this moment, we attribute power to A? I have said that we are referring not only to future events but also to other persons (usually unspecified). But we can easily see that this is an oversimplification. In addition to the aspects of power we have already pointed to — the character of the interrelated motives and desires of the actors, the presence or absence of a conflict situation, the mechanisms and bases of power — we must introduce still another aspect in order to explicate the concept, what we may call the "field," that on which the power holder operates or within which he produces his effects. Attributions of power are incomplete, and strictly meaningless, unless there is at least some specification of the "field."

Between persons and within social groups, power is, of course, distributed and diffused in infinitely complicated ways. And even with simple relations between two persons it will not be easy to find a case where the weaker is literally *powerless* in relation to the stronger. It seldom happens that B is so weak that he cannot compel A to pay a price he would rather not pay for the sake of enforcing his will. Because of the virtual omnipresence of power in human relations, our attributions of power to particular persons are comparative more often than we realize; they are quantitative judgments. A powerful man is like a moneyed man; most of us have some money, but not as much as the moneyed man. And when we look more closely at what these quantifications involve, we see the relevance of what I have called the "field."

There are a number of different dimensions that we are (usually implicitly) quantifying. I shall mention three by way of example. First, the power of a "powerful" man may relate to the number of men he can influence or coerce: Billy Graham is a more influential lecturer than I am, Menzies a more powerful man, because they can affect the behavior of far more men than I can. This dimension may be called the "range" of power. Second, the power that A has over B is relative also to the particular set of B's interests, desires, or activities that are amenable to A's influence or control. If I try to influence the views my students have about Marx, I may succeed; if I try to influence, still more to prescribe, their choice of wives, they will ignore me. Following Simon,[5] we call this dimension the "zone of acceptance," and clearly it is of fundamental importance in describing the distribution of political and social power: a government may have very great power within some "zone of acceptance," but its power can quickly evaporate if it attempts to operate outside that zone. Third, we find also that within the "zone of acceptance," and with respect to *one* particular segment of a man's interests or activities, there is a limit to the extent that another can influence or control this segment. A Fagin may have established a great influence or domination over an apprentice in crime, but the apprentice may rebel rather than be induced to attempt certain particular crimes. This dimension we call the "intensity" of power; it, too, is an extremely important one in the analysis of political power.[6] A commander may be able to compel his troops to endure a certain amount of suffering, but perhaps there is a limit beyond which mutiny will occur.

Thus, when we attribute power to a man, and especially when our attribution is comparative (as it usually is), we were referring to a "field" in which the power holder operates, and we are giving quantitative values to these and no doubt to other dimensions. There is no reason, of course, to suppose that these dimensions are commensurable. For this reason it does not seem likely that measurements of political and social power, including judgments about the distribution of power, have, or can ever have, any very exact meaning. In particular cases we might try to increase comparability by restricting comparisons to positions on a single dimension, but this will not often be very illuminating in dealing with the extremely intricate power relations of a political system or a complex social group.

V

Thus, it is usually easy to pick holes in empirical studies of the power structure of actual societies. Wright Mills's book, *The Power Elite*,[7] has been attacked on the ground that Mills does not define the criteria which in his opinion would have to be met before one could say that a particular group of men (say, the top men in the Pentagon) have the predominance of power in the U.S.A., and that consequently the assertions he makes about the distribution of power in the U.S.A. cannot be verified. As we have suggested, it is probably impossible for "logical" reasons for any global study of the structure of power within a society to meet these requirements.

R. A. Dahl, in an article which criticizes Mills's book on these grounds, outlines a method for the study of the distribution of power.[8] To abridge fiercely, what he proposes is something like this: one must start with a conflict situation or a cluster of conflict situations. One must identify in advance the conflicting interests and demands within the situation or situations. And one must then be able to show, over a period of time and in a specified proportion of cases, that the demands of interests of one group have prevailed or predominated in the decisions that are finally taken.

No doubt, some such method will often be applicable, yet there is much that could be said about this recipe for the empirical study of the distribution of power. In the first place, it will be noticed that Dahl has especially in mind what I have called the "domination" sector of the power continuum: his procedure would not be applicable to what I have called the "influence" sector, where there is no clearly identifiable conflict situation and where the defining characteristic of the situation is not that one man's demands or interests are forced to yield to those of another. In the second place, we must recognize that this is a rather important exclusion because of the concept of political and social change that is presupposed. Dahl concerns himself with cases in which *decisions* are debated and made. But social change is not only a matter of the taking of a series of discrete and distinguishable decisions. Equally important is slow, nondeliberate, unforeseen, and unintended change; and in *this* sort of change the influence that is exercised by elites or pace-setting minorities on the masses of men may be a crucial factor; here, however, we cannot begin by identifying opposing interests or assume that power is expressed in the solution of a conflict situation. At those points where, for instance, "power" and "prestige" interact, the methods of empirical analysis which may help in the study of situations of the "domination" type may be entirely useless.

But, third, suppose that we *do* confine ourselves to those cases where deliberate, discrete decisions are taken. Even so, the method we are examining will secure greater empirical rigor only at the cost of a great oversimplification of social reality. One thing that Mills appears to be saying is this, that certain groups (for instance, the military, the industrialists, and the top political men) constitute the "power elite" in the U.S.A. because the decisions *they* make affect most deeply, and throughout a very wide "zone," the lives of all the citizens of their country. This statement introduces all three of the dimensions I have just distinguished. But its interest for us at this point is that it brings us back to the question of *unintended* effects. I do not understand Mills to imply that all the effects of the decisions of his "power elite" are intended effects; it is quite intelligible to say that men whose decisions alter the lives of a great number of other men, continuously, deeply, and through a wide range of their interests and activities, are far more powerful than you and I whose decisions have effects in a very restricted "field." Thus, it is plausible to suppose that sometimes when we attribute great power to an individual or group we have in mind the range, the intensity, the extent of the zone of influence of the power that is exercised, but we may not think it highly relevant to consider whether the effects of decisions are intended or unintended. Political scientists and sociologists might well find it convenient to distinguish pretty sharply between power as the production of (or ability to produce) *intended* effects and all other forms or senses of power (including power to produce effects that are not intended); in studies of the distribution and mechanisms of political power, it might be convenient for them to concern themselves only with the first. Still, this would be at variance with the history of the term "power." For many important social theorists have habitually employed the concept as meaning simply power to produce effects on other men (intended *or* unintended); for instance, Marxist-inspired analyses of the power structure of capitalist society, with their emphasis on the power of the capitalist, the entrepreneur, and the investor, have certainly implicitly included the effect of their decisions in "determining" the fate of other men, not necessarily in intended or expected ways, in the calculation of the sum of their power. Similarly, the arguments which have been advanced in the present century in support of what is called "economic democracy"—

bringing the operation of the economy within the system of democratic control—have also usually appealed as much to the assumed power of "big business" to produce *unintended* effects as to its power to impose deliberate decisions. And it seems to me that no study of the nature of power and of its political and social significance can afford to exclude this meaning from its inquiries.

VI

I remarked earlier that one problem for an empirical study of a power structure is the problem of "identification"—to recognize the qualitative characters of the power relations present in the situation we are studying. I remarked also that we shall find, in any political system or social group, a great number of qualitatively different power relations most intricately intertwined. The discussion in the last section will have reinforced these points. When we are examining the power that may be said to be enjoyed by a particular social group, we are likely to be confronted by the whole gamut of power relations. For example, we will usually be able to discern the kind of "influence" I pointed to at the outset: the case where the presence of the conflict situation is not a crucial defining characteristic. We shall almost certainly find "influence" in the rather different sense: the power to affect the decisions or actions of others, which, however, falls short of being able to control or prescribe what those responses or decisions shall be; this is a concept of power which is very prominent in democratic formulations, in notions of popular participation, consultation, and the like. We shall find relations which do involve conflict situations of different sorts and degrees, and sanctions of different sorts. And we shall find decisions having both intended and unintended effects. It is not easy to make the necessary discriminations; it is so difficult in fact that very often the participants themselves, the man who exercises power and the man over whom it is exercised, do not themselves know whether sanctions are being employed or whether there is an element of what I have called "domination" in the relationship. That the quality of the relationship is often concealed from the actors themselves is often enough illustrated by interpersonal relations within the family—for instance, in the relations between husbands and wives, between parents and children. This is a commonplace with which psychoanalysts and novelists are very familiar. It is clear that the psychoanalytical theory of "internalization" or "introjection" would introduce some very nasty problems for analysts of power. It is a still more difficult problem to identify relationships within political or social situations. Abundant examples of this difficulty can be found in discussions of democracy; political scientists do not agree, nor are they likely ever to agree, about the role of "domination" in democratic societies like our own, the extent to which sanctions are brought into play in maintaining the stability of democracies, the extent to which the pattern of power (or structure of "powers") depends upon the consent of the governed, the voluntary acceptance of leadership, an ingrained respect for legitimate or constituted authority, and so on. Within recent years, political scientists and sociologists have been giving some attention to the problems connected with the *measurement* of power.[9] It appears to me, however, that a prior problem, and perhaps an even more important one, is what I call the problem of identification. At any rate it is a difficult enough task, apart from quantification, to discover what *kinds* of relationship confront us in any complex social situation; unless we can make these qualitative identifications and discriminations, we cannot begin to consider the significance of a power structure, its relation to problems about freedom, and many other issues.

I want to amplify this last point a little further by returning in conclusion to the "influence" pole of the continuum. Talcott Parsons, in another article attacking Mills's book about the power elite of the U.S.A.,[10] asserts that Mills works with a "zero sum" conception of power; that is, that Mills assumes, or tends to assume, that an increase in power at one point within a social system implies its diminution at another. I shall not ask whether this criticism really applies in this case; nevertheless, in our ordinary talk about power it is certainly true that the assumption is often made that there is, so to speak, a finite sum of power and that if A has become more powerful, then there is a B who has become less powerful. Yet it is easy to see that this is an assumption that cannot generally be made without considerable amplification and qualification.

Now, we can observe in many power relations that a man who enjoys power over others is endowed with the power that he has by those over whom it is exercised. One of the simplest and most familiar examples of this is the leadership situation—the situation where a group of men endow another man with power (including power over themselves) because they expect that by so doing their own power to satisfy some desire, demand, or interest they want to satisfy will be augmented. The power of the leader often survives (or continues to grow) so long as the expectations of those over whom power is exercised continue to be satisfied. Of this situation there are many variants; for instance, the power that the leader or ruler has conferred upon him by the followers or subjects may be the result of a conscious calculation of advantage, or it may come from nonrational belief or sentiment of one kind or another, such as a belief in the magical or nonnatural gifts of the leader. Some instances of what Weber calls "charismatic authority" belong here.

But there are features of all the variants that are worth pointing to. First, A's power does not flow merely from *his* exclusive possession of some power base (wealth, superior strength or knowledge, or whatever it may be); it is an aspect of the interaction between A and those over whom he has the power. Second, sanctions may be completely absent, or quite secondary. Third, and this is here the most relevant point, the power with which A is endowed need not entail what B, C, and D would consider to be a significant loss of power; on the contrary, the increase of A's power can contribute to an increase in their own power to satisfy certain of their own demands. In fact, one of the main functions of social power, one of the purposes of creating power structures and reservoirs of power and of experimenting with possible distributions of power, is to enlarge the available volume of power — the volume of power that is available not only to the leaders or governors of a group but to all its members.

And this appears with particular clarity in relationships at the extreme end of the "influence" pole of the continuum. We sometimes say of thinkers, writers, painters, or musicians that they possess unusual power; we appear to mean that they can produce effects in their work, or that they have a control over their medium, beyond the power of ordinary men — this is power simply as the "production of (intended?) effects." Now, a painter may not possess "by nature" the power of a Picasso, or a thinker the power of a Marx or a Freud, but it is not uncommon for them to develop a power that they could not otherwise have acquired by subordinating themselves to a master, following a discipline imposed upon them, and learning to work with the other man's skill and technique, to master his style. And in politics, as in all other forms of cooperative working, there are close analogies to this particular relationship.

But if we want to argue that a man can in certain circumstances increase his own power by subordinating himself to the authority or the power of another person, we can avoid paradox only by admitting further complexities in the power relation. During the war the English, let us say, increased their own power by conferring on Churchill an unusual degree of power and a set of unprecedented "powers": thereby they may be said to have increased their power to achieve an end they were pursuing in common, the defeat of Germany. To build up their power to achieve this end, they surrendered their power to act in certain other ways or to achieve certain other ends. The essential point is that the individuals who participate in a power relation possess many different interests and motives and are engaged in different sets of activity concurrently. Moreover, each person will often give different values to his different interests and activities; at least, he may in many cases rank them in an order of importance to himself.

It is at this point that one of the dimensions I distinguished, "the zone of acceptance," becomes of some importance. It is seldom that A who is said to have power or influence over B has the same power over all of B's interests or activities. In simple interpersonal relations it often happens that A's power to control certain of B's desires or activities (even sometimes to the point of being able to prevent their expression or indulgence) is a necessary or a sufficient condition of B's being able to satisfy other desires or carry out other activities. This, of course, is one of the familiar relationships between parents and children, and between teachers and pupils; the ordinary common-sense justification of the power of parents and of teachers assumes that this does happen. The influence or control which A exercises over B within the "zone of acceptance" may be experienced by B as unalloyed frustration or domination, without any compensating satisfaction or enlargement of potency (as of course it often is by children and school pupils); or B may rank his interests, desires, etc., in such an order that he may feel that the interests which gain in potency or facility are more important to him than those that are blocked. And, although I have spoken only of cases where these judgments are made by the actors themselves, we also habitually make such judgments for other persons; just as we do not make a rule of consulting the wishes of young children when we require them to submit themselves to educational discipline, so as political philosophers and as citizens we habitually make such judgments for other men: we do so whenever we take a position on questions of the legitimacy and illegitimacy of forms, distributions, modes of exercise, etc., of power. And, indeed, with power as with freedom, evaluations of the kind I have been referring to often affect our use or nonuse of the term "power" as a proper description of concrete situations.

VII

A survey of only a few of the different relations that may be intermingled and confused within any power situation warns us that the connections between one man's power and another's, between one form of power and another, or between power and freedom, may be extremely obscure, and their unraveling a very hazardous enterprise. One conclusion that is possibly suggested by these "Notes" is that the concept of power, for reasons implicit in this discussion, is not likely to be a fruitful concept in the explication of the "power structures" of actual societies; perhaps what is called for is a great deal of analysis in the sense of breaking up and discrimination, and the substitution of more manageable concepts for the portmanteau concept of power. I cannot pursue this question here. It is fair to say, I think, that both in ordinary discussion and in the discussions of social scientists there is a tendency to concentrate very heavily on certain manifestations of "power," and to ignore or minimize others. The power relations which lie toward the lower end of the scale tend to be emphasized; those lying toward the pure "influence" end tend to be played down. Furthermore, common sense does tend to assume a "zero sum" concept of power; everyday discussions (for instance, of the growth of the state's power or of the power of the bureaucracy) not only pay scant regard to the "dimensions" I have shown to be highly relevant but also tend to assume that if there is a building up of power at one point within the system there must be a diminution at others. Again, in thinking about power as a social phenomenon, we tend to be too much obsessed with problems of distribution, and perhaps we operate with very crude notions of distribution to boot. No one would be in danger of assuming that the wealth of a society is a fixed quantity or that the effects of a reallocation of wealth could be calculated by simple operations of addition and subtraction. Or, again, if we happen to be interested in moral issues connected with power and its operation, it is very obvious that such well-worn assertions as Acton's "power tends to corrupt and absolute power corrupts absolutely," or Reinhold Niebuhr's theme of the persistent tension between power and morality are not in an undissected form either illuminating or interesting. With power as with many other things, as Oakeshott has reminded us, *la vérité reste dans les nuances*.

Notes

1. Talcott Parsons, "Distribution of Power in American Society," *World Politics*, 10 (October 1957).
2. Robert Bierstedt, "The Problem of Authority," in M. Berger, T. Abel, and C. H. Page, eds., *Freedom and Control in Modern Society* (1954).
3. Bertrand Russell, *Power: A New Social Analysis* (1936), p. 35.

4. R. A. Dahl, "The Concept of Power," *Behavioral Science*, 2 (July 1957), 201–215.

5. H. A. Simon, "Notes on the Observation and Measurement of Political Power," *Models of Man* (1957).

6. In *one* popular usage, the distinction between "influence" and "power" seems to be related to a difference in "intensity." A man will often say about another: "I know that I cannot control him but I think I may be able to influence him" — that is, I know that I cannot get him to act exactly as I want him to act, but I can perhaps get him to come part of the way to meet my wishes. This, of course, is quite different from my own use of "influence."

7. C. Wright Mills, *The Power Elite* (1956).

8. R. A. Dahl, "A Critique of the Ruling Elite Model," *American Political Science Review*, LII:2 (June 1958), 463–469.

9. J. G. March, "Introduction to the Theory and Measurement of Influence," *American Political Science Review*, 49 (June 1955), 431–451, and references in Dahl's article, "Concept of Power."

10. Parsons, "Distribution of Power in American Society."

2

Power and Its Forms

Anthony de Crespigny

HUMAN beings may be said to have power in relation to themselves, to each other, and to the nonhuman world. This paper is concerned only with the power which is exercised in the context of human relations. Furthermore, it deals with a single type of social power — that which an actor[1] possesses insofar as he is able to move or alter the will of others so as to produce results in conformity with his own will.[2] People's bodies may be forcibly transferred from one place to another; they may be hypnotized and made to respond to another's wishes; their opinions may be altered without any intention to influence their behavior; they may be harmed for purely punitive reasons; and so on. In all these cases, social power may be said to be exercised, but in none of them has a conformity of wills been engendered.

When social scientists use the word "power" without qualification, they are commonly referring to the type of power which is here discussed. R. H. Tawney, for example, defines "power" as the "capacity of an individual, or group of individuals, to modify the conduct of other individuals or groups in the manner which he desires."[3] And David Easton says that power is "a relationship in which one person or group is able to determine the actions of another in the direction of the former's own ends."[4]

I want to begin by exploring this type of power and shall then investigate the principal forms which it can take. Whenever I employ the term "power," it should be taken, unless another use is specifically

From *Political Studies*, XVI (1968), 192–205.

indicated, as designating the capacity of an actor to affect the *actions*[5] of others in accordance with his own intentions.

I

When one actor exercises power in relation to another, the behavior of the latter is voluntary — "voluntary" in the sense that, in principle, it is subject to choice. This is indeed implied by the notion of an action, for human actions presuppose alternatives. If all alternatives are excluded, so that no choice is left, what occurs is not an action.[6] For example, frog-marching a person is not an exercise of power, save insofar as it leads to intended effects on the actions of others.

We do not ordinarily say that power is being exercised *whenever* one person acts as another intends him to act and in consequence of the latter's words or deeds. While we say this when actions are performed under duress, we tend not to do so when they result from requests or from rational persuasion, Nevertheless, a wider use of "power" can be justified as a desirable stipulation. For if it is wished to make "power" a technical term in the social sciences, it must be stripped of its emotive associations. It must be used without any limitations concerning the ways in which power may be said to be exercised. Power is not only exerted in conflict situations where there is a collision of wants and in which one actor "overpowers" another. It is not merely a capacity to impose one's will on others by reliance on negative sanctions;[7] it exists wherever one person or group is able to affect the conduct of others so as to produce results which accord with his intentions.

Some writers[8] have defined "power" in terms of actual causal connections. To have power in relation to others is to exercise power in relation to them; it is not merely to have the capacity to do so. But I cannot see that it matters much whether we talk of the "exercise" and "possession" of power or speak instead of "power" and "potential power." While the distinction between affecting and being capable of affecting actions is important, it appears to be largely a matter of indifference whether it is expressed in one terminology or the other. It may be that the former way of talking is the more natural and is to be preferred on that account. We frequently say that one actor has power in relation to another within a particular "field," but does not use it or does not use all the power he has. (This may be because he does not realize the fact or extent of his capacity or because he does not wish to employ it or to employ it fully.) On the other hand, it seems odd to say that a person is *powerful*, or has great power, simply because he is abundantly possessed of the things which, in his contemporary society, enable people to affect in important areas the activities of their fellows. To be called "powerful" he not only must possess these things — wealth, intelligence, knowledge, capacity for leadership, or whatever the sources of power may be — but must also use them in gaining the compliance of others.

A more important objection to my use of "power" comes from those who want to speak of unintended exercises of power. An actor is sometimes said to exercise power when he has an effect on another's actions, but not that which he intends. Felix Oppenheim, for example, says that an advertiser exercises power over those whom he dissuades from buying as well as over those whom he persuades to buy.[9] And Robert Dahl writes: "If, whenever I ask my son to stay home on Saturday morning to mow the lawn, my request has the inevitable effect of inducing him to go swimming, when he would otherwise have stayed home, I do have a curious kind of negative power over him."[10] But this is very curious indeed, for we would naturally say that both the advertiser and Professor Dahl had failed to exercise power, and failing to exercise power is not exercising negative power; it is not exercising power at all.[11] Dahl himself admits that "negative control of this kind is not ordinarily conceived of as power."[12] But if this is so, it would be much better not to talk about "negative power," at least not in Dahl's sense.

An actor is also sometimes said to exert power when he has an effect on another's actions, though *no* effects are intended. While P. H. Partridge would not wish to say that an actor exerts power whenever he produces unintended effects, he is critical of Russell's insistence on connecting power with intended effects only. He states that unintended effects can be equated with an exercise of power "when B becomes more like A — adopts his opinions or his preferences or his way of living."[13] Oppenheim also wants to talk of power being exercised when no effects are intended. He points out that the publication of the results of opinion polls may influence a reader's actions, yet the pollsters normally intend only to supply information, not to get anyone to do something.[14] He quotes approvingly an example drawn from a work by Dahl and Lindblom: "The boss who comes to work in a grumpy mood may not intend to induce his secretary to treat him gently; yet the responses of a good secretary are as definitely controlled as if the boss had deliberately asked her to smooth the way a little more than usual that day."[15]

If a person influences the conduct of another without having any intentions relating to the respect in which he exerts influence, he would not normally be said to exercise power. For instance, we would not say that a poet or scientist exercises power if he influences the way in which people versify or carry on research without intending to do so. While Partridge is on solid ground in speaking of *influence* unrelated to intention, it is misleading to do this in the case of *power*. Just as it is true that not all exercises of power are exercises of influence — we do not say that a gunman *influences* a shopkeeper to hand over the contents of the till — so it is also true that not all exercises of influence are exercises of power. The pollsters in Oppenheim's example would not be said to exert power over those whose behavior they influence simply because the notion of intention is absent. On the other hand, the grumpy boss in Dahl and Lindblom's example *would* be said to exert power, provided his secretary acts as she would not otherwise act. But this statement is not inconsistent with my analysis, for the boss *does* intend that his secretary should treat him gently. It is true that on this occasion he does not deliberately get her to act in this way, and may be unaware of the special treatment he is receiving, but nevertheless her conduct does accord with his intentions. For it may be assumed that those who employ secretaries possess intentions that cover this kind of behavior.

It is necessary in this connection to distinguish between "particular intentions," which refer to specific actions, and "general intentions," which refer to classes of actions. The grumpy boss has no particular intentions concerning the conduct of his secretary, but he has the general intention that she should act tactfully. This distinction should help to settle the long controversy over the relation between power and intention. It is confusing, because it is unnatural, to talk of an exercise of power when effects on conduct are produced which are not in conformity with an actor's intentions, whether because he has other intentions or because he has no relevant intentions at all. But an exercise of power need not be deliberate, nor need those who wield power be conscious of doing so. For example, A may exert power unwittingly when B acts in accordance with A's intentions, and as he would not otherwise act, because he hopes that A will benefit him if he does or fears that A will harm him if he does not.

There is a type of situation in which one might want to say that power is being exerted in spite of the fact that B *fails* to act in conformity with A's intentions. This is where B acts in accordance with what *he believes* to be A's intentions, and as he would not otherwise act, but where his belief is a mistaken one, either because A has other intentions or because he has no relevant intentions at all. I am uncertain whether one should speak of an exercise of power in this type of situation, or in all situations of this type, but if and insofar as it is thought desirable to do so, my definition of "power" would have to be reformulated. It would have to be widened to include those situations, or some of them, in which B acts in conformity with what are merely A's putative intentions.

This concludes my general discussion of power. I want now to explore the main forms which it can take. Forms of power will be distinguished on the basis of the mode of power involved — that is, according to the ways in which power can be exercised. I shall begin with *coercive power*.

II

Coercive power is the capacity of A to get B to act in conformity with his intentions, and contrary to B's wishes, by making things unpleasant for B in order to secure his compliance or by threatening to make things unpleasant for B if he does not comply. When A exercises coercive power, B complies with A's intentions because A has made doing so less unattractive to him, at the time of his compliance, than anything else. For example, a government extends the franchise in the face of a general strike because yielding to the demands of the strikers seems more eligible than standing firm. Or a person who is exposed to blackmail does what is wanted of him because compliance seems less unattractive than resistance.

It might be said that when A exercises coercive power, B regards himself, at the time of his compliance, as worse off then he would otherwise have been, but as likely to be better off than he would have been had he resisted or continued to resist. But this account would be unsatisfactory since B's compliance may be due to some attribute of character rather than to the belief that he is likely to be better off. B may comply and at the same time believe it would be more sensible to resist. (Equally, he may resist and think it wiser to comply.) It is more accurate, therefore, simply to say that in complying B does what seems least unattractive to him at the time.

The unpleasant consequences for B, actual or prospective, which are involved in an exercise of coercive power, may be consequences which directly affect him or they may be consequences which indirectly affect him by affecting others to whom he is attached by bonds of affection, sympathy, interest, responsibility, and so on.[16] Furthermore, they may be consequences which deprive him or another either of something he has or of something he expects to have. Unpleasant effects for B include the disappointment of his or another's expectations. If A regularly gives presents to B, so that B comes to expect them and to depend on them, then A may be able to exercise coercive power by making conditions for the continuance of the gifts.

Coercion may generate involuntary behavior or voluntary behavior or both. Physical coercion produces involuntary behavior at time "t," but it may produce voluntary behavior at "$t+$." For instance, the victim of a protection organization may begin to pay weekly "dues" as a result of being beaten up. If he pays for fear of similar treatment if he does not, he behaves voluntarily, though not freely. To apply physical coercion against the person of another is not in itself to exercise power, since an exercise of power occurs only when B behaves voluntarily. But an application of physical force which determines *actions* — though not directly and in the first instance — *is* an exercise of power. If some participants in a violent demonstration are killed to get the rest to disperse peacefully, then power is being wielded over those who abandon their previous activities.

There are several other things that may be said about an exercise of coercive power to clarify the notion. It clearly implies deliberate activity on the part of A. Second, it may occur, in specific circumstances, without A knowing so. The authorities of a state do not generally know when particular subjects are deterred by the penalties contained in a criminal statute, nor does a person who issues a face-to-face threat always know when it is responsible for the desired action of another. Third, it implies social conflict, since one actor is compelled to subordinate his wishes to those of another. Finally, it is incompatible with B's liberty, since it deprives him of freedom in respect of the choice which A constrains him to make.

Against my analysis it may be argued that we do not speak of an exercise of coercive power whenever unpleasant effects are produced or threatened in order to achieve an intended response. We do this only when B regards these effects as highly unfavorable. This view is advanced by Dahl, for example, in *Modern Political Analysis*.[17] But we do talk of "mild" and "severe" forms of coercion, and I can see no reason why we should not continue to do so. Indeed, it is sound procedure to limit the number of categories we employ, provided an important distinction is not thereby obscured.

It may also be said that coercive power can be exercised by means of benefits or advantages, actual or promised. H. D. Lasswell and A. Kaplan define coercion as "a high degree of constraint and/or inducement." They write: "We say that coercion is involved in an influence situation if the alternative courses of action are associated with severe deprivations *or* indulgences."[18] Leaving aside the qualification that inducements must be strong to be coercive, what is to be made of the view that coercion may involve the use of *positive* sanctions — rewards, benefits, advantages, etc.? It is clear that we may coerce an actor by depriving or threatening to deprive him of something which he values and which he has or expects to have. But it is neither customary nor useful to say that we can coerce him by improving or promising to improve his "value position."

It is arguable that the ultimate test of whether coercive power has been exercised is not in the mind of B. "Duress," writes S. I. Benn, "is not subjective in the sense that a man is under duress if he feels that he is. It presupposes standards that we apply irrespective of the subject's own feelings."[19] This is the language of the lawyer. A person does not act under duress when he can reasonably be expected to resist. For instance, I could not ordinarily be said to coerce a person if I threatened to pinch him, spit in his face, or tickle him. However, while there are obvious practical reasons for not employing a subjective notion of duress in the operations of the courts, this should not blind one to the fact that we usually regard a person as acting under duress when he feels that he is. It is true that in the case of the above examples, we would tend to disregard a claim that an action was performed under duress. But this is because such threats seem unlikely to be constraining, not because the recipient's own feelings are taken to be irrelevant.

An exercise of coercive power may be thought to involve threatened rather than actual harm. To coerce an actor successfully is to get him to make the choice you want him to make by threatening to make things unpleasant for him if he does not make it. It is true that people sometimes talk as if coercion always takes the form of a threat. But we also speak of coercion when the subject is actually harmed in order to secure his compliance — for example, when his property is damaged, his business boycotted, or his authority defied.

My second form of power is the capacity of A to get B to act in conformity with his intentions, and as B would not otherwise act, by providing or securing something attractive to B in order to gain his compliance or by undertaking to do this if B complies. I shall call this *inducive power*.

It is difficult to find suitable language to indicate this form of power. Some writers speak of "reward power,"[20] but the application of this term is too limited for my purpose. We talk of rewarding a person for having done something, not in order to get him to do it. I want a term which covers not only the situation where A influences B's present conduct by undertaking to "benefit" him in the future but also the situation where A influences B's future conduct by "benefiting" him in the present. "Inducive power" is not entirely satisfactory, for it is not uncommon to use "induce" and "coerce" interchangeably — for example, "Jack pulled out his revolver and induced John to get into the car."[21] However this may be, I wish to distinguish between inducement and coercion and between inducements and constraints.

Constraints are often made to look like inducements. If a government wants a political party banned in another country and, for the first time, offers its government aid, with the proviso that it do this, the offer is an inducement. On the other hand, if the second government had expected to receive aid because aid had been promised or had been regularly received in the past, then an offer of aid which was now made conditional upon the banning of a party would be a constraint.

The attractive consequences for B which are involved in an exercise of inducive power may affect him directly or they may affect him indirectly by affecting others. Moreover, as in the case of the previous form of power, an exercise of inducive power implies deliberate activity by A but may occur, in specific situations, without his knowledge. Unlike coercive power, however, it implies the absence of social conflict. B acts as he would not otherwise act, but he is not compelled to subordinate his wishes to those of A. This is not the case, for example, when an official grants a license as a result of receiving a bribe, when exports are promoted by subsidies, when an offer of money secures the release of a prisoner, or when a reduction of fares leads more people to use the train services. Nor does an exercise of inducive power typically involve a deprivation of B's liberty. If my action results from a threat, it would generally be said that I am unfree with respect to the behavior in question. But if it is done in consequence of a promise of "advantage," I would generally be considered to be free.[22] Nevertheless, there are circumstances in which an inducement *would* deprive a man of his freedom. This would be the case, for example, where his compliance was secured by an inducement which his psychological constitution was powerless to resist.

It may be said that the above examples would normally be called relations of influence rather than of power. I have already discussed this question, but shall restate my reason for using the term "power" to include these situations. I supported an extended use of "power" not on the ground that we possess an unlimited right to define terms as we please but as a desirable stipulation in the social sciences. I pointed out that if power is to serve as a technical concept, its emotive associations must be excluded. In particular, it must not be equated with the capacity to determine the actions of others by coercing them. Coercion is one way of exercising power, but there are other ways as well.

Exercises of coercive and inducive power imply deliberate activity by A. But there is a third form of power which is closely related to these two, but the exercise of which does not involve deliberate activity. It is the power which A exerts when B acts in conformity with A's intentions not because he has been induced or constrained to do so but because he nevertheless hopes that A will benefit him if he does or fears that A will harm him if he does not. I shall call this *reactional power* because its existence is a function of B's beliefs about A's reactions. It appears to be extremely important in social relationships.

Let me try to elucidate this category by means of examples. When we talk of the power of opinion, we are talking about reactional power. People sometimes use the term "coercive power" in this connection, but this is confusing. We do not say that a government is being coerced when it abandons a favored course of action because it is evident that it would be unpopular with the electorate. Nor would we say that a homosexual was being coerced if he concealed his condition for fear of the reactions of others. Reactional power is clearly important in hierarchical organizations. Hierarchical superiors often exercise power without employing inducements or constraints because their subordinates believe they may prosper if they comply with their superiors' intentions or may fail if they do not. It is also significant in the context of international relations, particularly in the relations between major and minor powers. The governments of small countries frequently refrain from acting as they desire because doing so would conflict with the policy of a powerful neighbor. To take some dramatic examples, reactional power has been evident in the relations between Cuba and the United States, Monaco and France, Finland and the U.S.S.R., Lesotho and South Africa.

There are a number of things to be noticed about an exercise of this form of power. The harmful or advantageous effects for B, which provide the motive for his compliance, may affect him either directly or indirectly. (To take an example of the latter alternative, the knowledge that he has relatives who are vulnerable may lead a political refugee to control his desire to seek the overthrow of his country's government.) But unlike the use of the previous forms of power, these effects are always prospective. Where harmful effects are feared, they may be such as would deprive B or another either of something he has or of something he expects to have. An exercise of reactional power often occurs unknown to A, particularly when B's beliefs about A's reactions lead him to *abstain* from doing what he would otherwise have done. Moreover, it may involve social conflict and a deprivation of B's liberty or it may not. Conflict would not exist, and B would not be said to be unfree, if B complied with A's intentions because he hoped to benefit thereby, though A had not undertaken to benefit him. On the other hand, conflict would exist, and B would suffer a loss of liberty, if B complied because he feared that A would harm him if he did not, though A had not threatened him.

This brings me to *impedimental power*. This form of power closely resembles coercive power, but it is useful to distinguish between them. Impedimental power is that which is exerted when A gets B to comply with his will by interposing obstacles between B and the attainment of his ends. These obstacles may be insuperable or they may not. A may make it impossible for B to act as he wishes, or he may make it difficult or more difficult for him to do so.

In the former case, impedimental power is exerted only when there are at least two remaining alternatives for B. Suppose, for example, that B wants to do x, A wants him to do y, and z is also open to him. If A makes it impossible for B to do x, and if B does y, preferring y to z, A would have exercised impedimental power. It is true that in this case B does not choose to abstain from doing x, but he does choose to do y. On the other hand, if there had been only one alternative to x, A would not have exerted power, since B's behavior would not then be subject to choice.

Exercises of coercive and impedimental power share several characteristics. They may both occur, in particular circumstances, without A's knowledge. Furthermore, they both imply that A acts deliberately, that he imposes his wishes on B, and that B is deprived of liberty. B is unfree in the sense and to the extent that he is prevented by other persons from doing what he wants. But there are also differences. A minor one is that an exercise of impedimental power, as the term suggests, always has a negative purpose — that of preventing an actor from doing something — though it may have a positive purpose as well — that of getting B to do y by preventing him from doing x. More important, the two forms of power involve different mechanisms. When impedimental power is exerted, A secures B's compliance not by harming or threatening him but by hindering him from achieving his goal. It is true, of course, that A makes things unpleasant for B when he impedes him and may harm B in the course of impeding him, but this is incidental to A's purpose. It may further be observed that B may not realize he has been impeded. I may prevent a person from keeping an engagement by tampering with his car without his realizing that some-one has interfered with his activity. (I am assuming here that he could still keep the engagement, but is now deterred from doing so.) But I cannot coerce a person without his knowing it.

Let me give some more illustrations. A minister may prevent a person from going abroad by withdrawing his passport; opponents of nuclear bomb tests may frustrate the occurrence of a test by entering the danger area; a government may reduce cigarette consumption by increasing taxation; the authorities of Oxford colleges may circumscribe the nocturnal life of undergraduates by erecting dangerous obstacles on the college walls; and governments may end a foreign war by denying arms to the belligerents. In all these cases, it is still possible, in theory at least, for the patient to continue the pursuit of his purposes.

I want now to examine a form of power that is quite different from those which have so far been discussed. It is the power which A exerts when he affects the actions of B because B regards him as *entitled* to do so. This form of power is usually called *legitimate power*.

An actor may exercise legitimate power because he is authorized by a set of rules to do certain things and because these rules are respected by those who fall under them. To exert this form of power, it is not sufficient that an actor should possess *de jure* "power"[23] since he may be authorized by a system of rules to issue commands or take decisions, and yet his commands or decisions may lack legitimacy. They may be ignored or obeyed from fear. In the former case, the actor has no power in the *de facto* sense; in the latter case, he has *de facto* power but not legitimate power.

The decisions or commands of those who possess rule-conferred "power" may be invested with legitimacy in different ways. Max Weber has said that in what he calls a legal-rational system, legitimacy rests on "a belief in the 'legality' of patterns of normative rules and the right of those elevated to authority under such rules to issue commands." On the other hand, in a traditional system, Weber saw legitimacy as "resting on an established belief in the sanctity of immemorial traditions and the legitimacy of the status of those exercising authority under them."[24]

It was stated above that to exert legitimate power it is not sufficient that a person should have rule-conferred "power." Nor is it necessary. A person may exercise this form of power not on the basis of any set of rules but because he is *an authority*. He is thought to have special knowledge or insight, a right to speak because "he knows what he is talking about." R. S. Peters says that "the notion of *an* authority...

implies, as it were, a self-generating system of entitlement which is confined to specific spheres of pronouncement and decision." He continues:

We speak of an authority on art, music, or nuclear physics. The grounds which entitle a man are directly connected with his *personal* history and achievements in a specific sphere. These grounds vary from extremes of revelation, initiation, and vocation, through less esoteric grounds like study of inaccessible material in history, to the more public and accessible training of a scientist. But in all these spheres success seems to be a usual ground of entitlement.[25]

Exercises of legitimate power have a number of features which are worth observing. They are typically initiated by commands or orders, but they may also stem from decisions, pronouncements, recommendations, and so on. Second, they imply that orders are obeyed, decisions or recommendations accepted, *simply because* they issue from a certain source, the attributes of which are regarded as investing them with legitimacy.[26] Third, they imply the absence of social conflict. It is sometimes said that when this form of power is used, the respondent complies willingly. But this may not be true, for the respondent may think it proper that he should comply, yet do so most reluctantly. In these circumstances, however, it would be wrong to say that A had *imposed* his wishes on B. Fourth, they are consistent with B's liberty, since he is not being subjected to another's will. The motive for his compliance is his respect for certain attributes which A possesses, such as an office, a status, or expert knowledge. Last, they imply deliberate activity on the part of A but may occur without his knowing so, whether because he is unaware that B has acted at all or because he cannot be certain of B's motives. This uncertainty may also extend to B himself.

My sixth form of power is that which A is able to exercise because B loves him, is impressed by his personality, desires to be as like him as possible, and so on. In naming it, I shall have recourse to a word which is no longer in use and shall call it *attrahent power,*[27] for the more usual alternatives are less satisfactory. "Attraction power" is a dreadful term. "Personal power" and "referent power" are commonly used, but they are both too narrow for my purpose, since the form of power I am now concerned with may be exercised by groups as well as by individuals and does not necessarily involve any process of identification.

An actor who exerts attrahent power does not do so because he is regarded as having a right or an entitlement to influence behavior. He exerts power because there is something about him in virtue of which people comply with his wishes simply because they are *his* wishes. B may comply because A is a favorite nephew, an adored mistress, an intimate friend, a hero, a "natural" leader, an arresting personality, a "reference group" or "reference individual," and so on. In all these relationships, B's behavior is affective rather than ratiocinative.

A person who possesses what Weber calls "charismatic authority" appears to combine legitimate and attrahent power. For Weber speaks of "charismatic authority" as "resting on devotion to the specific and exceptional sanctity, heroism, or exemplary character of an individual person, and of the normative patterns or order revealed or ordained by him."[28] The charismatic leader impresses his will both by the appeal of his personality and by generating a belief that he has exceptional powers which entitle him to shape the destinies of his followers. He does not justify his innovations but appeals to revelation or claims that he has a call. These are not really justifications; they are ways of emphasizing that he need give no reasons since he is a special sort of man.[29]

An exercise of attrahent power does not imply that the power holder acts deliberately, nor does it imply that the actors involved are conscious of its occurrence. Furthermore, it does not involve social conflict since A does not force B to submit to his will. This does not mean, however, that B complies willingly. For example, B's desire to identify with a particular group may lead him to conform to norms of conduct which, initially at least, are repugnant to him. Finally, an exercise of attrahent power is compatible with B's liberty in the "negative" sense though it may be inconsistent with his autonomy and, therefore, with his liberty in the "positive" sense.

The last form of power I shall discuss is the capacity of A to influence B's choices by the production of reasons. This may be called *persuasive power*. However, an exercise of persuasive power does not involve the production of any sort of reason, for threats and incentives are excluded. If I told a person that I would harm him if he ignored my wishes, and if this statement was not simply a prediction about my behavior but was designed to put pressure on him, I would be supplying him with a reason for conformity, but it would be euphemistic to say that I was attempting to persuade him. On the other hand, if I told him that somebody else would harm him if he ignored my wishes, and if this statement was intended to influence his behavior, I would then be seeking to persuade him, provided there was no suggestion of my getting the third person to do so.

Persuasive power is exerted only when the reasons which are produced in favor of some action are such as would be said to constitute the premises of an *argument*. If A threatened another or offered him a bribe, he would be providing B with a reason for compliance, but we would not say that he was engaging in argument. He would be supplying but not *advancing* a reason for compliance. A *would* be engaged in argument if, without loading alternatives by means of inducements or constraints, he tried to influence another's choices by making statements about the character or consequences of particular actions or courses of action. If B considered these reasons, weighed them in the light of his own values, and then accepted them as the basis of his actions, we would say that he had been persuaded to do what A intended him to do.

It is common to distinguish between rational and nonrational persuasion. I take it that persuasive activity in support of some action is rational insofar as (1) it is unmarked by concealment or deception of any kind — for instance, in respect to the motives or intentions of the would-be persuader or the means which he employs — and (2) the reasons which are produced are worthy of credence and constitute good reasons for doing the action in question. When I say that rational persuasion involves the production of "good reasons," I mean "logically good reasons." A reason for doing something is logically good when, once the reason has been granted, it would be logically odd, in the context in which it is given, to ask why it is a reason for doing the action.[30] For example, if A tried to persuade B to wear glasses on the ground that he would ruin his eyes if he did not, it would be logically odd if B accepted the proposition but asked why it was a reason for wearing glasses.

Exercises of persuasive power occur when and insofar as B's actions result from the reasons which A propounds rather than from the attributes or standing of the propounder. Moreover, they imply the absence of conflict and are consonant with B's liberty in the "negative" sense since he is not being prevented by others from acting as he pleases. However, some modes of nonrational persuasion are incompatible with the autonomy of a man and are therefore an infringement of his freedom, understood as rational self-mastery.

Notes

1. The word "actor" may refer to one person or to any human aggregate.
2. See Howard Warrender, *The Political Philosophy of Hobbes* (Oxford, 1957), p. 312.
3. *Equality* (London, 1931), pp. 175–176.
4. *The Political System* (New York, 1953), pp. 143–144.
5. I shall use "action" so as to include forbearances.
6. See Alasdair Macintyre, "A Mistake about Causality in Social Science,"

in Peter Laslett and W. G. Runciman, eds., *Philosophy, Politics and Society*, Second Series (Oxford, 1962), p. 60.

7. See George Schwarzenberger, *Power Politics — A Study of International Society* (New York, 1951), p. 14.

8. See, for example, Bertrand Russell, *Power — A New Social Analysis* (London, 1938), p. 35; Herbert Goldhamer and Edward A. Shils, "Types of Power and Status," *The American Journal of Sociology*, XLV (1939), 171; Harold Lasswell and Abraham Kaplan, *Power and Society* (New Haven, 1950), p. 76; and H. A. Simon, *Models of Man* (New York, 1957), p. 5.

9. Felix E. Oppenheim, *Dimensions of Freedom* (New York, 1961), p. 93.

10. Robert A. Dahl, "The Concept of Power," *Behavioral Science*, 2 (1957), 205.

11. I may appear to be inconsistent in criticizing Dahl for departing from ordinary usage when I have done this in my analysis of "power." But whereas I justify my unnatural usage, Dahl does not, and I do not see how he could.

12. Dahl, "The Concept of Power."

13. See p. 26 in this volume.

14. See Oppenheim, *Dimensions of Freedom*, p. 92.

15. Robert A. Dahl and Charles E. Lindblom, *Politics, Economics, and Welfare* (New York, 1953), p. 96.

16. The unpleasant consequences for B may be consequences for A. For instance, A may threaten to kill himself if B does not act as required.

17. Robert A. Dahl, *Modern Political Analysis* (Englewood Cliffs, N.J., 1963), p. 50.

18. Lasswell and Kaplan, *Power and Society*, pp. 97–98.

19. Unpublished manuscript.

20. See, for example, John R. P. French, Jr., and Bertram Raven, "The Bases of Social Power," in Dorwin Cartwright, ed., *Studies in Social Power* (Ann Arbor, 1959), p. 156.

21. It is also not uncommon to use "induce" and "persuade" interchangeably.

22. See J. Roland Pennock, "Hobbes's Confusing 'Clarity' — The Case of 'Liberty,' " in Keith C. Brown, ed., *Hobbes Studies* (Oxford, 1965), p. 113.

23. "Power" is used in two quite different senses — in the sense of actual ability and in a *de jure* sense. *De jure* power is the power prescribed by a system of rules. To attribute *de jure* power to an actor is not to say anything about what he can actually do; it is simply a statement about what the rules empower him to do.

24. Max Weber, *The Theory of Economic and Social Organization*, trans. A. M. Henderson and Talcott Parsons (Glencoe, Ill., 1947), pp. 300–301.

25. See p. 66 in this volume.

26. See p. 73 in this volume.

27. See *Oxford English Dictionary*.

28. *Theory of Economic and Social Organization*, p. 301.

29. See p. 65 in this volume.

30. For a discussion of the notion of logical oddness, see P. H. Nowell-Smith, *Ethics* (London, 1954), especially pp. 72–74, 83–85, 102–107.

Select Bibliography

Annales de Philosophie Politique. Vols. I and II: "Le Pouvoir" (Paris, 1956–1957).

BACHRACH, PETER, and BARATZ, MORTON. "Decisions and Non-decisions: An Analytical Framework," *American Political Science Review*, LVII (1963), 632–642.

BELL, RODERICK, EDWARDS, DAVID V., and HARRISON, WAGNER R., eds. *Political Power*. New York, The Free Press, 1969.

BIERSTEDT, ROBERT. "An Analysis of Social Power," *American Sociological Review*, XV (1950), 730–738.

DAHL, ROBERT A. "The Concept of Power," *Behavioral Science*, II (1957), 201–215.

EMMET, DOROTHY. "The Concept of Power," *Proceedings of the Aristotelian Society*, LIV (1953–1954), 1–26.

GOLDHAMER, HERBERT, and SHILS, EDWARD A. "Types of Power and Status," *American Political Science Review*, XLIX (1955). 431–451.

DE JOUVENEL, BERTRAND. *On Power*, trans. J. F. Huntington. New York: Viking Press, 1949.

LASSWELL, HAROLD, and KAPLAN, ABRAHAM. *Power and Society*. New Haven: Yale University Press, 1950.

MARCH, JAMES. "An Introduction to the Theory and Measurement of Influence," *American Political Science Review*, XLIX (1955), 431–451.

MINOGUE, K. R. "Power in Politics," *Political Studies*, VII (1959), 268–289.

NEUMANN, FRANZ L. "Approaches to the Study of Political Power," *Political Science Quarterly*, LXV (1950), 161–180.

OPPENHEIM, FELIX. "An Analysis of Political Control: Actual and Potential," *Journal of Politics*, XX (1958), 515–534.

————. *Dimensions of Freedom*. New York: St. Martin's Press, 1961.

PARTRIDGE, P. H. "Power and Politics," *Philosophy*, XXXVIII (1963), 117–135.

RUSSELL, BERTRAND. *Power — A New Social Analysis*. New York: W.W. Norton, 1938.

SIMON, HERBERT A. "Notes on the Observation and Measurement of Political Power," *Journal of Politics*, XV (1953), 500–516.

WALTER, E. V. "Power and Violence," *American Political Science Review*, LVIII (1964), 350–360.

AUTHORITY

POLITICAL scientists and political philosophers are rarely able to discuss authority without reference to Max Weber. Unlike Aristotle's classification of governments, Weber's typology of authority is still used extensively. But Weber was a socio-logical theorist, not primarily a political philosopher. While his analysis is useful in understanding and explaining the social and psychological basis of authority, it is not a philosophical analysis of the concept. Conceptual analysis is not, however, irrelevant to the concerns of the social scientist. Conceptual clarity is an essential ingredient in any sound empirical study. The articles by C. W. Cassinelli and R. S. Peters focus on the meaning of authority in terms of different dichotomies. Cassinelli contrasts the "exercise" and "possession of authority," whereas Peters contrasts *de jure* and *de facto* authority. Peters' dichoto-my was used by Anthony de Crespigny in his analysis of "legitimate power" in the previous section. Although their analyses are similar, the differences between Cassinelli and Peters are not wholly termino-logical.

Authority is not exclusively a political concept since it is present in many areas of life. But Cassinelli, unlike Peters, restricts his analysis to political authority. It might be thought that the concept of authority always remains the same, that only the sphere of reference changes. But that would depend upon one's understanding of politics, so Cassinelli sets out to define the scope of the political world. He finds it unsatisfactory to define politics in terms of the kinds of behaviors which are regulated, since political controls have been applied to almost all human activities. It is equally futile to define politics in terms of the scope of regulation. A nongovernmental directive may apply to a whole society whereas a governmental directive may not. After dismissing these definitions of politics, Cassinelli decides that politics can be understood in terms of its "method of regulation," i.e., the use of physical coercion. While governors may rarely need to use physical coercion, their directives always contain "at least an implicit reference to this ability to use physical coercion."

Cassinelli feels that much of the confusion about authority results from a failure to distinguish between its exercise and possession. He makes this distinction in terms of the two parties to the authoritative relation (authority is always a relation): the governor and the recipient. The motivations of both parties are crucial to the distinction. The exercise of authority requires that the governor does not intend to use coercion and that the citizen obeys without considering its use. Posses-sion of authority depends upon the acceptance of coercion, but unlike

57

the exercise of authority, it is compatible with occasional disobedience. The exercise of political authority requires that the governor intends to change only the governed's behavior, not his attitudes or beliefs. The governor's directive must always be accompanied by an implicit threat of physical coercion, while the actual use of force is a sign of the "breakdown" of authority. The exercise of authority requires several things of the recipient, too. He must know that he is being ordered to do something; if he unconsciously conforms to the governor's directive, authority has not been exercised. Second, the recipient must conform because he believes that the governor is (for some reason) entitled to issue such directives, not because he happens to agree with the substance of the directive. Weber's typology of legal-rational, traditional, and charismatic authority is useful in explaining why a recipient might believe that the governor is entitled to obedience.

The possession of authority depends upon the citizen's beliefs, whereas, according to Cassinelli, its exercise does not. (It seems that the exercise of authority does depend upon some minimal beliefs of the recipient.) The governor possesses political authority when the recipient believes he is entitled to his authority for some reason. He may attain this entitlement because of his office, status, or personal characteristics. But the citizen must believe that one or more of these factors gives the governor the right to issue binding directives.

Peters employs Weber's typology somewhat differently. He sets charismatic authority apart from traditional and legal-rational authority. Charismatic authority, because it concerns the traits of an individual, is intimately connected with the "exercise of authority in its *de facto* sense," while the other types of authority are *de jure*. Peters finds that our language contains a helpful distinction between a person "in" authority and one who is "an" authority. Someone is "in" authority if he has been authorized according to some system of rules. Someone is "an" authority when he possesses, or is thought to possess, special competence in a certain area. There is a connection between these two senses of authority (both *de jure*) and *de facto* authority, but the connection is contingent or empirical, not conceptual or logical. Empirically, it may be true that persons who are authorized or who possess special competence generally have *de facto* authority. But the two senses of authority are quite different, and it is by no means necessary that those who are authorized or who possess special competence are able to exercise authority.

Peters then approaches authority from a different angle, suggesting that all uses of authority (*de jure* and *de facto*) share certain characteristics. All uses of authority, he argues, are opposed to the use of power.

We say that a man exercises authority if he gets his way without using force, threats, incentives, or propaganda, "which are the usual ways of exercising power." This corresponds to several of de Crespigny's "forms of power," but there is an important difference. Peters contrasts authority with power, while de Crespigny suggests that authority is but one species of power. Peters actually seems more concerned to contrast authority with certain ways of exercising power, and in those terms his argument squares not only with de Crespigny's but with Cassinelli's too. Peters suggests that all uses of authority are irrelevant in science and morality. The appeal to an authoritative source is an inadequate defense of a scientific proposition or a moral argument. Scientific propositions must be validated by appeals to facts, while moral arguments must be defended by appeals to reason. The contrast between matters that are amenable to authoritative directives and those that are not is a problem worth pursuing in detail.

Peters and Cassinelli have one clear disagreement. Peters argues that *de facto* authority requires that the recipient not question or evaluate the substance of a directive. Cassinelli argues that the citizen may question or evaluate a directive, but, despite any disagreement with it, he must obey. In other words, the exercise of authority need not require the citizen to refrain from evaluating his governor's orders, but it does require that he recognize such orders as authoritative and obey them.

The concept of authority and the exercise of authority in political and social affairs are important problems for both the philosopher and the social scientist. Regardless of a person's occupational preferences, the following articles should provide much food for thought as well as a confirmation of the significance of conceptual analysis for the empirically oriented scholar.

3

Authority

R. S. Peters

Authority and Artifice

THERE are good reasons as well as personal excuses for ushering in Hobbes at the outset of a discussion on "authority," for Hobbes himself introduced the concept to deal with difficult problems connected with the analysis of human institutions. And there is little point in making a list of the different ways in which the term "authority" can be used unless the distinctions are made with an eye on the problem or cluster of problems that can be clarified by means of them.

Hobbes was impressed by the fact that a civil society is not a natural whole like a rook or a beehive, yet it is not a mere multitude of men. A multitude of men becomes an artificial person when each man *authorizes* the actions of a representative. "Of persons artificial, some have their words and actions owned by those whom they represent. And then the person is the *actor*; and he that owneth his words and actions is the AUTHOR: in which case the actor acteth by authority ... and as the right of possession, is called dominion; so the right of doing any action, is called AUTHORITY. So that by authority, is always understood a right of doing any act; and *done by authority*, done by commission, or licence, from him whose right it is" (*Leviathan*, ed. Oakeshott, pp. 105–106). De Jouvenel also uses the concept of "authority" in the context of the same type of problem. Having rejected the view that civil societies come into being through voluntary association or through

From *Proceedings of the Aristotelian Society*, suppl. vol. XXXII (1958), 207–224.

domination from without, he claims that authority is "the efficient cause of voluntary associations.... Everywhere and at all levels social life offers us the daily spectacle of authority fulfilling its primary function — of man leading man on, of the ascendancy of a settled will which summons and orients uncertain wills.... Society in fact exists only because man is capable of proposing and affecting by his proposals another's dispositions; it is by the acceptance of proposals that contracts are clinched, disputes settled and alliances formed between individuals.... What I mean by 'authority' is the ability of a man to get his proposals accepted" (*Sovereignty,* pp. 29–31).

The *de jure* and *de facto* senses of "authority"

I have chosen to start off with these quotations from Hobbes and de Jouvenel partly because they both introduce the concept of "authority" in the context of the attempt to elucidate what is meant by a society as distinct from a multitude of men, and partly because the two quotations illustrate an important difference in the ways in which the term "authority" is used in the context of the same sort of problem. For Hobbes "authority" is what might be called a *de jure* concept; for de Jouvenel it seems to be a *de facto* one. In other words, for Hobbes the term indicates or proclaims that someone has a *right* to do something. "Done by authority" means "done by commission or licence from him whose right it is." Now I am not concerned to defend Hobbes' odd conception of the handing over of rights or his account of "authorization." But, whatever the correct analysis of the connection between "authority" and "right," it is quite clear that there is a very important use of the term "authority," which is favored by Hobbes, which connects the two concepts. A man who is "in authority" for instance, clearly has a right to do certain sorts of things. This use of "authority" is to be contrasted with the *de facto* use favored by de Jouvenel. For he says "What I mean by 'authority' is the *ability* of a man to get his proposals accepted." The *Oxford English Dictionary* seems to permit both usages, for it gives "power or right to enforce obedience." It also speaks of "power to influence the conduct and actions of others;... personal or practical influence; power over the opinion of others; intellectual influence" as well as "moral or legal supremacy; the right to command or give an ultimate decision ... title to be believed." And in ordinary conversation the two senses can be used without danger of misunderstanding in one sentence when we say things like "The headmaster and others in authority had, unfortunately, no authority with the boys." The question quite naturally arises how these two senses of "authority" are related and whether both senses are important, as Hobbes and de Jouvenel maintain, for saying certain sorts of things about specifically human relationships and organizations.

Hobbes' rendering of the *de jure* sense

The *de jure* concept of authority presupposes a system of rules which determines who may legitimately take certain types of decision, make certain sorts of pronouncements, issue commands of a certain sort, and perform certain types of symbolic acts. Hobbes brings this out by saying that the actions of a representative are authorized. He relies on the sense of "authorize" which assimilates it to commissioning or giving a warrant to a man to do certain types of things. The subjects are conceived of as having words and actions which they own, of which they are the "authors," and to which they have a right. They then appoint a representative to whom they transfer their right. He is now commissioned or "authorized" to act on their behalf. "So that by authority is always understood a right of doing any act; and done by authority, done by commission or licence from him whose right it is." Now Hobbes, as is well known, and as Mr. Warrender has recently shown in such stimulating detail, had a very strange view of natural rights which permeates his picture of authority. He was led by it to conceive of authority *in general* in terms of the particular case where a man is the author of a word or act, to which he also has a right, and where he commissions someone else to act in this matter on his behalf. This is indeed a case of an authorized act, but there is a more general meaning of "authorize" which is to set up or acknowledge as authoritative, to give legal force or formal approval to. Similarly "authorized" in its most general meaning is equivalent to "possessed of authority." "Authorization" is better understood in terms of the general concept of "authority" rather than vice versa. Hobbes pictured "authority" in terms of "authorization," which is one of its derivatives. But he did bring out the obvious connection between "authority" and the existence of an "author" in the realm of acts and words, which is the key to seeing how the concept works.

"Auctoritas" as the key to "authority"

The concept of "authority" is obviously derived from the old concepts of "auctor" and "auctoritas." An "auctor" was, to quote Lewis and Short, "he that brings about the existence of any object, or promotes the increase or prosperity of it, whether he first originates it, or by his efforts gives greater permanence or continuance to it." "Auctoritas," which is a producing, invention, or cause, can be exercised in the spheres of opinion, counsel, or command. The point of this little excursion into philology is to stress not only the sphere of opinion, command, and so on, in which "auctoritas" is regarded as being exercised, but also the connection of the concept with "producing," "originating," "inventing" — in short, with there being an author.

Now in some spheres of social life it is imperative to have such "auctores" who are producers or originators of orders, pronouncements, decisions, and so on. It is also the case that in social life, whether we like it or not, there are such "auctores" to whom commands, decisions, and pronouncements are to be traced back in any factual survey of how social regulation is brought about. This is the sense of "authority" stressed by de Jouvenel. The notion of "authority" involves therefore either a set of rules which determines who shall be the "auctor" and about what, or, in its *de facto* sense, a reference to a man whose word in fact goes in these spheres. The *de jure* sense of "authority" proclaims that a man has a right to be an "auctor"; the *de facto* sense states that he is in fact one. Hobbes' account of "authorization" relates to the particular case where a man has a right to be an "auctor," as laid down by a set of rules, and where he commissions someone else to do what he himself has a right to do. Indeed, often, as in a bureaucratic system, there are subordinate sets of rules which lay down procedures for the granting of such warrants and commissions. But all authority cannot adequately be conceived in this fashion.

Weber's legal-rational and traditional rules
for determining who is *in* authority

Indeed, one of the great services done by the sociologist Max Weber has been to stress the *different* types of normative systems which are connected with different types of authority. For legitimacy may be bestowed in different ways on the commands or decisions or pronouncements issuing from an "auctor." In what he calls a legal-rational system, the claim to legitimacy rests on "a belief in the 'legality' of patterns of normative rules and the right of those elevated to authority under such rules to issue commands" (*Theory of Social and Economic Organization,* ed. Talcott Parsons, pp. 300–301). There is also, however, traditional authority "resting on an established belief in the sanctity of immemorial traditions and the legitimacy of the status of those exercising authority under them."

There are most important and interesting differences between these types of authority, but this is not the place to investigate the difference between traditional and legal rules or to comment on the adequacy of Weber's analysis. In both cases to speak of "the authorities" or "those in authority" or "those who hold authority" is to proclaim that on certain matters certain people are entitled, licensed, commissioned, or have a right to be "auctores." And the right is bestowed by a set pattern of rules.

Weber's charismatic authority

This type of authority is to be distinguished clearly from other types of authority where the right derives from personal history, personal credentials, and personal achievements, which, as will be argued later, are intimately bound up with the exercise of authority in its *de facto* sense. There is a gradation from the pure *de jure* sense of "authority" as when we say that "Wittgenstein held a position of authority in Cambridge," through the notion of "*an* authority" as when we say "Wittgenstein was an authority on William James," to the *de facto* sense as when we say "Wittgenstein exerted considerable authority over the Moral Science Club." Both the last two senses of "authority," unlike the first, imply something about the attributes or qualifications of the individual in question. But the details of this transition are very difficult to make explicit.

Weber, as a matter of fact, made much of authority deriving from personal characteristics when he spoke of "charismatic authority... resting on devotion to the specific and exceptional sanctity, heroism, or exemplary character of an individual person, and of the normative patterns or order revealed or ordained by him" (*Theory of Social and Economic Organization*, p. 301). He was thinking primarily of outstanding religious and military leaders like Jesus and Napoleon. He therefore pitched his account rather high, and personal "authority" is decked with the trappings of vocation, miracles, and revelation. Nevertheless, there is something distinctive about the charismatic leader which he shares in an exaggerated form with other "natural" leaders who exercise authority in virtue of personal claims and personal characteristics. For he is unlike the moral reformer who gives reasons of a general kind for his innovations, reasons which he expects everyone to appreciate. He appeals to revelation or claims that he has a call. These are not really justifications of his innovations; they are ways of stressing that he need give no justification because he is *a special sort of man.*

Gradations in the concept of *"an* authority"

This notion of presenting credentials of a *personal* sort is an intermediary between the purely *de jure* and the *de facto* senses of "authority." For the reference to personal characteristics is a way of establishing that a man has a right to make pronouncements and issue commands because he is a special sort of person. And, although in some societies a man who sees visions and goes into trance states is in danger of electric shock treatment, in other societies pointing to such peculiarities of personal biography are ways of establishing a man as *an* authority in certain spheres. In societies where the claim to vocation or revelation is acceptable there are also, usually, collateral tests for eliminating charlatans and the mentally deranged. But his claims rest, as it were, on some kind of personal initiation into mysteries that are a closed book to most men. In a similar way years of study on inaccessible manuscripts would establish a man as "an authority" on a special period of history, or years spent in Peru might establish a man as "an authority" on the Incas. Collateral tests would, of course, be necessary to vouch for his trustworthiness. But in many fields people become "authorities" by some process of personal absorption in matters that are generally held to be either inaccessible or inscrutable. Dodds suggested that the Forms were objects of this sort for Plato — objects which the initiated had to scrutinize by a kind of bilocation of personality as practiced by shamans. And the scrutiny of such objects gave the philosopher kings a right to make decisions and issue commands — in short, made them authorities (*The Greeks and the Irrational*, pp. 210–211).

Weber stresses the importance of success as a necessary condition for the maintenance of charismatic authority. If success deserts the leader he tends to think of his god as having deserted him or his exceptional powers as failing him. And his authority will be correspondingly reduced. The disciples, it is said, were in despair when Jesus had been crucified. It was only when he accomplished the supreme feat of rising from the dead that they recovered their faith in him and in his claims. To a certain extent the charismatic leader is in the position of a man who keeps spotting Derby winners without a system. His authority depends on always being right by virtue of a "flair" or a "hunch"—words which point to his inability to give grounds for his pronouncements. It is because his authority derives from such *personal* peculiarities that failure tends to be fatal. This is a very important empirical generalization about a necessary condition for the exercise of authority which applies at much more mundane levels.*

The point, however, is that in the case of these extreme types of charismatic authority revelation and success are not simply necessary conditions for the exercise of authority *de facto*. They are also *grounds* for establishing the right to be an "auctor." This can be shown, too, in more mundane spheres where we speak of a person being *an* authority. He has not been put *in* authority; he does not hold authority according to any system of rules. But because of his training, competence, and past success in this sphere he comes to be regarded as *an* authority. He has a right to speak. It may be the case that people do not exercise authority in various spheres unless they are competent and successful *as a matter of fact*, but it is also the case that they come to be regarded as authorities because these necessary conditions come to be regarded as grounds for a right. The notion of *an* authority, therefore, implies, as it were, a self-generating system of entitlement which is confined to specific spheres of pronouncement and decision. We speak of an authority on art, music, or nuclear physics. The grounds which entitle a man are directly connected with his *personal* history and achievements in a specific sphere. These grounds vary from the extremes of revelation, initiation, and vocation, through less esoteric grounds like study of inaccessible material in history, to the more public and accessible training of a scientist. But in all these spheres success seems to be a usual ground of entitlement.

De facto authority: its necessary conditions and meaning

It was suggested by reference to the Wittgenstein example that there was a gradation from the purely *de jure* sense of "authority," through the concept of "an authority" to the *de facto* sense of "authority." The analysis of *de facto* authority must now be tackled and the question faced whether the term "authority" can ever be used properly if there is no suggestion of a *right* to make decisions and issue commands or pronouncements. Does the exercise of authority *de facto* presuppose that the person who exercises it must be in authority or an authority?

---

*Ernest Gellner has pointed out to me that in many societies there are institutional devices for covering up failure so that the authority *can't* be wrong.

In the Admirable Crichton situation the butler, in fact, exercised authority, though the lord was in authority. Are we to assume that, in some sense, the butler had a right to make decisions? Or does saying that the butler had authority over the lord mean simply that the lord accepted the butler's decisions just because they issued from a particular man in whose presence his "genius was rebuked"?

Of course most people who exert authority *de facto* do so because of the deference paid to their office or status rather than because of any outstanding personal characteristics. But there is often a mixture of both, as in the case of Julius Caesar or Queen Elizabeth the First. Indeed there is subtle interweaving of these institutional and personal conditions for the exercise of authority *de facto*. For, as we say, the office makes the man, and often the man gives dignity to the office. The same tendency is to be observed in cases where it is more appropriate to speak of there being *an* authority. The entitlement accorded has a snowball effect. Often the outcome is disastrous—portentous pronouncements which are unquestionably accepted but which turn out to be erroneous. The generalization to other spheres is also a well-known phenomenon—one which Socrates spent so much time attacking.

There is, therefore, a widespread connection between being in authority or an authority and the *de facto* exercise of authority. But this is a contingent connection, not a necessary one. And as Admirable Crichton situations are not unusual, it looks as if being in authority or an authority are only frequently conditions for exercising authority; it does not look as if they are even necessary conditions.

What then of the cases where a man exercises authority *de facto* purely because of certain personal characteristics — either when there is no deference paid to his office if he is an official or when he is not in a position of authority at all? There are two questions here which need to be distinguished. The first is about the conditions other than being in authority or an authority which are necessary to the exercise of authority *de facto*. The second is the logical question of what it *means* to exercise authority *de facto* in this tenuous sense. Is it the case that the exercise of authority always implies that in *some* sense a man must be regarded as entitled to command, make decisions, and so on? Are there necessary conditions which, as in the case of "an authority," come to be regarded as grounds for a right? To answer this it will be as well to deal briefly with the sorts of things which might be suggested as necessary conditions.

A variety of generalizations can be made about necessary conditions for bringing about unquestioning conformity—for instance, that a man's decisions tend to be accepted in proportion to the extent to which he has been proved right before. Success, too, strengthens another necessary condition for the exercise of authority — the expectation of being believed, followed, or obeyed. People will tend to accept decisions and obey orders in proportion as the man who makes them or gives them expects that they will. The more successful he is, the less questioning there will be and the greater will be the confidence with which he utters them. We have phrases like "an air of authority," "an authoritative voice," and Jesus, it is said, produced consternation because as a boy he spoke "with authority" in the temple. Such descriptions draw attention to the outward signs of the inner certitude which is usually necessary for the exercise of authority. For it is not sufficient for a man to be in fact wise or shrewd or a felicitous prophet if he is to exercise authority. He must also be known to be so. It is said that Attlee's authority in the country suffered in his early days as Prime Minister because he did not have a good public relations officer. A man cannot exercise authority if he hides his light under a bushel.

Such empirical generalizations are the province of the social psychologist. The question of philosophical interest is whether any such empirical conditions must come to be regarded as *grounds* for a right if a man is to be said properly to exercise authority without being in authority or an authority. A concrete case will help here. Suppose there is an explosion in a street or a fire in a cinema. Someone comes forward who is not a policeman or a fireman or manager of the cinema and who is quite unknown to all present — i.e., he is not regarded as "an authority" in virtue of his personal history or known competence in an emergency. Suppose he starts issuing orders and making announcements. And suppose that he is unquestioningly obeyed and believed. Would we say that such a man exerted authority in a crisis? I think we would only say so if we thought that his orders were obeyed *simply because they were his*. There would have to be something about him in virtue of which his orders or pronouncements were regarded as being in some way legitimately issued. Maybe it would be his features; maybe it would be the tone of his voice.* Maybe he would have a habit of command. But those who heard him would have to think in an embryonic way that he was the sort of man who could be trusted. It would put the matter altogether too strongly to say that they thought he had a right to take control. For obviously, in any useful sense of "right," he has not got a right. He has not been appointed; he is not a status-

---

*Compare *King Lear*, Act 1, Scene IV. *Lear*: Who wouldst thou serve? *Kent*: You. *Lear*: Dost thou know me fellow? *Kent*: No sir: but you have in your countenance which I would fain call master. *Lear*: What's that? *Kent*: Authority.

holder; he possesses no credentials of a more personal sort. All that can be said is that there is something about him which people recognize in virtue of which they do what he says simply because he says it. Perhaps the word "faith" is required here, for, as Hobbes put it, the word "faith" is required when our reasons for assent derive "not from the proposition itself but from the person propounding."

It may be, however, that the search for some vague ground for the acceptance of orders in this unquestioning way is to approach the analysis of "authority" in its *de facto* sense in too positive a manner. Perhaps the use of the term "authority" is to *deny* certain characteristic suggestions rather than to assert a positive ground for unquestioning obedience. People often do what they are told because they are threatened or bribed or physically forced. After all, obedience in a crisis can be produced by a fire hose or machine gun, irrespective of who is manning it. Maybe the term "authority" is necessary for describing those situations where conformity is brought about *without* recourse to force, bribes, incentives, or propaganda and *without* a lot of argument and discussion, as in moral situations. We describe such situations by saying that an order is obeyed or a decision is accepted *simply because* X gave it or made it. This is a way of excluding *both* that action was taken on moral grounds *and* that the person acted under constraint or pressure or influence. The use of authority, in other words, is a manner of regulating human behavior which is an intermediary between moral argument and the use of force, incentives, and propaganda.

Common features of all uses of "authority"

There are, therefore, features which all uses of the term "authority" have in common. In so far as the *de facto* sense implies that, in an indeterminate and embryonic sense, the person who exercises authority is regarded as "having a right" to be obeyed, and so on, the *de facto* sense is parasitic on the *de jure* sense. But the common features of both senses are, perhaps, best brought out by summarizing and making explicit the peculiar nature and role of authority in the regulation of human behavior—the point at which I embarked on this analysis in the company of Hobbes and de Jouvenel.

In contrast to "power." The first feature to stress is the connection between "authority" and the use of certain types of regulatory utterances, gestures, and symbolic acts. A person *in* authority has a right to make decisions, issue pronouncements, give commands, and perhaps perform certain sorts of symbolic significant· acts. To *have* authority with another man is to get him to do things by giving orders to him, by making pronouncements and decisions.

The main function of the term "authority" in the analysis of a social situation is to stress these ways of regulating behavior by certain types of utterance *in contrast* to other ways of regulating behavior. This is to reject the more usual attempts to analyze "authority" in terms of "power" as exemplified by Weldon, for instance, who claims that "authority" means power exercised with the general approval of those concerned (*Vocabulary of Politics*, p. 56). This, of course, is not to deny that it may be important, as Warrender stresses, to distinguish physical power from political power, the latter being confined to cases where an element of "consent" is involved, as when a man does something because he is threatened, cajoled, or duped, in contrast to when he is physically coerced — e.g., bound and put into prison. (See *The Political Philosophy of Hobbes*, pp. 312–313.) It might, therefore, be tempting to regard the exercise of authority as a species of the exercise of political power distinguished by approval as opposed to mere acceptance on the part of the victim. But this, surely, is an oversimplification. For often what we want to bring out when we say that men are in authority or exert authority over other men is that they get their way or ought to get their way by means *other than those* of force, threats, incentives, and propaganda, which are the usual ways of exercising *power*. It is only when a system of authority breaks down or a given individual loses his authority that there must be recourse to power if conformity is to be ensured. The concept of "authority" is necessary to bring out the ways in which behavior is regulated *without* recourse to power — to force, incentives, and propaganda. These ways are intimately bound up with issuing pronouncements, making decisions, and giving commands. I suppose the concept of "power" can be extended to cover these ways of influencing people. But my claim is that "power" usually has meaning by contrast with "authority" rather than as a generic term of which "authority" is just one species.

In so far as there is a *positive* connection between "power" and "authority," it is better conceived along other lines. For instance, it might well be true that a common condition for the exercise of authority *de facto* is the ability to dispose of overwhelming power, if necessary. Or, alternatively, power might be regarded as a ground of entitlement. The old saying that there can be no legitimacy without power might be interpreted in this second way — as claiming that one of the grounds which give a man a right to command must always be, directly or indirectly, the ability to dispose of power, if necessary. Or it could be interpreted in the first way as an assertion that the possession of power is a necessary condition for the *de facto* exercise of authority, the legitimacy of which might be established in other ways. And, of course, this necessary condition, like others which I have mentioned before, can come to be regarded as a ground of entitlement. There is, however, no need to explore this positive connection in detail. For my claim is that these are answers to other questions — questions about the grounds of entitlement or about the necessary conditions for the exercise of authority, not questions about the meaning of "authority."

There is little mystery about why authority should be so intimately connected with the problem of the analysis of human institutions. For men, *pace* Aristotle, are rule-following animals; they talk and regulate their own behavior and that of others by means of speech. Men perform predictably in relation to each other and form what is called a social system to a large extent because they accept systems of rules which are infinitely variable and alterable by human decision. Such systems can only be maintained if there is general acceptance of procedural rules which lay down who is to originate rules, who is to decide about their concrete application to concrete cases, and who is entitled to introduce changes. In other words, if this peculiarly human type of order is to be maintained there are spheres where it is essential that decisions should be accepted simply because *somebody*, specified by rules of procedure, has made them. It is very difficult to play cricket without an umpire just as it is difficult to conceive of an army working without a hierarchical system of command. The term "authority" is essential in those contexts where a pronouncement, decision, or command must be accepted simply because some person, conforming to specifications laid down by the normative system, has made or given it — where there must be a recognized "auctor." More liberal societies, of course, guard against injustice and stupidity by instituting further procedures for appealing against decisions of those in authority. But this is merely a device whereby a higher authority is instituted to correct the mistakes of a lower one. It is still a regulatory device which relies on the institution of authority and in no way abrogates the duty of obedience to the lower authority, provided that the lower authority is acting *intra vires*.

In contrast to moral and scientific regulation of conduct and opinions. This analysis of "authority" accounts also for a long tradition which stresses the incompatibility between authority and certain specific human enterprises like science and morality. For it would be held that in science the importance of the "auctor" or originator is at a minimum, it never being justifiable in scientific institutions to set up individuals or bodies who will either be the originators of pronouncements or who will decide finally on the truth of pronouncements made.

The procedural rules of science lay it down, roughly speaking, that hypotheses must be decided by looking at the evidence, not by appealing to a man. There are also, and can be, no rules to decide who will be the originators of scientific theories. In a similar way, it would be held that a rule cannot be a moral one if it is to be accepted just because someone has laid it down or made a decision between competing alternatives. Reasons must be given for it, not originators or umpires produced. Of course, in both enterprises provisional authorities can be consulted. But there are usually good reasons for their choice and their pronouncements are never to be regarded as final just because they have made them. In science and morality there are no appointed lawgivers or judges or policemen. This is one of the ways in which life in the laboratory differs from life in the army and law courts.

This analysis of "authority" readily explains, too, the connections so often made between "authority" and "command." For commands, roughly speaking, are the sorts of regulatory utterances for which no reasons need to be given. A man can only give a command if he is in a position of authority or if he exerts authority in a *de facto* sense. For as an occupant of an office or as a status holder he has a right to make decisions which are binding and to issue orders. Similarly, if the *de facto* sense of authority is being used, to say that a man has authority over other men is to say, among other things, that they will do what they are told without questioning the prudence, wisdom, and good sense of the decision. They may, of course, question its legality, for questions can be raised about a man's right to issue commands in general or in a particular sphere. These are questions about his right to an office or status, or about the sphere of its competence or his prerogative. But once it is granted that he occupies an office or holds a status legitimately, and once it is made clear that he is not straying from its sphere of competence or exceeding his prerogative, there can be no further question of justifying his commands. For commands just are the type of regulatory utterance where questions of justification are ruled out.

Authority, however, is not exercised *only* in the giving of commands. There are also the spheres of making pronouncements and decisions and the performance of symbolic acts. Behavior or opinion in these spheres is regulated by the utterance of a man which carries with it the obligation for others to accept, follow, or obey. The claim put forward by Hobbes and Austin, that law is command, is right in stressing the connection between law and authority but wrong in conceiving of commands as the only form of authoritative utterance. Similarly, those who speak of the "authority of the individual conscience" cannot be supposed merely to be saying that in moral matters a man must give himself orders, which sounds, in any case, a little quaint; rather they are saying that in moral matters a man must decide himself between conflicting claims and principles and not accept the pronouncements and decisions of others simply because they issue from determinate sources. In morals a man must be his own "auctor."

Conclusion

To conclude: my thesis is that the concept of "authority" can be used in a *de jure* and a *de facto* sense. Among the former uses it is very important to distinguish the kind of entitlement implied in being *in* authority from that implied in being *an* authority. Authority in a *de facto* sense is parasitic on the *de jure* sense in that it implies that decisions are in fact accepted or commands obeyed simply because they issue from a certain person whose attributes are in some way regarded as bestowing legitimacy on them. The grounds for this legitimacy are often much more indeterminate than those more impersonal grounds characteristic of *de jure* authority. There are, however, more general negative features which all senses of "authority" share. The term is always used to speak of ways in which conduct is regulated as distinct from the mere use of power — e.g., the giving of commands, the making of decisions and pronouncements, as distinct from the use of force, incentives, and propaganda. Second, within the sphere of decisions, pronouncements, and other such regulatory utterances, authority is confined to those which are or must be obeyed simply because someone has made them. This second feature of "authority" brings out the contrast between laws, commands, and religious utterances, on the one hand, and those of science and morality on the other. Both these features of "authority" are rooted in the Latin word "auctoritas" which implies an originator in the sphere of opinion, counsel, and command.

4

Political Authority: Its Exercise and Possession

C. W. Cassinelli

THE concept of authority is central to the study of politics, since descriptions of governmental institutions, public policy, and patterns of political power must assume at least a distinction between the presence and absence of authority, while broader issues like the nature of the state, the law, and political obedience require a clear definition of authority for their satisfactory treatment. Political theorists have always recognized this, but the modern disciplines of sociology and public administration have provided much new information and many new insights regarding authority. Nevertheless, the theory of authority still contains certain weaknesses stemming from lack of information and analysis.

The present essay will be concerned with one of these ambiguities of analysis. It appears to me that the failure to distinguish between what I shall call the "exercise" of political authority and its "possession" has impeded our understanding of the relationship between political authority on the one hand and obedience, coercion, and popular attitudes on the other. Moreover, if the distinction is made and kept in mind, many apparent discrepancies of evidence and disagreements of argument about political authority itself seem to disappear. The exercise of political authority requires the citizen to obey uncritically and without considering the possibility of coercion; the possession of political authority depends upon his critical acceptance of the use of coercion, and it is compatible with his occasional disobedience.

From *Western Political Quarterly*, XIV (1961), 635–646. Copyright 1961 by the University of Utah.

The Function of the Governor

Although political authority — the authority possessed and exercised by the governor[1] — may be fundamentally similar to the authority of the expert, cleric, or parent, it still differs from these other authorities because it is political and they are not. An analysis of political authority must therefore begin by defining "political."

The governor exercises and possesses political authority only when his special competence is specifically related to ordering, regulating, shaping, or determining the behavior of a limited group of human beings. Since this statement also applies to other "authorities," his special competence and thus his particular function must be more or less precisely described. Social theorists have defined the function of governing by reference to the aspects of human behavior the governor regulates, the scope of his regulation, or the methods which he may use.

Defining the governor's function in terms of the kind of behavior he regulates is unsatisfactory, for it founders on the obvious fact that all governments, from totalitarian to democratic, control and direct practically every activity in which men normally engage. The statement that government has a limited sphere of competence is usually normative rather than descriptive.

The second type of definition says that the governor makes decisions which apply to the whole society, in contrast to the limited scope of the decisions of other possessors of influence.[2] This definition is also unsatisfactory. In the first place, decisions by people who are not governors successfully regulate the behavior of the whole society. The theological and moral pronouncements of clerics in single-faith societies are the most obvious examples, but decisions by "experts" in matters such as dress and "manners" may also have a similar scope. Second, not all decisions by government "allocate values for the whole society"; they may deal with special subgroups (like the inhabitants of the Tennessee Valley) or even with individuals (like the subjects of "relief" bills of the United States Congress).[3] Finally, the notion of the "whole society" is extremely vague. On first glance it seems to refer to all the people of the state, but since the state is usually defined by reference to the scope of governmental control, the "whole society" must be something else. If the "whole society" is defined in terms of relatively intensive human interaction,[4] then no account is taken of the fact that the governor's jurisdiction stops at the boundaries of his state, no matter how socially and economically artificial these boundaries may be.

The method of regulation which the governor may use provides, on the contrary, a useful definition of his function. His ability to attach to his directives the threat to utilize physical coercion against those who do not comply with them clearly distinguishes his function from that of any other regulator of human behavior.[5] This statement is not affected by pointing out that this threat may be only a minor factor in the governed's motivation to comply with the governor's directives, or that in order to accomplish certain purposes the latter may rely extensively upon nondirective techniques like persuasion.[6] The increasing importance of the governor's new "positive" tasks — social welfare, public works, aid to foreigners, etc. — also does not affect the issue, because they are all based upon his old task of raising revenue which is always connected with his ability to use coercion.

Moreover, every act of the governor in his capacity as governor is accompanied by at least an implicit reference to this ability to use physical coercion. Any of his acts which do not imply such coercion are performed in some other capacity, such as "leading citizen," party politician, or symbol of the national community. Therefore, political authority, the authority attached to the function of governing, is always conjoined with the governor's ability to use physical coercion. The principal analytical problem is to clarify the relationship between political authority and coercion and to relate both to the behavior and attitudes of those subject to regulation. Making a distinction between exercising and possessing political authority seems to solve at least some aspects of this problem.

The "Exercise" of Political Authority

The concepts of "exercising" and "possessing" political authority are introduced to take account of a more or less implicit distinction often made in discussions of authority and to correspond to certain facets of authority which upon analysis are seen to have different characteristics. The possession of authority and its exercise are both necessary and sufficient for one another, but the tendency to refer to them as if they were identical — or, more usually, to fail to distinguish between them — has led to some confusion.

When the governor exercises political authority he performs an overt act aimed at regulating his governed's behavior. In order to perform such an act, he must (as we say) have authority, but his possession is clearly not the same thing as his act. The latter, when authoritative, is a relationship containing a communication, its issuer, and its recipient, each of which should be described in some detail.

The Actions and Motivations of the Governor. An exercise of political authority is initiated when the governor issues a communication to the governed with the definite intention of predictably changing the latter's behavior. This communication is an imperative[7] normally designed to regularize behavior, but often dealing with specific and unique cases. The governor is concerned with behavior and not with beliefs; in his capacity as governor, he never intends to convince the governed of his communication's desirability, in any sense of the latter word. He may hope that they consider it desirable, but he makes no attempt to persuade them.[8] The governor also has no intention of bargaining with the governed; he may bargain before he makes his decision, but once stated his communication is not subject to amendment.[9] Finally, the governor does not intend to use coercion to achieve his purpose, and he expects people to follow his directions while being physically able to ignore them. If he wishes to collect revenue, for example, he does not intend that money be taken from taxpayers at gunpoint, but he expects them to give it to the collector although nothing literally prevents them from withholding it.[10]

Nevertheless, the governor always accompanies his communication with a least an implicit threat to use physical coercion either to obtain its intended results — e.g., to get revenue by forcibly taking money from tax-dodgers — or to punish those who ignore it in (presumably) the hope that they and others will be deterred from future disobedience.[11] When the governor actually applies coercion for either of these purposes, he is not exercising authority; we say that in this instance his authority has "broken down" or is "inoperative."[12] When he applies coercion his intentions and expectations, as pointed out above, are quite different from when he exercises authority, and the reactions of the governed are also quite different in the two cases.

The Reactions and Motivations of the Governed. The recipient of the communication is the second element in an exercise of political authority. The governed,[13] whose behavior is to be regulated by the governor's directive, have special reactions and motivations when the governor exercises authority.[14]

The recipient's first reaction is to become aware that the communication is directing him to do something, to take or refrain from some action. If the governor regulates the governed's behavior without the latter's knowing it, his influence is not an exercise of authority but rather a "manipulation."[15] The recipient must also realize that the communication is an imperative, that the governor does not intend to convince, persuade, or bargain. However, he need not understand precisely what the communication is saying, and he can even misinterpret it to the extent that he believes it to say something which the governor did not at all intend. The governor's exercise of authority over the citizen is not undermined by obscureness and misunderstanding. The recipient must only be aware that he is being told to do something.

The recipient's second reaction is to try to conform to the stipulations of the communication as he understands them. Strict compliance is clearly not necessary; we do not hesitate to say that a governor exercises authority over a citizen who makes a serious but misguided or unsuccessful attempt to comply with his directives.

In an exercise of political authority the citizen reacts as he does because he is consciously aware that the governor's communication specifies a certain reaction. If he "unthinkingly" conforms, authority is not being exercised. For example, most people refrain from murder not because they know it is prohibited by the governors, although they do have this knowledge, but because it is inconsistent with their education, their nonpolitical values, and the mores of the people with whom they associate and identify. Such law-abidingness does not result from the exercise of political authority.

When the governor exercises authority over the governed, the latter recognizes the former's communication as "authoritative," that is, he recognizes it as coming from a source which possesses special attributes entitling it to be obeyed. (These attributes — position, status, and charisma — will be described below; they are the links between the exercise of authority and the possession of authority.) The recipient connects the communication with the source by hearing the former directly from a heroic leader or a village elder or a uniformed policeman, or by seeing certain symbols attached to it, or by being assured by one whose judgment he trusts — a lawyer, for example — that it issues from the proper source. His reaction to this source or its symbolic representation may be either habitual or conscious; that is, he may either act directly upon receiving the properly characterized communication or he may take the intermediate step of acknowledging that it comes from the proper source. The exercise of authority clearly does not include compliance without awareness of the issuer's identity, a reaction compatible only with acute fear or excitement.

In an exercise of authority the governed are not motivated to compliance by any kind of agreement with the communication's contents. It has been said that the recipient conforms to the communication without evaluating it in terms of his own standards, without contemplating its merits,[16] but this is not entirely accurate. He may quite thoroughly evaluate it in terms of "justice" or of his own selfish interests, and still "accept its authority"; the only requirement for an exercise of authority is that his decision to comply does not result from a favorable evaluation. He must conform to the communication despite any evaluation of it, and indeed one of the most common variations of the exercise of authority occurs when the recipient has decided that the communication is factually, rationally, or ethically incorrect and still does not reject it.[17]

The relative insignificance of the truth, goodness, or rationality of the communication's contents is probably the most striking feature of the exercise of political authority.[18] The recipient complies because of the source of the communication, not because of its contents. It is true that the governed believe that the governor has attributes which are connected with unusual degrees of truth or goodness or rationality, whether or not they believe the latter characteristics are manifested in any given communication: this means that the governor possesses authority and it will be discussed below. But the point to be stressed here is that the exercise of authority does not depend on the recipient's appraisal of the communication in terms of its worthiness to be obeyed.

Fear of Coercion and the Recipient's Motivation. Writers have disagreed about the relationship of physical coercion to the recipient's motivation for compliance in an exercise of authority. Authority cannot be exercised when the recipient is "restrained,"[19] because under restraint compliance is not a motivated action, and some kind of motivation is undoubtedly implied by the notion of authority. However, it is less clear whether an exercise of authority is compatible with compliance motivated by the recipient's fear that his failure to comply will result in personal disadvantage. Some theorists say that authority is exercised whenever an imperative is obeyed, including of course those cases where obedience is motivated by the fear of physical coercion.[20] This position seems to conflict with ordinary usage, and it is clearly incompatible with the traditional conception of governors without authority — usurpers, conquerors, and "tyrants" in general. This disagreement, however, may be only terminological; those who hold fear of physical coercion to be consistent with authority must admit that different kinds of governors have different kinds of authority, and it should be obvious to all that obedience motivated by fear of coercion differs rather sharply from other kinds of obedience.

The relationship between fear and authority may be unclear in part because two kinds of fear have not been distinguished. When an individual receives an imperative, he ignores it or unthinkingly complies with it or asks himself in effect, "Why should I comply?" His answers based on his fear not to comply involve many possible disadvantages which he expects to accompany noncompliance. These disadvantages are basically of two kinds, according to whether or not they involve punishment willed by human beings. When they do involve punishment, they are called "sanctions," and traditionally sanctions have been classified as legal, social, moral, and religious.[21] Fines and imprisonment, withdrawal of deference, disapproval and censure, and penance and excommunication are disadvantages which the issuers of imperatives can impose upon the recipient who fails to comply. All these sanctions play an important part in motivating the governed to obey the governor,[22] but among authorities only the governor can apply sanctions involving physical coercion. Fear of these so-called legal sanctions is the fear normally held incompatible with the exercise of political authority.

The second kind of disadvantage is not a punishment to be effected by the "authority" in question, but rather a disadvantage independent of his will. For example, disobedience of traffic laws may lead to bodily injury, of norms of etiquette to boorishness, of principles of morality to immorality, and of religious precepts to damnation. That is to say, in this type of case disobedience seems likely to involve one in error or irrationality or evil. This kind of disadvantage is quite different from a sanction, but it also aids in promoting law-abidingness.[23]

Although both kinds of fear operate as reasons for law-abidingness, the latter, in contrast to the former, can be the motivation for compliance in an exercise of authority. The recipient often defers to the governor and complies with the governor's communication because he believes his own sources of information and powers of reasoning inferior to those of the governor. This kind of motivation is particularly evident in the case of military authority: the field officer believes the general officer to be better equipped than he is to understand and exploit the entire battle-situation. The general, because of his position, is considered very likely to be right, even though his individual communication may appear peculiar or even incorrect. The ultimate motivation for compliance in any exercise of political authority is the belief that the source of the communication is capable of giving rational directions.[24] This belief and the fear of error in case of noncompliance are the same thing: If I follow someone's advice because I believe he is right, I am at the same time complying with his recommendation because I fear that otherwise I will be in error.

The Exercise of Political Authority: Summary. The overt act of X's exercising political authority over Y occurs when and only when: (1) X addresses to Y a communication which is an imperative consciously designed to influence the actions of Y; (2) this communication is accompanied by the explicit or implicit intention to utilize physical coercion (for one reason or another) against Y if he fails to comply; X, however, does not intend to use coercion to bring about the desired behavior of Y; (3) Y attempts to comply with the terms of the communication as he understands them (or attempts to get them changed so that compliance is, as he sees it, possible), and he does so in full knowledge that X has intended to influence his behavior; (4) Y complies with the communication because and only because it comes from X, whom he recognizes as possessing certain attributes which justify giving orders; he can approve of the communication's contents, but this approval is not his motivation for compliance.

The preceding analysis has led to a rather strange conclusion. Although political authority is inseparable from the function of governing, which in turn is inseparable from the governor's ability to use physical coercion in his attempt to regulate the governed's behavior, when a governor exercises political authority over a citizen the former does not intend to use physical coercion and the latter is not motivated by any consideration of its possible use. In its exercise, political authority appears fundamentally similar to other authorities. Its difference from them, and its connection with the function of governing, are aspects of what I have called the "possession" of political authority.

The "Possession" of Political Authority

A governor "possesses" authority when he is able to exercise authority, as the latter is described above. Although the relationship between exercise and possession is obviously very close, a governor can possess authority at the moment his communication is not being complied with, or when the citizen obeys because he agrees with its contents or fears the punishment attached to disobedience. The possession of authority, unlike the exercise of authority, depends upon the citizens' attitudes rather than upon their actions. One can have the ability to exercise authority without being invariably successful in his attempts to exercise it.

Characteristics Necessary for the Possession of Authority. The possessor of political authority must have certain special characteristics. He may, in the first place, occupy a "position" or "office"; that is, he may belong to a formal organization which operates according to rules specifying the human behavior its members may regulate and defining its own membership. For example, the United States Constitution says that "the Congress shall have the power to lay and collect taxes," and it also describes how one becomes a member of the Congress. This situation of the governor corresponds to what Max Weber called "rational-legal authority."[25]

Rather than occupying an office, the governor may have a status. When having political authority depends upon a status, the rules regarding possession of the status are usually fairly clear but the area of human behavior to be regulated is normally only vaguely defined. Nevertheless, the status-order, like the governmental organization, is institutionalized. For example, in gerontocracy or hereditary monarchy individuals acquire the requisite status by a regularized procedure, and everyone recognizes that the general function of governing is connected with this status. This type of situation corresponds to Weber's "traditional authority."[26]

Both status and position are indirectly connected with their possessor's political authority. The assumption is that elections will supply sound and farsighted congressmen, that senior bureaucrats will select and promote competent subordinates, that the old men will be wise, and that the heir to the throne will receive an appropriate education. The third special characteristic, however, is directly connected with the possession of authority. It consists solely of certain personal attributes — a commanding appearance, an ability to create enthusiasm and articulate grievances, the personification of norms of honor or trustworthiness or expertise, in general "a raw capacity of obtaining compliance"[27] — which appear as immediately qualifying their possessor to regulate human affairs. This is Weber's "charismatic authority"; and, as he points out, because of this direct connection between personal characteristics and the presumed ability to govern, it is the least institutionalized and tends to develop into one of the others.[28]

In themselves position, status, and charisma have nothing in common. Holding an office, having a noble ancestry, and being "dynamic" have no similar essential properties; they all accompany the possession of political authority only because they are reacted to similarly by various citizenries. Moreover, the three do not coexist as concomitants of authority. For example, in a democracy the greatest amount of charisma and the highest possible status do not by themselves bring any political authority whatever, and in an aristocracy only a noble birth qualifies one to be a governor.[29]

The Governed's Attitude toward the Governor's Characteristics. The governor's position, status, or charisma is sufficient for possessing authority when those whom he regulates believe it to provide the knowledge, judgment, virtue, or trustworthiness required for controlling certain human activities considered so important that their regulation necessitates the ability to threaten physical punishment. These activities vary widely, ranging from the simplest to the most subtle. Men recognize other agencies as qualified to direct their activities, but only the governor is conceded the right to use physical coercion in the event of non-compliance.

The governor possesses political authority because the governed believe in three connections: the first between his position, status, or charisma on the one hand, and his knowledge, judgment, virtue, or trustworthiness on the other; the second between the latter qualities and the right to regulate their behavior; and the third between the kind of regulation for which the governor is suited and the instrumental necessity of physical coercion. It is difficult to say precisely who among the governed believes in these connections, because every society has some people who either believe that knowledge, judgment, and virtue are associated with other positions or statuses or charismas, or refuse to recognize anyone's right to control their own behavior, or deny that any regulation of human beings requires physical coercion. It can be said only that "most of the people" under the governor's control recognize his right to rule; the belief that he has this right "predominates throughout the state."

A citizen can believe in these three connections while disobeying his governor's directives or complying with them for reasons incompatible with the exercise of authority, but a governor cannot possess authority if no one at all complies with his directives or if no one complies for the right reasons. Consequently, the governor must have a certain proportion of his directives duly obeyed, but this proportion also can be described only in a most general way: when a governor possesses authority "most of the people most of the time" properly abide by his decisions. However, the governed's belief in the governor's right to rule and their obedience to him can probably be connected empirically. If a people are reasonably law-abiding, if it is reasonably certain that this obedience is not motivated by the fear of punishment, and if the society is too complex to suppose that the reasons behind most laws can be widely understood, then most of the people probably believe their governors to have a right to obedience.[30]

The governed believe that the governor's position or status or charisma gives him a right to regulate at least some of their affairs, if necessary by means of physical coercion. This right depends upon the results they expect from his governing, which range from the provision of simple physical protection to the realization of complex notions of justice. The point is that the governor's right is based upon something he is presumably able to do for the governed; he thus does not possess political authority because his governed fear him, but he may possess it because they fear that undirected they are incapable of acting correctly or morally or rationally.

This right of the governor, which is identical with his possession of political authority, may be either practical or moral. The people may believe that his rule is simply expedient, or they may believe that it is morally good. These two beliefs differ significantly, for when the latter prevails the position, status, or charisma of the governor is much more thoroughly integrated with the whole pattern of mores characterizing the society in question, and as a result the governor's authority is more deeply founded and his success in receiving obedience more likely. Authority based on a moral right to rule is often called "legitimacy," and it is no doubt the most important variety of political authority.[31] Nevertheless, a governor whom the people consider only a means of providing protection against internal "anti-social" elements or external aggressors also has authority, even though he is not believed to have a moral right to rule. The people recognize his usefulness and probably are thus quite willing to obey him, but they consider him only temporary or only the best available under the circumstances.

The Possession of Political Authority: Summary. The attitudes and beliefs of those who receive authoritative communications are the foundation of the governor's possession of authority. The popular approval and acceptance generally believed characteristic of all authority relate not to the communication when political authority is exercised, but to its source, the possessor of political authority. In an exercise of political authority evaluation of the communication can be only incidental, but the possession of political authority can be constantly evaluated in terms of its consistency with the practical needs or moral postulates it is supposed to satisfy. The average citizen usually assumes the governor's right to rule, which means that the possession, as well as the exercise, of authority can rest upon habit. The average man becomes critical only when the presuppositions justifying the governor's rule come in conflict with his own basic sense of practical or moral correctness — when, that is, a revolutionary situation is at hand. The intellectual, on the other hand, may frequently question whether the governor deserves to be obeyed, and each time he answers in the affirmative the governor's authority is further strengthened.[32]

The governor's authority is always an implication of the basic norms of his society.[33] It is based on reason and justice, but on reason and justice as conceived by the society — and the society may be mistaken.[34] Thus the political moralist always has the right to say that in a given society a governor incorrectly possesses political authority.

The governor's exercise of political authority is always accompanied by his implicit threat to punish disobedience, and his possession of political authority is always accompanied by his governed's belief that he should have this coercive power.[35] However, the threat of physical coercion must be quite divorced from the situation where political authority is exercised, while the governor would not possess political authority at all if he were not recognized as having the right to make such a threat. Political authority therefore seems to differ from the other authorities which characterize human interaction only in this latter respect. It is the purely political aspect of the governor's function which makes his authority unique.

Notes

1. When we say that someone other than a governor has political authority, we mean either that he has political influence in general or, more likely, that he has influence upon those who have governmental authority. In either case, however, the word "authority" does not seem to be applied properly.
2. E.g., David Easton, *The Political System* (New York: Knopf, 1953), p. 133. Easton's concept of politics as the "authoritative allocation of values" means, when developed, "making decisions which bind the whole society."
3. See Anthony Downs, *An Economic Theory of Democracy* (New York: Harper, 1957). pp. 14–17, and the references there cited.
4. Society is "the broadest grouping of human beings who live together and collectively undertake to satisfy all the minimum prerequisites of group life" (Easton, *Political System*, p. 135).
5. Cf. Hans Kelsen, *General Theory of Law and State*, trans. Anders Wedberg (Cambridge, Mass.: Harvard University Press, 1945), p. 18; and Frederick M. Watkins, *The State as a Concept of Political Science* (New York: Harper, 1934), pp. 47–49.
6. Cf. David Easton, "The Perception of Authority and Political Change," in Carl J. Friedrich, ed., *Authority* (Cambridge, Mass.: Harvard University Press, 1958), p. 183.
7. The principal attack on the theory of law as command has been given by Kelsen, *General Theory*, pp. 30–35. This position, however, creates more difficulties than it solves: see Alan Gewirth, "The Quest for Specificity in Jurisprudence," *Ethics*, LXIX (1959), 162–163.
8. Governmental personnel may engage in "public relations campaigns" to

86 | AUTHORITY

convince the governed of the desirability of a law, either before or after it is passed; but in doing so they do not differ from any "civic-minded" group which may wish to increase law-abidingness, and the passing of the law is an act logically quite independent of any attempt to inform people of its meaning or convince them of its desirability.

9. Bargaining may occur when law-enforcement agencies attempt to apply a generalized statute, but in this case the agency has been delegated authority to make adjustments, and its final decision is not open to bargaining.

10. On the use of coercion, see Felix E. Oppenheim, "An Analysis of Political Control," *The Journal of Politics*, XX (1958), 515–534. Oppenheim's concept of "restraint" includes situations where an individual is literally unable to pursue a course of action and where his pursuing it would involve "extremely disvaluable" consequences (p. 521). Being at gunpoint comes within the latter category.

11. On the theory of the legal penalty, see Carl J. Friedrich, *The Philosophy of Law in Historical Perspective* (Chicago: University of Chicago Press, 1958), chap. 22, and especially pp. 212–213.

12. Robert Bierstedt has said that when, in a voluntary association, a member refuses to resign after having broken its rules, there occurs another exercise of authority to compel his resignation: "The Problem of Authority," in Morroe Berger *et al.*, eds., *Freedom and Control in Modern Society* (New York: Van Nostrand, 1954), pp. 79–80. See also Chester I. Barnard, *The Functions of the Executive* (Cambridge, Mass.: Harvard University Press, 1938), p. 183. An official can *have* authority to compel resignation, but it does not follow that an act of compulsion is an *exercise* of authority.

13. The governed must be distinguished from governmental subordinates who are "under the authority" of their superiors. There is a difference between, for example, the American Congress and President's directives to the general citizenry and their directives to the governmental bureaucracy. The latter situation depends upon the principle of hierarchy within a single organization, and since it does not involve the possible application of physical coercion it is not political. The usual penalty for a bureaucrat's failure to comply with his superior's directives is dismissal, as it is in any organization.

14. Barnard, *Functions of the Executive*, p. 163, has said that authority is the character of a communication by virtue of which it is accepted by a member of an organization as governing his action. While this statement emphasizes quite properly the importance of the recipient's motives, it is misleading because his particular reaction is only necessary for an exercise of authority; it is not sufficient as well.

15. This is Easton's term: "The Perception of Authority and Political Change," p. 179.

16. *Ibid.*, pp. 179–180; see also Herbert A. Simon, *Administrative Behavior* (New York: Macmillan, 1947), pp. 125–126.

17. Another variation occurs when the recipient, on evaluation of the com-

munication, decides that it cannot be complied with, and thereupon attempts to get it altered. In this case the governor will exercise authority as long as the recipient does not decide that he will not comply with the communication because of its impropriety or incorrectness. If he decides that he cannot comply, the exercise of authority does not necessarily disappear.

18. Carl J. Friedrich has argued that "authority" is a characteristic of a communication and does not at all depend upon the recipient; the communication possesses the "potentiality of reasoned elaboration," it is "worthy of acceptance"; and if the recipient mistakenly believes it to have this characteristic, the situation is one of false or faked authority ("Authority, Reason, and Discretion," in Friedrich, ed., *Authority*, pp. 35–37). Jerome Hall has said that authority fills a gap where reason and investigation fall short, and that it can always be challenged on rational or empirical grounds: "Authority and the Law," *ibid.*, pp. 64–65. However, both authors seem to be describing an ideal authority rather than analyzing what we call "political authority": see Friedrich, n. 15; I am here interested in "false" as well as "true" authority. Their remarks are also more applicable to the possession of authority than to its exercise.

19. In Oppenheim's sense; see note 10 above.

20. E.g., Easton, "The Perception of Authority and Political Change," pp. 180–182; and Robert Michels, "Authority," *Encyclopedia of the Social Sciences*, II, 319–321. Although it is admitted that obedience because of fear differs from obedience for other reasons, these writers wish to emphasize obedience rather than the different kinds of obedience. They are interested in the operation of political systems, not in the differences between them, and they say that all governors, by definition, possess authority: see Easton, "Perception of Authority."

21. Cf. J. S. Mill, *Utilitarianism* (New York: Dutton, 1940), pp. 25–26. "Sanctions of the conscience" are of a different order, since they do not involve the will of another person.

22. See R. M. MacIver, *The Web of Government* (New York: Macmillan, 1947), pp. 76–77.

23. *Ibid.*

24. This resembles Friedrich's conception of the "capacity of reasoned elaboration." However, it depends upon the belief of the recipient rather than upon any "objective" standards of rationality, and it focuses on the issuer rather than on the communication.

25. *The Theory of Social and Economic Organization*, trans. Henderson and Parsons (Glencoe, Ill.: Free Press, 1947), pp. 329 ff. As Talcott Parsons has pointed out, Weber classifies authority on the basis of the "level of differentiation of the social system with reference to political function" and the "stability of institutionalization of the value system" regarding this differentiation: "Authority, Legitimation, and Political Action," in Friedrich, ed., *Authority*, p. 213.

26. *Theory of Social and Economic Organization*, pp 341 ff., and Parsons' "Introduction," pp. 60–61; see also *ibid.*, pp. 212–213.
27. Bertrand de Jouvenel, "Authority: the Efficient Imperative," in Friedrich, ed., *Authority*, p. 163.
28. Weber, *Theory of Social and Economic Organization*, pp. 358 ff.
29. What we call "aristocracies" may well contain offices. When they do an aristocrat without an office has no political authority; that is, a noble birth is necessary but not sufficient for possessing political authority.
30. Cf. Kelsen's discussion of the relationship between the "validity" and the "efficacy" of the law: *General Theory*, pp. 29–44. As seen above, the obscureness of an individual communication, the recipient's misunderstanding of its contents, and the failure of the recipient to comply with it successfully do not by themselves prevent an exercise of authority. To possess authority, however, the governor must have a fairly large proportion of his directives more or less successfully carried out. Otherwise his authority would disappear through confusion.
31. For a discussion of legitimacy, see C. W. Cassinelli, "The 'Consent' of the Governed," *Western Political Quarterly*, XII (1959), 391–409.
32. Cf. Hall, "Authority and the Law," p. 65: "it is always possible on rational-empirical grounds to challenge authority in any specific area." Friedrich's idea of the potentiality of reasoned elaboration also applies to the possession of authority. If the source is supposed to possess rationality, then its communications are supposed to be rational. If one of them is not, however, the governor does not thereby lose his authority. If he is constantly wrong, then his authority will no doubt dissipate.
33. The rationale of authority "is in the very factors which induce men to form associations in the first place..." Bierstedt, "Problem of Authority," p. 77.
34. A society might genuinely believe, for example, that "might is right," and thus accord legitimacy to whoever possesses the largest amount of coercive power. Ideally authority should be based upon perfect reason and the ultimate social good — "The final authority is truth and right, valid values..." Frank H. Knight, "Authority and the Free Society," in Friedrich, ed., *Authority*, p. 77. However, where such authority could be realized, *political* authority would probably be unnecessary.
35. "Authority" itself, which I have not discussed, is probably to be defined as a sub-set of the norms of human behavior which characterize every society. For accounts of these norms, see Parsons, *Theory of Social and Economic Organization*, William C. Mitchell, "The Polity and Society: A Structural-Functional Analysis," *Midwest Journal of Political Science*, II (1958), 403–420, which follows Parsons' scheme; and E. Abramson *et al.*, "Social Power and Commitment: A Theoretical Statement," *American Sociological Review*, XXIII (1958), 15–22.

Select Bibliography

ARENDT, HANNAH. "Authority in the Twentieth Century," *Review of Politics*, XVIII (1956), 403–417.

————. "What Is Authority?" In *Between Past and Future*. Cleveland: World Publishing Co., 1963. Pp. 91–141.

BENN, S. I., and PETERS, R. S. *Principles of Political Thought*. New York: Macmillan, 1964. Chapter 14.

BLAU, PETER. "Critical Remarks on Weber's Theory of Authority," *American Political Science Review*, LVII (1963), 305–316.

DAY, JOHN. "Authority," *Political Studies*, XI (1963), 257–271.

FRIEDRICH, C. J., ed. *Authority: Nomos I*. New York: Liberal Arts Press, 1958.

DE GRAZIA, S. "Authority and Rationality," *Philosophy*, XXVII (1952), 99–109.

DE GRAZIA, S. "What Authority Is Not," *American Political Science Review*, LIII (1959), 321–331.

HANDCOCK, W. D. "The Function and Nature of Authority in Society," *Philosophy*, XXVII (1953), 99–112.

DE JOUVENEL, BERTRAND. *Sovereignty*. Chicago: University of Chicago Press, 1957.

KIM, YOUNG C. "Authority: Some Conceptual and Empirical Notes," *Western Political Quarterly*, XIX (1966), 223–234.

MICHELS, ROBERTO. "Authority," *Encyclopedia of the Social Sciences*, 1930.

PETERS, R. S., WINCH, P. G., and DUNCAN-JONES, A. E. "Symposium: Authority," *Proceedings of the Aristotelian Society*, XXXII, suppl. (1958), 207–260.

WEBER, MAX. *The Theory of Social and Economic Organization*, trans. A. M. Henderson and Talcott Parsons. New York: Oxford University Press, 1947.

LIBERTY

TWO MEN are engaged in a debate about a law which would prohibit those selling homes from discriminating on the basis of race. One claims that the law would give men freedom; the other claims that it would deny men freedom. The first argues that since it would allow men to live where they wish, it gives them freedom; the second argues that since it prohibits men from selling their own property to whom they wish, it deprives them of freedom.

Political philosophers do not always take stands on such moral issues. Instead, they may analyze or clarify a particular concept or ideal that is involved. The next two articles are examples of conceptual analysis. Neither takes a side on any moral or political issue. Yet an understanding of the concept of freedom, for example, does make moral discussions involving freedom much more meaningful and fruitful. After reading these articles, the reader will see that in the case above both men are using the commendatory force of "freedom" to support their cases. The differences do not concern the nature of freedom, but only the importance of particular freedoms.

Professors Scott and MacCallum believe that previous analyses of freedom have been confused or mistaken. Scott especially criticizes those who have defined or analyzed freedom so as to include only those freedoms which they approve. MacCallum criticizes those who have tried to make a distinction between negative and positive freedom, asserting that they involve distinct concepts of freedom. (For background, the reader may wish to consult Sir Isaiah Berlin's *Two Concepts of Liberty*.) But since the aim of both articles is to offer a satisfactory analysis of the concept of freedom, the target of their criticisms is not crucial.

While their conclusions are often similar, the articles use different philosophical techniques. Scott relies on "everyday usage" because he believes that the layman's understanding of freedom is superior to the social theorist's. Ordinary language is useful because "freedom is one of the things on whose characteristics the generations who have shaped our language have had few doubts, and usage consequently offers virtually unequivocal guidance." Scott abandons this approach only when ordinary language is confusing, which is rare. MacCallum is not convinced of this. He finds that our "idioms of freedom" usually obscure its fundamental character (that it is a triadic relation). Therefore, we should look not at what we say (ordinary language), but at "the conditions under which what we say is intelligible." The difference between Scott and MacCallum on this point raises several important questions. How does one determine if a particular usage is ordinary? How does one determine if such usage is philosophically fruitful or confusing?

Scott stresses that freedom is a "nonmoral thing," that it is not intrinsically good or bad. Moral disagreements about freedom should be decided on the basis of the facts involved and not by definition. One could argue that it is immoral to grant men a "freedom to gamble," but it is not permissible to argue that it does not truly constitute a freedom and therefore that men ought not to have it.

Scott thinks that ordinary language is clear about the nonmoral character of freedom but confusing about the relation between moral obligation (or moral constraints) and freedom. One might say that a man is not free to do something if he has a moral obligation to do otherwise. But is he really unfree? Scott says no. He suggests that ordinary usage implies that a moral obligation renders us unfree only when that obligation results from a voluntary promise. In all other cases, "a moral obligation does not render us unfree." Since this problem cannot be settled in terms of his favored approach, Scott turns to other criteria. It is clear, he says, that legal obligations can render us unfree while most moral obligations cannot. Since obligations resulting from a voluntary promise are more akin to moral obligations than to legal obligations, they cannot render us unfree. This position will be examined again at a later point.

Scott distinguishes cases of "unfreedom" from cases in which the "question of freedom does not arise" or is irrelevant. The question of freedom arises only when "we are able to do a thing and want to do it." For example, if A is unable to do X, the question of his freedom to do X does not arise. Surely, there is a distinction between ability and freedom. I cannot claim that I am unfree to do something merely because I am unable to do it. However, it does not necessarily follow that the question of freedom arises only when we are able to perform an act. A person may be unable to buy a home in a suburb but may be legitimately concerned about his legal freedom to do so. A similar point can be made regarding the assertion that the question of freedom arises only when we want to do something. Scott solves this problem himself (although by contradiction) when he argues that freedom of action in a certain field is "the freedom to do whatever we *may* want to do," not what we do want to do.

MacCallum's article attacks the notion that there are two distinct concepts of freedom, one positive and one negative. Generally, the notion of negative freedom is concerned with the area within which a subject is left alone, while the notion of positive freedom is concerned with the presence of opportunities for realizing desires. Accordingly, a hungry man lying on a street may be "negatively free" if no one helps him, but he would not be "positively free." The nature of this distinction is made clear within the context of MacCallum's article. Those who advocate negative liberty usually do so by asserting that positive liberty is not truly liberty, and vice versa. MacCallum demonstrates that the difference does not concern the meaning of liberty, but rather the specifications of certain "term variables."

Freedom is always a "triadic relation." Freedom is always "*of* something (an agent or agents), *from* something, *to do*...something." Statements about freedom are intelligible only in terms of these three term variables, i.e., the agent, the constraint, and the goal. Other statements about freedom are intelligible when the missing term variables are understood. For example, if a man leaving a divorce court says, "I'm free," he is understood to be saying, "I am free from the constraints of marriage to do what I please in certain areas." MacCallum argues that disagreements over the meaning of freedom are actually (or can be best understood as) disagreements over the "range" of one or more of the term variables. Advocates of the notions of negative and positive freedom have different views as to what constitutes an agent or a constraint. They do not have a different understanding of the meaning of freedom. Disputes over the meaning of freedom arose because philosophers tried to answer the question: "When are men *really* free?" "These questions *invite* confusion and misunderstanding, largely because of their tacit presumption that persons can be free or not free *simpliciter*." Men are free or unfree in specific circumstances and situations; they are not free or unfree in general.

MacCallum's argument can be used to examine Scott's contention that a moral obligation leaves a man free. This contention can be understood simply as one that restricts the range of theoretically possible constraints so as to exclude moral constraints. Certainly moral obligations may be constraints on human action. There is no reason to exclude moral constraints from cases involving freedom. In other words, Scott holds a certain view as to what constitutes a constraint on an agent's freedom. This is not to say that this is the only possible view. But how do we determine whether or not a man's actions are constrained? It might be argued that if a man feels unfree, i.e., if he perceives himself as subject to constraints, then he is unfree. The verification of constraints is an important problem for the political scientist and the philosopher. These articles suggest this problem, but they do not provide an answer.

5

Liberty, License, and not being Free

K.J. Scott

Liberty and License

EVERYDAY usage of the word "free" recognizes no distinction between
liberty and license, as in "Young people have too much freedom today."
But most social theorists who describe freedom do so in such a way as
to exclude license. This sophisticated usage becomes self-conscious in
some stipulative definitions of the word "freedom," and is reflected in
some lexical definitions of the word. I have no criticism to offer of
these definitions, so long as their lexical or stipulative nature is clear.
But sometimes what is in form a lexical or a stipulative definition of
the word "freedom" is in effect an analysis of freedom, i.e., a definition
of the thing freedom.[1] (Freedom the thing, though I so describe it to
distinguish it from "freedom" the word, is not an entity; it is a relation –
a relation between a desiring person and a permitting social environment.) My purpose in this paper is to criticize analyses of the thing
freedom that exclude license, whether the analyses are couched as such
or take the form of stipulative or lexical definitions of the word "freedom." The writers who give these analyses begin by deciding that
freedom is something of which they approve, and then go on to analyze
it in such a way as to exclude the freedoms of which they disapprove.
The correct procedure for a writer who wants to express his disapproval
of some freedoms is the reverse: he should first analyze freedom without
moral preconceptions (and I hope to show that he would have to

From *Political Studies*, IV (1956), 176–185.

include license), and should then go on to say that some freedoms should not be allowed, or that some freedoms should not be exercised. Statements of fact, such as that I am free to gamble, may be denied on factual grounds but should not be denied on moral grounds. The function of morals is to judge facts, not to deny them.

To make a claim of pre-emptive right for everyday usage of the word "free," I must establish, first, that the thing freedom is capable of analysis, and, second, that everyday usage is the criterion on which we should base our analysis. Some would say that since the word "freedom" can be used in different ways, the thing freedom is incapable of being analyzed.

> When we ask what the thing x is, believing it to be analysable but not possessing the analysis, a certain type of person replies, "you are free to make the word 'x' mean anything you like," as if there were nothing at issue but a choice of nomenclature. There is at issue, however, the achievement of an increased insight into the nature of some thing.[2]

And freedom would be incapable of being analyzed if it were not a distinct thing.

> Many things have never been analysed to the satisfaction of all.... And though this may be in some cases... because the supposed thing is really a bundle of things held together by nothing better than an ambiguous word, it seems overwhelmingly probable that there remain cases in which analysis is possible but not yet achieved.[3]

A thing can be analyzed when it differs in kind from all other things or when the members of the class to which it belongs differ in kind from all other things. Thus the thing human being can be analyzed. In social theory we are more familiar with differences in degree. As these are necessarily arbitrary, things that differ from one another only in degree are not distinct things capable of being analyzed. Thus, what we call "democracy" differs only in degree from some other systems of government, and while we can give lexical and stipulative definitions of the word "democracy" we cannot analyze the thing democracy. But free relations (which we can call "freedom" for convenience) differ in kind from all other relations. Free relations need to be distinguished from only two other kinds of relations: unfree relations, and relations where the question of freedom does not arise. In analyzing freedom, we do not have to draw an arbitrary line on a scale. The relation freedom is something with a distinct existence, and is thus a thing capable of being analyzed.

The kind of problem that arises in analyzing freedom is how to classify a marginal class of relations that have distinct and identical characteristics—for instance, whether we are free to do a thing if we want to do it and are physically compelled to do it. It is instructive to compare the way questions as to such characteristics arise in the process of defining the word "democracy." When we are defining "democracy," there are questions as to characteristics to settle before we draw the arbitrary lines. One of the arbitrary decisions we may have to make at least in broad terms, whether we are giving a lexical or a stipulative definition of "democracy," is what unfreedoms must exist before we say that what we call political freedom ceases to exist. But this arbitrary decision has to be made only if we have already made another decision: that political freedom is an essential element of "democracy." Now this is a decision that we may well decide to make if we are giving one of the lexical definitions of "democracy," or if we are giving a stipulative definition of "democracy." But we cannot decide that political freedom is or is not an essential element of the thing democracy. In fact, the point at which we discover that there is no thing democracy capable of being analyzed is the point at which we find that we cannot answer questions as to the characteristics of the thing democracy. But questions as to the characteristics of the thing freedom can be answered by examination of everyday usage (at least, this is true of everyday English usage).

Freedom is a thing of which all men have experience, and usage embodies their beliefs as to its characteristics. Fortunately freedom is one of the things on whose characteristics the generations who have shaped our language have had few doubts, and usage consequently offers virtually unequivocal guidance. Usage is uniform in statements as to whether a particular person is free to do a particular thing. Laymen are more expert at recognizing freedom than social theorists are at analyzing it. In the rare cases where usage appears to result from confused thinking (as when an idiom appropriate to one meaning of "free" is transferred to another meaning to which it is inappropriate), recourse must be had to a second criterion: the importance with respect to freedom of the similarities and differences between the class of relations we are considering and other classes of relations that are clearly either free or unfree or relations where the question of freedom does not arise. This second criterion should be used only where the confusion behind everyday usage is clearly discernible.

Only one element of the analysis of the thing freedom is germane to this paper: that freedom is a nonmoral thing. On this point everyday usage is clear. We do not say that a person is not free (meaning, is unfree) to do a thing because in our opinion he should not be allowed to do it or because in our opinion he should not do it. If we live in a country where gambling is allowed and we wish to say that in our opinion it should not be allowed, we do not say: "People are not free (meaning, are unfree) to gamble." Neither do we say this if we live in a country where gambling is allowed and we wish to say that in our opinion people should not gamble.

But most social theorists who analyze freedom say that people are not free in these cases. They work out their analyses either to express the political view that people should not be allowed to do certain things or to express the moral view that people should not do certain things they are allowed to do. I propose to examine two examples expressing the political view and two expressing the moral view. Of each pair of examples the first is clearly a statement of an ideal (political or moral) and the second is on first appearances an unprejudiced analysis.

When the analysis is clearly a statement of political opinion as to the desirability of certain social arrangements, no confusion results.

By freedom I mean a system of society in which every man can discharge the infinite duty he owes to God and his fellow men.[4]

But when the analysis is apparently unprejudiced and is only covertly a statement of political opinion as to the desirability of certain social arrangements, then analysis and advocacy are being confused.

And, if I were asked to define freedom, I do not think I could do better than the definition of Berdyaev (which is indeed not altogether new): "The opportunity for creative activity."[5]

The context of this sentence clearly indicates that it is offered as analysis. But freedom includes not only the opportunity for creative activity; it includes also the opportunity for uncreative activity, for instance gambling.

Again the analysis may clearly be a statement of a moral ideal. Where this is the case, there is no confusion.

For man is not free but enslaved when he seeks merely the satisfaction of his own unrestrained desires. He becomes free when and in so far as he endeavours to act as a moral being.[6]

But when the analysis is apparently unprejudiced, and is only covertly a statement of a moral ideal, analysis and advocacy are being confused.

I am free to do A if I am not physically prevented, have the ability and opportunity to do A, am not obliged to do something contrary to A, and am not exposed, by doing A, to disproportionately hurtful consequences.[7]

The context clearly indicates that the contrary obligation referred to is any moral obligation contrary to *A*. But if I am not physically prevented from gambling, have the ability and opportunity to gamble, and am not exposed, by gambling, to disproportionately hurtful consequences, then I am free to gamble even if I am under a moral obligation to refrain from gambling. Professor Duncan-Jones imports the moral element into his analysis quite deliberately; he adduces two arguments in support, both based on usage.

> Suppose a friend invites me to dinner, and I reply in good faith that I can't come, or am not free to come.... Nine times out of ten I plead a previous engagement.[8]

> Recognition that the issue is of this nature (*sc.* a moral nature) appears in ordinary language when those who allege a contrary obligation say "I am not *morally* free to act in such and such a way."[9]

To deal first with the second of these passages, I cannot agree that it is ordinary language to say "I am not *morally* free to act in such and such a way." This is the technical language of philosophy, and the only semantic inference that can be drawn from a philosophical use of words is that a certain philosopher attaches a certain meaning to certain words.

The first passage raises a more difficult question. It gives an illustration of the one kind of case where everyday usage suggests that we can be rendered unfree by a moral obligation: when we have placed ourselves under a moral obligation by making a voluntary promise we say that we are not free to do the thing we have promised not to do. The moral obligation to keep a previous engagement is not the only one we discuss in these terms. Thus we say that we are not free to disclose confidential information that we have promised not to disclose and that we are not free to sell goods on which we have given a gratuitous option that has not yet expired. In all other kinds of case, everyday usage recognizes that a moral obligation does not render us unfree. Where we are subject to a moral obligation, everyday usage thus bases the distinction between freedom and unfreedom on the adventitious nature of the source of the moral obligation: according to usage, moral obligations arising from gratuitous promises render us unfree and moral obligations arising from all other sources leave us free.

This is so surprising a distinction that one wonders whether usage in respect to moral obligations created by promises has been distorted by some confusion. On examination, two sources of confusion are revealed. First, there is a confusion between legal obligation and moral obligation. If we are prohibited by law from disclosing confidential information, we are not free to disclose it; and, when we discuss the analogous case of moral prohibition of disclosure, we confusingly do so in terms of freedom. If we have granted an option over goods and have been paid for it, we are not free to sell the goods to a third party; and, when we discuss the analogous case of a gratuitous option that is only morally binding, we confusingly do so in terms of freedom. A previous engagement of a legally binding nature renders us unfree, and this is what prompts us to say that we are "not free to come" when we are under a moral obligation to keep a previous engagement. We cannot infer from this usage that we are in fact unfree. The second confusion is between different senses of the world "free." A promisee can free a promisor from his promise in the sense of releasing him from it, and if we have not been freed in the sense of being released we come by a confusion of thought to speak of ourselves as not being free in the sense of being able to act without restraint. Either or both of these analogies could have caused the linguistic quirk of discussing one and only one kind of moral obligation in terms of freedom. Everyday usage could thus well be misleading; we have now to examine whether it is in fact misleading.

Since everyday usage in respect to moral obligations created by gratuitous promises is a confusing one, we need to fall back on the other criterion of analysis and decide whether relations in this marginal class are more like the most similar free relation, i.e., those involving other moral obligations, or the most similar unfree relations, i.e., those involving legal obligations. The issue has only to be stated in these terms for it to be apparent that moral obligations created by gratuitous promises have a much closer affinity to some relations that are clearly free than to any relations that are clearly unfree. Everyday usage is misleading. A moral obligation created by a gratuitous promise leaves us free.

I have thought it best to consider this question on its merits, but there is a shorter answer to the case as put by Professor Duncan-Jones. He does not open up the general question of gratuitous promises that I have discussed. His argument is the specific one that when we have a previous engagement we say we are "not free to come" to dinner. In this specific case there is a further source of confusion from a different meaning of the word "free": having time uncommitted. If we have committed our time, but without putting ourselves under any moral obligation, we still say that we are not free to come. We may not say *tout court* that we are not free to come, but we might say: "I'm not free to come that evening — my wife and I were looking forward to going to the ballet together before the season ends, but it looks as though she's not going to be well enough, so I'm going on my own, and I've reserved a seat for that evening." The reason why we are "not free to come" to dinner is merely that we have decided to do something else and cannot conveniently change our plans. Similarly if we have arranged to go to the ballet with friends and say that we are not free to come to dinner we may mean only that we have committed our time, and not that we are unable to act without restraint because we have entered into a moral obligation. The usage of saying that we are not free to come to dinner proves nothing about the nature of freedom in the sense of ability to act without restraint.

The four passages I have examined are not unprejudiced analyses of freedom; they are expressions of political or moral opinion. The word "freedom" is used in them as the name for various things that are similar to freedom. Recognition of the existence of such things may furnish concepts that are useful in social theory. But recognition of the existence of things that are similar to freedom neither disproves the existence of freedom nor justifies denying it its traditional name. Freedom is what it is, and not another thing. License is one kind of liberty.

On not being Free

When we say that we are not free to do something, we mean that we are unfree to do it. We could also say this (though it would not be idiomatic) when we are neither free nor unfree to do the thing. For, in respect of many things that we could do or could imagine ourselves doing, the question of freedom does not arise, and we are neither free nor unfree. There are, as I show later in this paper, two kinds of things we are neither free nor unfree to do: those we are unable to do, and those we do not want to do. "Not free" is thus a term that can have any one of three meanings:

> He is not free to do it = he is unfree to do it.
> He is not free to do it = he is unable to do it.
> He is not free to do it = he does not want to do it.

In everyday speech the term has only the first of these meanings, but in social theory it is used with all three meanings. Thus in everyday speech there is no confusion: we never talk in terms of freedom except of a person who is either free or unfree. But in social theory there is confusion. The term "not free" may have any one of three meanings; what is worse, writers use the term in more than one sense without being aware that they are doing so. They allow the term to slide from one meaning into another. And, beginning from the false premise that we must be either free or not free in the sense of unfree, they reach false conclusions about things we are unable to do and about things we do not want to do. What is false about these conclusions is that they are couched in terms of freedom. Thus the scope of the problem of the nature of freedom is obscured — and most often in papers that are devoted to this very subject.

First, we are neither free nor unfree to do things we are unable to do. Inability is to be distinguished from restraint on ability. If we are able to do something but natural laws deter us, for instance if fear of a hangover deters us, we are free. If we are able to do something but positive laws deter us, for instance if fear of imprisonment deters us, we are unfree. And there is one kind of situation where inability constitutes unfreedom. This is where the inability is the result of a conscious human intention to render us unfree. Thus a prisoner is unfree to escape from a locked cell. But this is a rare kind of unfreedom; restraints on our freedom almost always operate through deterrence, not prevention. Inability that is not the result of a conscious human intention to render us unfree, for instance inability to fly like a bird, does not raise the question of freedom.

Everyday usage recognizes that inability does not raise the question of freedom except where the inability is the result of a conscious human intention to render us unfree. It is only situations where this conscious human intention exists that we ever discuss in terms of freedom, though we sometimes discuss even them in terms of ability. Other situations of inability we always discuss in terms of ability, never in terms of freedom. Thus we say of the prisoner in the locked cell either that he is not able to escape from it or that he is not free (meaning, is unfree) to do so. But in none of the following situations typical of other kinds of inability do we ever talk in terms of freedom. Human impossibility: we say of a man shipwrecked on an island that he is not able to escape from it, not that he is not free to do so. Want of personal skill: we say that we are unable to play chess, not (if we are unable to play it) that we are not free to do so. Inability resulting from the action of an animal: when we find a stable door blocked by a recalcitrant horse we say that we are not able to get through, not that we are not free to do so. Inability resulting from conscious human action that is not intended to render us unfree: when we find our favorite park bench occupied we say that we are not able to have our lunch there, not that we are not free to do so. Inability resulting from the operation of impersonal social forces: we are consciously straining language when we say that a penniless man is not free to buy a meal.

Unfreedom and inability are thus distinct though overlapping terms.

We are not unable to commit murder, though we are unfree to do so. We are not unfree to fly like birds, though we are unable to do so. It is common in social theory to overlook the second of these kinds of situation and to suppose that wherever there is inability there is unfreedom. The following is an instance.

The idea of liberty is, primarily, a negative one, the removal of restraints upon doing what one wishes. Such restraints may be imposed by the actions of other persons or may be due to natural obstacles.[10]

Neither does the question of freedom arise in respect of anything we do not want to do and do not do. John Stuart Mill pointed out that in respect of freedom there is something peculiar about such a situation, though he did not go so far as to say that the question of freedom does not arise.

Now, there are two kinds of freedom, which perhaps have not yet been sufficiently distinguished, even by those eminent thinkers and writers who have given their attention to this subject. These are — the freedom to do what we wish to do — and the freedom to do what we do *not* wish to do."[11]

Everyday usage shows that where we are able to do something and do not want to do it, the question of freedom does not arise. I shall consider first something we are not allowed to do and then something we are allowed to do. We feel that it is straining language to say: "Neither the rich man nor the poor man is free to steal a loaf of bread." Analyzing why we feel uneasy about this statement, we find it is because we are departing from everyday usage in saying of the rich man that he is not free (meaning, is unfree) to do something that we assume he does not want to do. Similarly when we are allowed to do the thing. We say: "Any normal man can carry a twenty-pound weight for a hundred yards." As we assume that a man would not want to do so except to enable him to achieve some other purpose, so long as we are not thinking of some such purpose we do not say: "Any normal man is free to carry a twenty-pound weight for a hundred yards." But if we contemplate the possibility that the man may want to carry the weight, for instance if we are thinking that he may want to carry a suitcase along a station platform, then we speak in terms of freedom and we say: "He's free to carry his suitcase himself if he wants to." The very wording of this last statement shows that it is only if he wants to carry his suitcase himself that he is free.

The following argument is typical of those that assume that the question of freedom arises in respect of doing a thing that we do not want to do.

It is no limitation on a man's freedom that he has not the power to do something that he has no desire to do. We can increase our freedom, therefore, by limiting our desires, without any change in the means of action at our disposal. The free man is the man whose means are adequate to his ends. We can gain freedom by increasing our power while our ends remain constant, or by limiting our ends to the means at our disposal.[12]

But increasing our power does not necessarily increase our freedom. It does so only if we want to exercise the particular kind of power. If we do not want to, then the question of freedom does not arise, whether or not we possess the particular kind of power. Again, while the renunciation of our frustrated desires decreases our unfreedom, it does not increase our freedom. It converts our situation from one where we are unfree to one where the question of freedom does not arise. The view that we should exorcize insatiable desires, a commonplace of religious morality, should not be advocated under the banner of freedom. We can compare the view of an economic historian.

Human wants are infinite in their variety: progress consists, indeed, in creating new wants just as enlightened progress consists in elevating the nature of our wants.[13]

There is an important corollary to the view that if we do not want to do a thing the question of freedom does not arise. It is always assumed that our freedom of action throughout a field of activity over a period of time is an aggregation of particular freedoms. Conventionally the problem of analysis is the nature of a particular freedom, and the problem of political philosophy is the value of a general freedom, and it assumed that the subject matter of these problems is the same qualitatively though not quantitatively. This, however, is not so. Our freedom of action throughout a field of activity over a period of time is more than the freedom to do whatever we want to do in that field, for what we want to do will emerge only as concrete situations develop; it is freedom to do whatever we *may* want to do in that field, and, as there is no knowing what we *may* want to do, it is freedom to do everything in that field whether or not we *will* want to do it. Similarly, freedom for the members of a group to do identical particular things differs qualitatively from freedom for a single person, except where each member of the group wants to do the thing in question. Thus political freedom is more than a sum of freedoms.

It remains to consider things we are unable to do and in any case do not want to do. Here there are two respects in which the question of freedom does not arise. Take the case of a man who does not want to buy a Rolls-Royce and in any case cannot afford to do so. There is seldom any reason to discuss the fact that he does not buy a Rolls-Royce. If the subject does arise, we would not normally discuss it in terms of freedom, but would say perhaps that he does not want to buy a Rolls-Royce, or that he does not care that he cannot afford one. If somebody who is keen to score a point about economic inequality says that the man is not free to buy a Rolls-Royce we feel uneasy about the statement, though we may not at first notice why it is that we feel uneasy. The reason we feel uneasy is that the term "not free" is being made to slide from one of its meanings to another. The man is not free to buy a Rolls-Royce, but neither is he unfree to do so.

We shall think more clearheadedly if we remember that the question of freedom arises only when we are able to do a thing and want to do it. Freedom and unfreedom are categories that have only a limited range of utility in social analysis.

Notes

1. The term "analysis" seems preferable for the reasons given by Richard Robinson in *Definition* (Oxford, 1950), pp. 177–178.
2. *Ibid.*, p. 173.
3. *Ibid.*, p. 175.
4. Lionel Curtis, "When I Look Back," *The Listener*, May 8, 1952, p. 750.
5. E. H. Carr, *The New Society* (Macmillan, 1951), p. 118.
6. R. Bassett, *The Essentials of Parliamentary Democracy* (Macmillan, 1935), p. 110.
7. Austin Duncan-Jones, "Freedom to Do Otherwise," *The Cambridge Journal*, III: 12 (September 1950), 754.
8. *Ibid.*, p. 752.
9. *Ibid.*, p. 753. Italics in original.
10. D. Daiches Raphael, "Justice and Liberty," *Proceedings of the Aristotelian Society*, N.S., LI (1950–1951), 191.
11. John Stuart Mill, *On Social Freedom*, reprinted from *The Oxford and Cambridge Review*, June 1907, with an introduction by Dorothy Fosdick (Columbia University Press, 1941), p. 36. Italics in original.
12. John Macmurray, *Conditions of Freedom* (Faber, 1950), p. 21.
13. E Lipson, *A Planned Economy or Free Enterprise*, 2d ed. (A. and C. Black, 1946), p. 242.

6

Negative and Positive Freedom

Gerald C. MacCallum, Jr.

THIS paper challenges the view that we may usefully distinguish between two kinds or concepts of political and social freedom — negative and positive. The argument is not that one of these is the only, the "truest," or the "most worthwhile" freedom, but rather that the distinction between them has never been made sufficiently clear, is based in part upon a serious confusion, and has drawn attention away from precisely what needs examining if the differences separating philosophers, ideologies, and social movements concerned with freedom are to be understood. The corrective advised is to regard freedom as always one and the same triadic relation, but recognize that various contending parties disagree with each other in what they understand to be the ranges of the term variables. To view the matter in this way is to release oneself from a prevalent but unrewarding concentration on "kinds" of freedom, and to turn attention toward the truly important issues in this area of social and political philosophy.

I

Controversies generated by appeals to the presence or absence of freedom in societies have been roughly of four closely related kinds — namely, (1) about the nature of freedom itself, (2) about the relationships holding between the attainment of freedom and the attainment

From *The Philosophical Review*, LXXVI (1967), 312–334.

of other possible social benefits, (3) about the ranking of freedom among such benefits, and (4) about the consequences of this or that policy with respect to realizing or attaining freedom. Disputes of one kind have turned readily into disputes of the other kinds.

Of those who agree that freedom is a benefit, most would also agree that it is not the *only* benefit a society may secure its members. Other benefits might include, for example, economic and military security, technological efficiency, and exemplifications of various aesthetic and spiritual values. Once this is admitted, however, disputes of types (2) and (3) are possible. Questions can be raised as to the logical and causal relationships holding between the attainment of freedom and the attainment of these other benefits, and as to whether one could on some occasions reasonably prefer to cultivate or emphasize certain of the latter at the expense of the former. Thus, one may be led to ask: *can* anyone cultivate and emphasize freedom at the cost of realizing these other goals and values (or vice versa) and, second, *should* anyone ever do this? In practice, these issues are often masked by or confused with disputes about the consequences of this or that action with respect to realizing the various goals or values.

Further, any of the above disputes may stem from or turn into a dispute about what freedom *is*. The borderlines have never been easy to keep clear. But a reason for this especially worth noting at the start is that disputes about the nature of freedom are certainly historically best understood as a series of attempts by parties opposing each other on very many issues to capture for their own side the favorable attitudes attaching to the notion of freedom. It has commonly been advantageous for partisans to link the presence or absence of freedom as closely as possible to the presence or absence of those other social benefits believed to be secured or denied by the forms of organization advocated or condemned. Each social benefit is, accordingly, treated as either a result of or a contribution to freedom, and each liability is connected somehow to the absence of freedom. This history of the matter goes far to explain how freedom came to be identified with so many different kinds of social and individual benefits and why the status of freedom as simply one among a number of social benefits has remained unclear. The resulting flexibility of the notion of freedom, and the resulting enhancement of the value of freedom, have suited the purposes of the polemicist.

It is against this background that one should first see the issues surrounding the distinction between positive and negative freedom as two fundamentally different kinds of freedom. Nevertheless, the difficulties surrounding the distinction should not be attributed solely to the interplay of Machiavellian motives. The disputes, and indeed the distinction itself, have also been influenced by a genuine confusion concerning the concept of freedom. The confusion results from failure to understand fully the conditions under which use of the concept of freedom is intelligible.

II

Whenever the freedom of some agent or agents is in question, it is always freedom from some constraint or restriction on, interference with, or barrier to doing, not doing, becoming, or not becoming something.[1] Such freedom is thus always *of* something (an agent or agents), *from* something, *to* do, not do, become, or not become something; it is a triadic relation. Taking the format "*x* is (is not) free from *y* to do (not do, become, not become) *z*," *x* ranges over agents, *y* ranges over such "preventing conditions" as constraints, restrictions, interferences, and barriers, and *z* ranges over actions or conditions of character or circumstance. When reference to one of these three terms is missing in such a discussion of freedom, it should be only because the reference is thought to be understood from the context of the discussion.[2]

Admittedly, the idioms of freedom are such that this is sometimes not obvious. The claim, however, is not about what we say, but rather about the conditions under which what we say is intelligible. And, of course, it is important to notice that the claim is only about what makes talk concerning the freedom of agents intelligible. This restriction excludes from consideration, for example, some uses of "free of" and "free from" — namely, those not concerned with the freedom of agents, and where, consequently, what is meant may be only "rid of" or "without." Thus, consideration of "The sky is now free of clouds" is excluded because this expression does not deal with agents at all, but consideration of "His record is free of blemish" and "She is free from any vice" is most probably also excluded. Doubt about these latter two hinges on whether these expressions might be thought claims about the freedom of agents; if so, then they are not excluded, but neither are they intelligible *as* claims about the freedom of agents until one is in a position to fill in the elements of the format offered above; if not, then although probably parasitic upon talk about the freedom of agents and thus perhaps viewable as figurative anyway, they fall outside the scope of this investigation.

The claim that freedom, subject to the restriction noted above, is a triadic relation can hardly be substantiated here by exhaustive examination of the idioms of freedom. But the most obviously troublesome cases — namely, those in which one's understanding of the context must in a relevant way carry past the limits of what is explicit in the idiom — may be classified roughly and illustrated as follows:

(a) *Cases where agents are not mentioned.* For example, consider any of the wide range of expressions having the form "free x" in which (1) the place of x is taken by an expression not clearly referring to an agent — as in "free society" or "free will" — or (2) the place of x is taken by an expression clearly not referring to an agent — as in "free beer." All such cases can be understood to be concerned with the freedom of agents and, indeed, their intelligibility rests upon their being so understood; they are thus subject to the claims made above. This is fairly obvious in the cases of "free will" and "free society." The intelligibility of the free-will problem is generally and correctly thought to rest at least upon the problem's being concerned with the freedom of persons, even though the criteria for identification of the persons or "selves" whose freedom is in question have not often been made sufficiently clear.[3] And it is beyond question that the expression "free society," although of course subject to various conflicting analyses with respect to the identity of the agent(s) whose freedom is involved, is thought intelligible only because it is thought to concern the freedom of agents of some sort or other. The expression "free beer," on the other hand (to take only one of a rich class of cases some of which would have to be managed differently), is ordinarily thought intelligible because thought to refer to beer that *people* are free *from* the ordinary restrictions of the market place *to* drink without paying for it.

For an expression of another grammatical form, consider "The property is free of (or from) encumbrance." Although this involves a loose use of "property," suppose that the term refers to something like a piece of land; the claim then clearly means that *owners* of that land are free *from* certain well-known restrictions (for example, certain types of charges or liabilities consequent upon their ownership of the land) *to* use, enjoy, dispose of the land as they wish.

(b) *Cases where it is not clear what corresponds to the second term.* For example,"freedom of choice," "freedom to choose as I please." Here, the range of constraints, restrictions, and so forth is generally clear from the context of the discussion. In political matters, legal constraints or restrictions are most often thought of, but one also sometimes finds, as in Mill's *On Liberty*, concern for constraints and interferences constituted by social pressures. It is sometimes difficult for persons to see social pressures as constraints or interferences; this will be discussed below. It is also notoriously difficult to see causal nexuses as implying constraints or restrictions on the "will" (the person?) in connection with the free-will problem. But the very fact that such difficulties are the focus of so much attention is witness to the importance of getting clear about this term of the relation before such discussions of freedom can be said to be intelligible.

One might think that references to a second term of this sort could always be eliminated by a device such as the following. Instead of saying, for example, (1) "Smith is free *from* legal restrictions on travel *to* leave the country," one could say (2) "Smith is free *to* leave the country *because* there are no legal restrictions on his leaving." The latter would make freedom appear to be a dyadic, rather than a triadic, relation. But we would be best advised to regard the appearance illusory, and this may be seen if one thinks a bit about the suggestion or implication of the sentence that nothing hinders or prevents Smith from leaving the country. Difficulties about this might be settled by attaching a qualifier to "free" — namely, "*legally* free." Alternatively, one could consider which, of all the things that might still hinder or prevent Smith from leaving the country (for example, has he promised someone to remain? will the responsibilities of his job keep him here? has he enough money to buy passage and, if not, why not?), could count as limitations on his freedom to leave the country; one would then be in a position to determine whether the claim had been misleading or false. In either case, however, the devices adopted would reveal that our understanding of what has been said hinged upon our understanding of the range of obstacles or constraints from which Smith had been claimed to be free.

(c) *Cases where it is not clear what corresponds to the third term.* For example, "freedom from hunger" ("want," "fear," "disease," and so forth). One quick but not very satisfactory way of dealing with such expressions is to regard them as figurative, or at least not really concerned with anybody's freedom; thus, being free from hunger would be simply being rid of, or without, hunger — as a sky may be free of clouds (compare the discussion of this above). Alternatively, one might incline toward regarding hunger as a barrier of some sort and claim that a person free *from* hunger is free *to* be well fed or to do or do well the various things he could not do or do well if hungry. Yet again, and more satisfactory, one could turn to the context of the initial bit of Rooseveltian rhetoric and there find reason to treat the expression as follows. Suppose that hunger is a feeling and that someone *seeks* hunger; he is on a diet and the hunger feeling reassures him that he is losing weight.[4] Alternatively, suppose that hunger is a bodily condition and that someone seeks it; he is on a Gandhi-style hunger strike. In either case, Roosevelt or his fellow orators might have wanted a world in which these people were free from hunger, but this surely does not mean that they wanted a world in which people were not hungry despite a wish to be so. They wanted, rather, a world in which people were not victims of hunger they did not seek; that is, they wanted a world without barriers keeping people hungry despite efforts to avoid hunger — a world in which people would be free *from* barriers constituted by various specifiable agricultural, economic, and political conditions *to* get enough food to prevent hunger. This view of "freedom from hunger" not only makes perfectly good and histori- cally accurate sense out of the expression, but also conforms to the view that freedom is a triadic relation.

In other politically important idioms the *range* of the third term is not always utterly clear. For example, does freedom of religion include freedom *not* to worship? Does freedom of speech include *all* speech no matter what its content, manner of delivery, or the circumstances of its delivery? Such matters, however, raise largely historical questions or questions to be settled by political decision; they do not throw doubt on the need for a third term.

That the intelligibility of talk concerned with the freedom of agents rests in the end upon an understanding of freedom as a triadic relation is what many persons distinguishing between positive and negative freedom apparently fail to see or see clearly enough. Evidence of such failure or, alternatively, invitation to it is found in the simple but conventional characterization of the difference between the two kinds of freedom as the difference between "freedom from" and "freedom to" — a characterization suggesting that freedom could be either of two dyadic relations. This characterization, however, cannot distinguish two genuinely different kinds of freedom; it can serve only to emphasize one or the other of two features of *every* case of the freedom of agents. Consequently, anyone who argues that freedom *from* is the "only" freedom, or that freedom *to* is the "truest" freedom, or that one is "more important than" the other, cannot be taken as having said anything both straightforward and sensible about two distinct kinds of freedom. He can, at most, be said to be attending to, or emphasizing the importance of, only one part of what is always present in any case of freedom.

Unfortunately, even if this basis of distinction between positive and negative freedom as two distinct kinds or concepts of freedom is shown to collapse, one has not gone very far in understanding the issues separating those philosophers or ideologies commonly said to utilize one or the other of them. One has, however, dissipated one of the main confusions blocking understanding of these issues. In recognizing that freedom is always *both* freedom from something *and* freedom to do or become something, one is provided with a means of making sense out of interminable and poorly defined controversies concerning, for example, when a person really is free, why freedom is important, and on what its importance depends. As these, in turn, are matters on which the distinction between positive and negative freedom has turned, one is given also a means of managing sensibly the writings appearing to accept or to be based upon that distinction.

III

The key to understanding lies in recognition of precisely how differing styles of answer to the question "When are persons free?" could survive agreement that freedom is a triadic relation. The differences would be rooted in differing views on the ranges of the term variables — that is, on the ("true") identities of the agents whose freedom is in question, on what counts as an obstacle to or interference with the freedom of such agents, or on the range of what such agents might or might not be free to do or become.[5] Although perhaps not always obvious or dramatic, such differences could lead to vastly different accounts of when persons are free. Furthermore, differences on one of these matters might or might not be accompanied by differences on either of the others. There is thus a rich stock of ways in which such accounts might diverge and a rich stock of possible foci of argument.

It is therefore crucial, when dealing with accounts of when persons are free, to insist on getting *quite* clear on what each writer considers to be the ranges of these term variables. Such insistence will reveal where the differences between writers are, and will provide a starting point for rewarding consideration of what might justify these differences.

The distinction between positive and negative freedom has, however, stood in the way of this approach. It has encouraged us to see differences in accounts of freedom as resulting from differences in concepts of freedom. This in turn has encouraged the wrong sorts of questions. We have been tempted to ask such questions as "Well, who *is* right? Whose concept of freedom *is* the correct one?" or "Which *kind* of freedom do we really want after all?" Such questions will not help reveal the fundamental issues separating major writers on freedom from each other, no matter *how* the writers are arranged into "camps."

It would be far better to insist that the same concept of freedom is operating throughout and that the differences, rather than being about what *freedom* is, are for example about what persons are, and about what can count as an obstacle to or interference with the freedom of persons so conceived.

The appropriateness of this insistence is easily seen when one examines prevailing characterizations of the differences between "positive" and "negative" freedom. Once the alleged difference between "freedom from" and "freedom to" has been disallowed (as it must be; see above), the most persuasive of the remaining characterizations appear to be as follows:[6]

1. Writers adhering to the concept of "negative" freedom hold that only the *presence* of something can render a person unfree; writers adhering to the concept of "positive" freedom hold that the *absence* of something may also render a person unfree.

2. The former hold that a person is free to do *x* just in case *nothing due to arrangements made by other persons* stops him from doing *x*; the latter adopt no such restriction.

3. The former hold that the agents whose freedom is in question (for example, "persons," "men") are, in effect, identifiable as Anglo-American law would identify "natural" (as opposed to. "artificial") persons; the latter sometimes hold quite different views as to how these agents are to be identified (see below).

The most obvious thing to be said about these characterizations, of course, is that appeal to them provides at best an excessively crude justification of the conventional classification of writers into opposing camps.[7] When one presses on the alleged points of difference, they have a tendency to break down, or at least to become less dramatic than they at first seemed.[8] As should not be surprising, the patterns of agreement and disagreement on these several points are in fact either too diverse or too indistinct to support any clearly justifiable arrangement of major writers into two camps. The trouble is not merely that some writers do not fit too well where they have been placed; it is rather that writers who are purportedly the very models of membership in one camp or the other (for example, Locke, the Marxists) do not fit very well where they have been placed[9]—thus suggesting that the whole system of dichotomous classification is futile and, even worse, conducive to distortion of important views on freedom.

But, even supposing that there were something to the classification and to the justification for it in terms of the above three points of difference, what then? The differences are of two kinds. They concern *(a)* the ("true") identities of the agents whose freedom is in question, and *(b)* what is to count as an "obstacle" or "barrier" to, "restriction" on, or "interference" with the freedom of such agents. They are thus clearly about the ranges of two of the three term variables mentioned earlier. It would be a mistake to see them in any other way. We are likely to make this mistake, however, and obscure the path of rewarding argument, if we present them as differences concerning what "freedom" means.

Consider the following. Suppose that we have been raised in the "libertarian" tradition (roughly characterized as that of "negative" freedom). There would be nothing unusual to us, and perhaps even nothing troubling, in conventional accounts of what the adherent of negative freedom treats as the ranges of these variables.

1. He is purported to count persons just as we do — to point to living human bodies and say of each (and only of each), "There's a person." Precisely what we ordinarily call persons. (And if he is troubled by nonviable fetuses, and so forth, so are we.)

2. He is purported to mean much what we mean by "obstacle," and so forth, though this changes with changes in our views of what can be attributed to arrangements made by human beings, and also with variations in the importance we attach to consenting to rules, practices, and so forth.[10]

3. He is purported to have quite "ordinary" views on what a person may or may not be free to do or become. The actions are sometimes suggested in fairly specific terms — for example, free to have a home, raise a family, "rise to the top." But, on the whole, he is purported to talk of persons being free or not free "to do what they want" or (perhaps) "to express themselves."[11] Furthermore, the criteria for determining what a person wants to do are those we customarily use, or perhaps even the most naïve and unsophisticated of them — for example, what a person wants to do is determined by what he *says* he wants to do, or by what he manifestly *tries* to do, or even *does* do.[12]

In contrast, much might trouble us in the accounts of the so-called adherents of "positive" freedom.

1. They sometimes do not count, as the agent whose freedom is being considered, what inheritors of our tradition would unhesitatingly consider to be a "person." Instead, they occasionally engage in what has been revealingly but pejoratively called "the retreat to the inner citadel"[13]; the agent in whose freedom they are interested in identified as the "real" or the "rational" or the "moral" person who is somehow sometimes hidden within, or has his seed contained within, the living human body. Sometimes, however, rather than a retreat to such an "inner citadel," or sometimes in addition to such a retreat, there is an

expansion of the limits of "person" such that the institutions and members, the histories and futures of the communities in which the living human body is found are considered to be inextricable parts of the "person."

These expansions or contractions of the criteria for identification of persons may seem unwarranted to us. Whether they are so, however, depends upon the strength of the arguments offered in support of the helpfulness of regarding persons in these ways while discussing freedom. For example, the retreat to the "inner citadel" may be initiated simply by worries about which, of all the things we want, will give us lasting satisfaction — a view of our interests making it possible to see the surge of impulse or passion as an obstacle to the attainment of what we "really want." And the expansion of the limits of the "self" to include our families, cultures, nations, or races may be launched by awareness that our "self" is to some extent the product of these associations; by awareness that our identification of our interests may be influenced by our beliefs concerning ways in which our destinies are tied to the destinies of our families, nations, and so forth; by the way we see tugs and stresses upon those associations as tugs and stresses upon us; and by the ways we see ourselves and *identify* ourselves as officeholders in such associations with the rights and obligations of such offices. This expansion, in turn, makes it possible for us to see the infringement of the autonomy of our associations as infringement on our freedom.

Assessing the strengths of the various positions taken on these matters requires a painstaking investigation and evaluation of the arguments offered — something that can hardly be launched within the confines of this paper. But what should be observed is that this set of seemingly radical departures by adherents of positive freedom from the ways "we" ordinarily identify persons does not provide us with any reason whatever to claim that a different concept of *freedom* is involved (one might as well say that the shift from "The apple is to the left of the orange" to "The seeds of the apple are to the left of the seeds of the orange" changes what "to the left of"-means). Furthermore, that claim would draw attention away from precisely what we should focus on; it would lead us to focus on the wrong concept — namely, "freedom" instead of "person." Only by insisting àt least provisionally that all the writers have the same concept of freedom can one see clearly and keep sharply focused the obvious and extremely important differences among them concerning the concept of "person."

2. Similarly, adherents of "positive" freedom purportedly differ from "us" on what counts as an obstacle. Will *this* difference be

revealed adequately if we focus on supposed differences in the concept of "freedom"? Not likely. Given differences on what a person is, differences in what counts as an obstacle or interference are not surprising, of course, since what could count as an obstacle to the activity of a person identified in one way might not possibly count as an obstacle to persons identified in other ways. But the differences concerning "obstacle" and so forth are probably not due solely to differences concerning "person." If, for example, we so-called adherents of negative freedom, in order to count something as a preventing condition, ordinarily require that it can be shown to be a result of arrangements made by human beings, and our "opponents" do not require this, why not? On the whole, perhaps, the latter are saying this: if one is concerned with social, political, and economic policies, and with how these policies can remove or increase human misery, it is quite irrelevant whether difficulties in the way of the policies are or are not *due to* arrangements made by human beings. The only question is whether the difficulties can be removed by human arrangements, and at what cost. This view, seen as an attack upon the "artificiality" of a borderline for distinguishing human freedom from other human values, does not seem inherently unreasonable; a close look at the positions and arguments seems called for.[14] But again, the issues and arguments will be misfocused if we fail to see them as about the range of a term variable of a single triadic relation (freedom). Admittedly, we *could* see some aspects of the matter (those where the differences do not follow merely from differences in what is thought to be the agent whose freedom is in question) as amounting to disagreements about what is meant by "freedom." But there is no decisive reason for doing so, and this move surely threatens to obscure the socially and politically significant issues raised by the argument suggested above.

3. Concerning treatment of the third term by purported adherents of positive freedom, perhaps enough has already been said to suggest that they tend to emphasize conditions of character rather than actions and to suggest that, as with "us" too, the range of character conditions and actions focused on may influence or be influenced by what is thought to count as agent and by what is thought to count as preventing condition. Thus, though something more definite would have to be said about the matter eventually, at least some contact with the issues previously raised might be expected in arguments about the range of this variable.

It is important to observe here and throughout, however, that close agreement between two writers in their understanding of the range of one of the variables does not make *inevitable* like agreement on the ranges of the others. Indeed, we have gone far enough to see that the kinds of issues arising in determination of the ranges are sufficiently diverse to make such simple correlations unlikely. Precisely this renders attempts to arrange writers on freedom into two opposing camps so distorted and ultimately futile. There is too rich a stock of ways in which accounts of freedom diverge.

If we are to manage these divergences sensibly, we must focus our attention on each of these variables and on differences in views as to their ranges. Until we do this, we will not see clearly the issues which have in fact been raised, and thus will not see clearly what needs arguing. In view of this need, it is both clumsy and misleading to try to sort out writers as adherents of this or that "kind" or "concept" of freedom. We would be far better off to insist that they all have the same concept of freedom (as a triadic relation) — thus putting ourselves in a position to notice how, and inquire fruitfully into why, they identify differently what can serve as agent, preventing condition, and action or state of character vis-à-vis issues of freedom.

IV

If the importance of this approach to discussion of freedom has been generally overlooked, it is because social and political philosophers have, with dreary regularity, made the mistake of trying to answer the unadorned question, "When are men free?" or, alternatively, "When are men *really* free?" These questions *invite* confusion and misunderstanding, largely because of their tacit presumption that persons can be free or not free *simpliciter*.

One might suppose that, strictly speaking, a person could be free *simpliciter* only if there were no interference from which he was not free, and nothing that he was not free to do or become. On this view, however, and on acceptance of common views as to what counts as a person, what counts as interference, and what actions or conditions of character may meaningfully be said to be free or not free, all disputes concerning whether or not men in societies are ever free would be inane. Concerning such settings, where the use and threat of coercion are distinctively present, there would *always* be an air of fraud or hocus-pocus about claims that men are free — just like that.

Yet one might hold that men can be free (*simpliciter*) even in society because certain things which ordinarily are counted as interference or barriers are not actually so, or because certain kinds of behavior ordinarily thought to be either free or unfree do not, for some reason, "count." Thus one might argue that at least in certain (conceivable) societies there is no activity in which men in that society are not free to engage, and no possible restriction or barrier from which they are not free.

The burden of such an argument should now be clear. Everything *from* which a person in that society might ordinarily be considered unfree must be shown not actually an interference or barrier (or not a relevant one), and everything which a person in that society might ordinarily be considered not free to *do* or *become* must be shown irrelevant to the issue of freedom. (Part of the argument in either or both cases might be that the "true" identity of the person in question is not what it has been thought to be.)

Pitfalls may remain for attempts to evaluate such arguments. For example, one may uncover tendencies to telescope questions concerning the *legitimacy* of interference into questions concerning genuineness *as* interference.[15] One may also find telescoping of questions concerning the *desirability* of certain modes of behavior or character states into questions concerning the *possibility* of being either free or not free to engage in those modes of behavior or become that kind of person.[16] Nevertheless, a demand for specification of the term variables helps pinpoint such problems, as well as forestalling the confusions obviously encouraged by failure to make the specifications.

Perhaps, however, the claim that certain men are free *simpliciter* is merely elliptical for the claim that they are free in every important respect, or in most important respects, or "on the whole." Nevertheless, the point still remains that when this ellipsis is filled in, the reasonableness of asking both "What are they free from?" and "What are they free to do or become?" becomes apparent. Only when one gets straightforward answers to these questions is he in any position to judge whether the men *are* free as claimed. Likewise, only then will he be in a position to judge the *value* or *importance* of the freedom(s) in question. It is important to know, for example, whether a man is free from legal restrictions to raise a family. But of course social or economic "arrangements" may be such that he still could not raise a family if he wanted to. Thus, merely to say that he is free to raise a family, when what is meant is only that he is free from legal restrictions to raise a family, is to invite misunderstanding. Further, the *range* of activities he may or may not be free from this or that to engage in, or the range of character states he may or may not be free to develop, should make a difference in our evaluations of his situation and of his society; but this too is not called for strongly enough when one asks simply, "Is the man free?" Only when we determine what the men in question are free *from*, and what they are free to do or become, will we be in a position to estimate the value for human happiness and fulfilment of being free from *that* (whatever *it* is), to do the *other thing* (whatever *it* is). Only then will we be in a position to make rational evaluations of the relative merits of societies with regard to freedom.

V

The above remarks can be tied again to the controversy concerning negative and positive freedom by considering the following argument by friends of "negative" freedom. Freedom is always and necessarily *from* restraint; thus, insofar as the adherents of positive freedom speak of persons being made free *by means of* restraint, they cannot be talking about freedom.

The issues raised by this argument (which is seldom stated more fully than here) can be revealed by investigating what might be done to make good sense out of the claim that, for example, Smith is (or can be) made free by restraining (constraining, coercing) him.[17] Use of the format of specifications recommended above reveals two major possibilities:

1. Restraining Smith by means *a* from doing *b* produces a situation in which he is now able to do *c* because restraint *d* is lifted. He is thereby, by means of restraint *a*, made free from *d* to do *c*, although he can no longer do *b*. For example, suppose that Smith, who always walks to where he needs to go, lives in a tiny town where there have been no pedestrian crosswalks and where automobiles have had right of way over pedestrians. Suppose further that a series of pedestrian crosswalks is instituted along with the regulation that pedestrians must use only these walks when crossing, but that while in these walks pedestrians have right of way over automobiles. The regulation restrains Smith (he can no longer legally cross streets where he pleases) but it also frees him (while in crosswalks he no longer has a duty to defer to automobile traffic). Using the schema above, the regulation (*a*) restrains Smith from crossing streets wherever he likes (*b*), but at the same time is such as to (make it practicable to) give him restricted right of way (*c*) over automobile traffic. The regulation (*a*) thus gives him restricted right of way (*c*) because it lifts the rule (*d*) giving automobiles general right of way over pedestrians.

This interpretation of the assertion that Smith can be made free by restraining him is straightforward enough. It raises problems only if one supposes that persons must be either free or not free *simpliciter* and that the claim in question is that Smith is made free *simpliciter*. But there is no obvious justification for either of these suppositions.

If these suppositions *are* made, however, then the following interpretation may be appropriate:

2. Smith is being "restrained" only in the ordinary acceptance of that term; actually, he is not being restrained at all. He is being helped to do what he really wants to do, or what he *would* want to do if he were reasonable (moral, prudent, or such like); compare Locke's words: "that ill deserves the name of confinement which hedges us in only from bogs and precipices."[18] Because of the "constraint" put upon him, a *genuine* constraint that *was* upon him (for example, ignorance, passion, the intrusions of others) is lifted, and he is free from the latter to do what he really wishes (or would wish if...).

This interpretation is hardly straightforward, but the claim that it embodies is nevertheless arguable; Plato argues it in the *Republic* and implies such a claim in the *Gorgias*. Furthermore, insistence upon the format of specifications recommended above can lead one to see clearly the kind of arguments needed to support the claim. For example, if a person is to be made free, whether by means of restraint or otherwise, there must be something *from* which he is made free. This must be singled out. Its character may not always be clear; for example, in Locke's discussion the confinement from which one is liberated by law is perhaps the constraint produced by the arbitrary uncontrolled actions of one's neighbors, or perhaps it is the "constraint" arising from one's own ignorance or passion, or perhaps it is both of these. If only the former, then the specification is unexceptionable enough; that kind of constraint is well within the range of what is ordinarily thought to be constraint. If the latter, however, then some further argument is needed; one's own ignorance and passion are at least not unquestionably within the range of what can restrain him and limit his freedom. The required argument may attempt to show that ignorance and passion prevent persons from doing what they want to do, or what they "really" want to do, or what they *would* want to do if.... The idea would be to promote seeing the removal of ignorance and passion, or at least the control of their effects, as the removal or control of something preventing a person from doing as he wishes, really wishes, or would wish, and so forth, and thus, plausibly, an increase of that person's freedom.

Arguments concerning the "true" identity of the person in question and what *can* restrict such a person's freedom are of course important here and should be pushed further than the above discussion suggests.

For the present, however, one need observe only that they are met again when one presses for specification of the full range of what, on interpretation (2), Smith is made free to *do*. Apparently, he is made free to do as he wishes, really wishes, or *would* wish if....But, quite obviously, there is also something that he is *prima facie not* free to do; otherwise, there would be no point in declaring that he was being made free *by means of* restraint. One may discover how this difficulty is met by looking again to the arguments by which the claimer seeks to establish that something which at first appears to be a restraint is not actually a restraint at all. Two main lines may be found here: (*a*) that the activities being "restrained" are so unimportant or minor (relative, perhaps, to what is gained) that they are not worth counting, or (*b*) that the activities are such that no one could ever want (or really want, and so forth) to engage in them. If the activities in question are so unimportant as to be negligible, the restraints that prevent one from engaging in them may be also "not worthy of consideration"; if, on the other hand, the activities are ones that no one would conceivably freely choose to engage in, then it might indeed be thought "idle" to consider our inability to do them as a restriction upon our freedom.

Admittedly, the persons actually making the principal claim under consideration may have been confused, may not have seen all these alternatives of interpretation, and so forth. The intention here is not to say what such persons did mean when uttering the claims, but only more or less plausibly what they might have meant. The interpretations provide the main lines for the latter. They also provide a clear picture of what needs to be done in order to assess the worth of the claims in each case; for, of course, no pretense is being made here that such arguments are always or even very often ultimately convincing.

Interpretation (2) clearly provides the most difficult and interesting problems. One may analyze and discuss these problems by considering them to be raised by attempts to answer the following four questions:

(*a*) What is to count as an interference with the freedom of persons? (*b*) What is to count as an action that persons might reasonably be said to be either free or not free to perform? (*c*) What is to count as a legitimate interference with the freedom of persons? (*d*) What actions are persons best left free to do?

As was mentioned above, there is a tendency to telescope (*c*) into (*a*), and to telescope (*d*) into (*b*). It was also noted that (*c*) and (*d*) are not distinct questions: they are logically related insofar as criteria of legitimacy are connected to beliefs about what is best or most desirable. (*a*) and (*b*) are also closely related in that an answer to one will affect what can reasonably be considered an answer to the other. The use of these questions as guides in the analysis and understanding of discussions of freedom should not, therefore, be expected to produce always a neat ordering of the discussions. But it *will* help further to delimit the alternatives of reasonable interpretation.

VI

In the end, then, discussions of the freedom of agents can be fully intelligible and rationally assessed only after the specification of each term of this triadic relation has been made or at least understood. The principal claim made here has been that insistence upon this single "concept" of freedom puts us in a position to see the interesting and important ranges of issues separating the philosophers who write about freedom in such different ways, and the ideologies that treat freedom so differently. These issues are obscured, if not hidden, when we suppose that the important thing is that the fascists, communists, and socialists on the one side, for example, have a different concept of freedom from that of the "libertarians" on the other. These issues are also hidden, of course, by the facile assumption that the adherents on one side or the other are never sincere.

Notes

1. The need to elaborate in this unwieldy way arises from the absence in this paper of any discussion of the verification conditions for claims about freedom. The elaboration is designed to leave open the issues one would want to raise in such a discussion.
2. Of writers on political and social freedom who have approached this view, the clearest case is Felix Oppenheim in *Dimensions of Freedom* (New York, 1961); but, while viewing social freedom as a triadic relation, he limits the ranges of the term variables so sharply as to cut one off from many issues I wish to reach. Cf. also T. D. Weldon, *The Vocabulary of Politics* (Harmondsworth, 1953), especially pp. 157 ff.; but see also pp. 70–72.
3. Indeed, lack of clarity on just this point is probably one of the major sources of confusion in discussions of free will.
4. I owe this example to Professor James Pratt.
5. They might also be rooted in differing views on the verification conditions for claims about freedom. This issue would be important to discuss in a full-scale treatment of freedom but, as already mentioned, it is not discussed

in this paper. It plays, at most, an easily eliminable role in the distinction between positive and negative freedom.

6. Yet other attempts at characterization have been offered — most recently and notably by Sir Isaiah Berlin in *Two Concepts of Liberty* (Oxford, 1958). Berlin also offers the second and (more or less) the third of the characterizations cited here.

7. A fair picture of that classification is provided by Berlin (*Two Concepts*) who quotes from various writers in such a way as to suggest that they are in one camp or the other. Identified in this manner as adherents of "negative" freedom one finds Occam, Erasmus, Hobbes, Locke, Bentham, Constant, J. S. Mill, Tocqueville, Jefferson, Burke, Paine. Among adherents of "positive" freedom one finds Plato, Epictetus, St. Ambrose, Montesquieu, Spinoza, Kant, Herder, Rousseau, Hegel, Fichte, Marx, Bukharin, Comte, Carlyle, T. H. Green, Bradley, Bosanquet.

8. For example, consider number 1. Perhaps there is something to it, but the following cautionary remarks should be made. (*a*) The so-called adherents of "negative" freedom might very well accept the *absence* of something as an obstacle to freedom. Consider a man who is not free because, although unguarded, he has been locked in chains. Is he unfree because of the *presence* of the locked chains, or is he unfree because he *lacks* a key? Are adherents of "negative" freedom prohibited from giving the latter answer? (*b*) Even purported adherents of "positive" freedom are not always straightforward in their acceptance of the lack of something as an obstacle to freedom. They sometimes swing toward attributing the absence of freedom to the presence of certain conditions causally connected with the lack, absence, or deprivation mentioned initially. For example, it may be said that a person who was unable to qualify for a position owing to lack of training (and thus not free to accept or "have" it) was prevented from accepting the position by a social, political, economic, or educational "system" the workings of which resulted in his being bereft of training.

Also, insofar as this swing is made, our view of the difference mentioned in number 2 may become fuzzy, for adherents of "positive" freedom might be thought at bottom to regard those "preventing conditions" counting as infringements of freedom as most often if not always circumstances due to human arrangements. This might be true even when, as we shall see is sometimes the case, the focus is on the role of "irrational passions and appetites." The presence or undisciplined character of these may be treated as resulting from the operation of certain specifiable social, educational, or moral institutions or arrangements. (Berlin, e.g., seems to acknowledge this with respect to the Marxists. See *Two Concepts*, p. 8, n. 1, and the text at this point.) Thus one might in the end be able to say no more than this: that the adherents of "negative" freedom are on the whole more inclined to require that the *intention* of the arrangements in question have been to coerce, compel, or deprive persons of this or that. The difference here, however, is not very striking.

9. Locke said: "liberty...is the power a man has to do or forbear doing any particular action according...as he himself wills it" (*Essay Concerning Human Understanding*, Bk. 11, ch. xxi, sec. 15). He also said, of law, "that ill deserves the name of confinement which hedges us in only from bogs and precipices," and "the end of law is, not to abolish or restrain, but to preserve and enlarge freedom" (*The Second Treatise of Government*, sec. 57). He also sometimes spoke of a man's consent as though it were the same as the consent of the majority. Why doesn't all this put him in the camp of "positive" freedom vis-à-vis at least points 2 and 3 above? Concerning the Marxists, see n. 8, *supra*.

10. The point of "consent theories" of political obligation sometimes seems to be to hide from ourselves the fact that a rule of unanimity is an unworkable basis for a system of government and that government does involve coercion. We seem, however, not really to have made up our minds about this.

11. These last ways of putting it are appreciably different. When a person who would otherwise count as a libertarian speaks of persons as free or not free to express themselves, his position as a libertarian may muddy a bit. One may feel invited to wonder which of the multitudinous wants of a given individual *are* expressive of his nature — that is, which are such that their fulfillment is conducive to the expression of his "self."

12. The possibility of conflicts among these criteria has not been much considered by so-called libertarians.

13. See Berlin, *Two Concepts*, pp. 17 ff. (though Berlin significantly admits also that this move can be made by adherents of negative freedom; see p. 19).

14. The libertarian position concerning the borderline is well expressed by Berlin in the following passage on the struggle of colonial peoples: "Is the struggle for higher status, the wish to escape from an inferior position, to be called a struggle for liberty? Is it mere pedantry to confine this word to the main ('negative') senses discussed above, or are we, as I suspect, in danger of calling any adjustment of his social situation favored by a human being an increase of his liberty, and will this not render this term so vague and distended as to make it virtually useless" (*Two Concepts*, p. 44)? One may surely agree with Berlin that there may be something of a threat here; but one may also agree with him when, in the passage immediately following, he inclines to give back what he has just taken away: "And yet we cannot simply dismiss this case as a mere confusion of the notion of freedom with those of status, or solidarity, or fraternity, or equality, or some combination of these. For the craving for status is, in certain respects very close to the desire to be an independent agent." What first needs explaining, of course, is why colonial peoples might believe themselves freer under the rule of local tyrants than under the rule of (possibly) benevolent colonial administrations. Berlin tends to dismiss this as a simple confusion of a desire for freedom with a hankering after status and recognition. What need more careful evaluation than he gives them are (a) the strength of reasons for regarding rule by one's racial and religious peers as self-rule and (b) the strength of

claims about freedom based on the consequences of consent or authorization for one's capacity to speak of "self-rule" (cf. Hobbes's famous chap. xvi in *Leviathan*, "Of Persons and Things Personated"). Cf. n. 10, *supra*.

15. Cf. notes 10 and 14, *supra*.
16. E.g., is it logically possible for a person to be free to do something immoral? Cf. Berlin, *Two Concepts*, p. 10, n.
17. This presumes that the prospect of freeing Smith by restraining *someone else* would be unproblematic even for the friends of negative freedom.
18. *The Second Treatise of Government*, sec. 57. As is remarked below, however, the proper interpretation of this passage is not at all clear.

Select Bibliography

ADLER, MORTIMER. *The Idea of Freedom*, 2 vols. Garden City, N.Y.: Doubleday, 1958–1961.

ANSHEN, RUTH N., ed. *Freedom: Its Meaning*. New York: Harcourt, Brace, 1940.

BAY, CHRISTIAN. *The Structure of Freedom*. Stanford, Calif.: Stanford University Press, 1958.

BERLIN, ISAIAH. *Two Concepts of Liberty*. Oxford: Clarendon Press, 1958.

BERLIN, ISAIAH. *Four Essays on Liberty*. New York: Oxford University Press, 1969.

CRANSTON, MAURICE. *Freedom*. New York: Basic Books, Third Edition, 1967.

DILMAN, ILHAN. "The Freedom of Man," *Proceedings of the Aristotelian Society*, LXII (1961–1962), 39–62.

DRYER, D. P. "Freedom," *Canadian Journal of Economics and Political Science*, XXX (1964), 444 448.

FRIEDRICH, CARL J., ed. *Liberty: Nomos IV*. New York: Atherton Press, 1962.

FULLER, LON. "Freedom: A Suggested Analysis," *Harvard Law Review*, LXVIII (1955), 1305–1325.

GRAHAM, A. C. "Liberty and Equality," *Mind*, LXXIV (1965), 59–65.

HAYEK, F. A. *The Constitution of Liberty*. Chicago: University of Chicago Press, 1960.

MCCLOSKEY, H. J. "A Critique of the Ideals of Liberty," *Mind*, LXXIV (1965), 483–508.

OPPENHEIM, FELIX. *Dimensions of Freedom*, New York: St. Martin's, 1961.

RYAN, ALAN. "Freedom," *Philosophy*, XL (1965), 93–112.

EQUALITY

THE ARTICLES on freedom were exercises in conceptual analysis, and the authors avoided stating their views on moral and political issues. While the focus of the articles in this chapter is largely conceptual (especially the article by Charvet), the authors' arguments contain definite views on the nature of human society and the adequacy of egalitarian ideals. While both articles find that the idea of equality or equality of opportunity is either inadequate, incoherent, or self-contradictory, their similarity stops there. While the authors do not criticize each others' arguments directly, they have quite different reasons for being disenchanted with the idea of equality.

Children are usually not very old when they realize that all men are not equal. But they are then told that the words of the Declaration of Independence "really mean" that men should be given equal opportunity. This seems to be a perfect solution in that it enables them to believe in equality in the face of obvious inequalities among men. John Schaar is not convinced. He believes not only that the equal opportunity doctrine is a poor response to the fact of inequality but also that the doctrine and its implications are not morally desirable. Ostensibly a critique of the equal opportunity principle, Schaar's article is a wide-ranging critique of the liberal, bourgeois, capitalist model of society, its ideological assumptions, its understanding of human psychology, and its model of politics. Schaar probes the "inner spirit" of the equal opportunity principle while simultaneously offering a critique of American society in the Marxian tradition. Without specifically referring to Marx, Schaar enlists some of Marx's most acute thoughts on capitalist society as contained in the *Economic and Philosophic Manuscripts of 1844,* and focuses those thoughts on one of our most widely accepted and cherished ideals.

It is important to note that Schaar criticizes equality of opportunity as an "operative doctrine" which holds that "each man should have equal rights and opportunities to develop his own talents." He focuses on how Americans understand that principle and on how it seems to work in our society. Of course, the principle could be understood in several different ways, and one could attempt to provide a reconstruction of the ideal which would avoid Schaar's criticisms. But if Schaar is to be criticized on his own terms, it must first be shown that his analysis of equal opportunity as an operative doctrine is not valid.

Schaar asserts that the doctrine is basically conservative because it supports equal opportunities to develop only those talents and abilities which society considers worth developing. Since some abilities and

131

talents are always more highly regarded than others, those who advocate equality of opportunity are indirectly supporting the existing hierarchy of values. To support equal opportunity in America may entail supporting opportunities to develop scientific abilities but not opportunities to develop a talent for socialist-revolutionary thought. The distinctions are rarely that extreme, but they are nevertheless significant. Second, the application of the principle will increase the inequalities among men. In a complex, technologically sophisticated society, these inequalities will become even more pronounced. Rather than leading to equality, the principle seems to provide men with the opportunity to become unequal, and increases their natural inequality. The outcome would be a society ruled by a meritocracy, and Professor Schaar agrees with those who find such a model of society morally obnoxious. The equal opportunity principle is, however, only one of many liberal ideals which are founded on a competitive, antagonistic model of society, where human relations are viewed as mere contests. This model of society is based on a conception of human psychology which "reduces man to a bundle of abilities, an instrument valued according to its capacity for performing socially valued functions with more or less efficiency." Men become "winners or losers" in the contest for scarce goods, and the result, says Schaar, is "humanly disastrous" for both.

When Schaar applies his understanding of the equal opportunity principle to politics, he finds that the outcome would be an oligarchy based on merit. This, he feels, is anathema to the democrat. For while such an oligarchy may be preferable to an oligarchy based on birth, wealth, or status, it is still an oligarchy, and the true democrat rejects "oligarchy as such." An oligarchy of merit is not defensible because it is based in part on an extremely narrow and inadequate model of politics. For in capitalist society, politics is understood in economic terms: a competitive struggle for power for the satisfaction of private interests. (The recent application of economic models to politics may support Schaar's contention.) But an alternative view of politics is possible and ethically superior. Politics can be understood as the pursuit of a common good. "Men, acting together, define the ideal aims of the common life and try to bend realities toward them. Through acting with others...each realizes part of his own meaning and destiny." Schaar's attempt to recapture the Aristotelian view of politics may seem strange to us, but it certainly merits our consideration.

If Schaar is disenchanted because a principle of equality seems to lead to inequality, and thus does not serve its purpose, John Charvet is disenchanted because egalitarian ideals are essentially incoherent and/or self-contradictory. Whereas Schaar examines the ideal by focusing on its effects and implications, Charvet examines the ideal by going back to its root assumptions. That their different avenues of approach should lead to different conclusions is not surprising.

The title of Charvet's article suggests a distinction between a "substantive principle" and a "formal principle." Equality can be understood in purely formal terms, which tells us only that equals ought to be treated equally. This, according to Charvet, is perfectly coherent but does not give us any clues as to how specific members of a society ought to be treated. So, while satisfactory as a concept, it is, "trivial and uninteresting" as a principle of society. This latter assertion is subject to question, but its validity is not crucial to Charvet's argument.

According to Charvet, the principle of equality of opportunity is but a derivative of the principle of equality. Equality of opportunity is required because of the assumption that human society will require certain inequalities. But because it is a derivative, and because the assumption seems quite reasonable, the problem with the principle of equality of opportunity is identical to the problem with the principle of equality. Charvet proceeds by looking at four arguments for equality: the "state of nature" argument as developed by Hobbes and others; the idea of "justice as fairness" as developed by John Rawls, which was designed to resolve the inadequacies in the "state of nature" model; the theory of inequality as developed by Rousseau; and the idea of equality of respect. In examining these various arguments, Charvet offers us more than an analysis of equality. He offers us important criticisms of these various doctrines, their models of society, and their assumptions about man. The reader may want to return to Charvet's article after reading Rawls' article in the section on justice.

Charvet's examination of these various arguments is detailed and complex. But in each case the conclusion is essentially the same. He finds that the ideal of equality was formulated in a nonsocial setting and that it really has coherence only in such a setting. But if the principle of equality is to function as a "substantive principle for society," it must be meaningful in a social context. Charvet finds, however, that when it is applied in a social context it is self-contradictory. He finds that the principle of equality of opportunity ultimately requires that men not be dependent on other human beings; in other words, that there be no society. But then these men would not be men.

The articles by Schaar and Charvet can be used to examine each other. While Schaar argues that equality of opportunity is incompatible with the "good society," Charvet argues that it is incompatible with any form of society. But Schaar may wish to point out that when Charvet speaks of "society" he is implicitly employing an unsatisfactory model of society. And Charvet might wish to suggest that Schaar could find the problems with the doctrine not in its effects but in its assumptions.

7

Equality of Opportunity, and Beyond

John H. Schaar

I

EQUALITY is a protean word. It is one of those political symbols —
liberty and fraternity are others — into which men have poured the
deepest urgings of their hearts. Every strongly held theory or conception
of equality is at once a psychology, an ethic, a theory of social relations,
and a vision of the good society.

On the many conceptions of equality that have emerged over time,
the one that today enjoys the most popularity is equality of opportunity.
The formula has few enemies — politicians, businessmen, social
theorists, and freedom marchers all approve it — and it is rarely
subjected to intellectual challenge. It is as though all parties have
agreed that certain other conceptions of equality, and notably the radical
democratic conception, are just too troublesome to deal with because
they have too many complex implications, too broad a scope perhaps,
and a long history resonant of violence and revolutionary fervor.
Equal opportunity, on the other hand, seems a more modest proposal.
It promises that the doors to success and prosperity will be opened
to us all yet does not imply that we are all equally valuable or that all
men are really created equal. In short, this popular and relatively
new concept escapes many of the problems and pitfalls of democratic
equality and emphasizes the need for an equal opportunity among

From *Equality: Nomos IX*, ed. J. Roland Pennock and John W. Chapman (New York:
Atherton Press, 1967), pp. 228–249. Copyright © 1967 by Atherton Press.

men to develop and be paid for their talents, which are of course far from being equal.

The doctrine itself is attractively simple. It asserts that each man should have equal rights and opportunities to develop his own talents and virtues and that there should be equal rewards for equal performances. The formula does not assume the empirical equality of men. It recognizes that inequalities among men on virtually every trait or characteristic are obvious and ineradicable, and it does not oppose differential evaluations of those differences. Nor is the formula much concerned with complex chains of normative reasoning: It is practical and policy-oriented. In addition, equal opportunity is not, in principle, confined to any particular sector of life. It is held to be as applicable to politics as to law, as suitable for education as for economics. The principle is widely accepted as just and generous, and the claim is often made that application of the principle unlocks the energies necessary for social and economic progress.

Whereas this conception of equality answers or evades some questions, it raises others. Who is to decide the value of a man's talents? Are men to be measured by the commercial demand for their various abilities? And if so, what happens to the man whose special gifts are not recognized as valuable by the buying public? And most important, is the resulting inequality, based partly on natural inequalities and partly on the whims of consumers, going to bury the ideal of democratic equality, based on a philosophy of equal human worth transcending both nature and economics?

These are serious questions, and it is my intention in this essay to probe their deeper meanings as well as to clarify some major assumptions, disclose the inner spirit, and explore some of the moral and political implications of the principle of equal opportunity.

II

The first thing to notice is that the usual formulation of the doctrine — equality of opportunity for all to develop their capacities — is rather misleading, for the fact always is that not all talents can be developed equally in any given society. Out of the great variety of human resources available to it, a given society will admire and reward some abilities more than others. Every society has a set of values, and these are arranged in a more or less tidy hierarchy. These systems of evaluation vary from society to society: Soldierly qualities and virtues were highly admired and rewarded in Sparta, while poets languished. Hence, to be accurate, the equality of opportunity formula must be revised to read: equality of opportunity for all to develop those talents which are highly valued by a given people at a given time.

When put in this way, it becomes clear that commitment to the formula implies prior acceptance of an already established social-moral order. Thus, the doctrine is, indirectly, very conservative. It enlists support for the established pattern of values. It also encourages change and growth, to be sure, but mainly along the lines of tendency already apparent and approved in a given society. The doctrine is "progressive" only in the special sense that it encourages and hastens progress within a going pattern of institutions, activities, and values. It does not advance alternatives to the existing pattern. Perhaps we have here an example of those policies that Dwight D. Eisenhower and the theorists of the Republican Party characterized as the method of "dynamic conservatism."

If this argument is correct, then the present-day "radicals" who demand the fullest extension of the equal-opportunity principle to all groups within the society, and especially to Negroes and the lower classes, are really more conservative than the "conservatives" who oppose them. No policy formula is better designed to fortify the dominant institutions, values, and ends of the American social order than the formula of equality of opportunity, for it offers *everyone* a fair and equal chance to find a place within that order. In principle, it excludes no man from the system if his abilities can be put to use within the system. We have here another example of the repeated tendency of American radicals to buttress the existing framework of order even while they think they are undermining it, another example of the inability of those who see themselves as radical critics of the established system to fashion a rhetoric and to formulate ends and values that offer a genuine alternative to the system. Time after time, never more loyally than at the present, America's radicals have been her best conservatives.

Before one subscribes to the equality of opportunity formula, then, he should be certain that the dominant values, institutions, and goals of his society are the ones he really wants. The tone and content of much of our recent serious literature and social thought — thought that escapes the confines of the conservative-radical framework — warn that we are well on the way toward building a culture our best men will not honor. The facile formula of equal opportunity quickens that trend. It opens more and more opportunities for more and more people to contribute more and more energies toward the realization of a mass, bureaucratic, technological, privatized, materialistic, bored, and thrill-seeking, consumption-oriented society — a society of well-fed, congenial, and sybaritic monkeys surrounded by gadgets and pleasure-toys.

Second, it is clear that the equal opportunity policy will increase the inequalities among men. In previous ages, when opportunities were restricted to those of the right birth and station, it is highly probable, given the fact that nature seems to delight in distributing many traits in the pattern of a normal distribution, and given the phenomenon of regression toward the mean, that many of those who enjoyed abundant opportunities to develop their talents actually lacked the native ability to benefit from their advantages. It is reasonable to suppose that many members of ascribed elites, while appearing far superior to the ruck, really were not that superior in actual attainment. Under the regime of equal opportunity, however, only those who genuinely are superior in the desired attributes will enjoy rich opportunities to develop their qualities. This would produce, within a few generations, a social system where the members of the elites really were immensely superior in ability and attainment to the masses. We should then have a condition where the natural and social aristocracies would be identical — a meritocracy, as Michael Young has called it.[1]

Furthermore, the more closely a society approaches meritocracy, the wider grows the gap in ability and achievement between the highest and the lowest social orders. This will happen because in so many fields there are such huge quantities of things to be learned before one can become certified as competent that only the keenest talents, refined and enlarged by years of devoted study and works, can make the grade.[2] We call our age scientific, and describe it further as characterized by a knowledge explosion. What these labels mean from the perspective of equalitarianism is that a handful of men possess a tremendous fund of scientific knowledge, while the rest of us are about as innocent of science as we have always been. So the gap widens: The disparity between the scientific knowledge of an Einstein and the scientific knowledge of the ordinary man of our day is greater than the disparity between a Newton and the ordinary man of his day.

Another force helps widen the gap. Ours is an age of huge, complex, and powerful organizations. Those who occupy positions of command in these structures wield enormous power over their underlings, who, in the main, have become so accustomed to their servitude that they hardly feel it for what it is. The least efficient of the liberal-social welfare states of our day, for example, enjoys a degree of easy control over the ordinary lives of its subjects far beyond the wildest ambitions of the traditional "absolute" rulers. As the commanding positions in these giant organizations come to be occupied increasingly by men who have been generously endowed by nature and, under the equal opportunity principle, highly favored by society, the power gap between the well- and the poorly-endowed widens. The doctrine of equality of opportunity, which in its origins was a rather nervous attempt to forestall moral criticisms of a competitive and inequalitarian society while retaining the fiction of moral equality, now ironically magnifies the natural differences among men by policies based on an ostensibly equalitarian rationale. The doctrine of equal opportunity, social policies and institutions based on it, and advances in knowledge all conspire with nature to produce more and more inequality.

This opens a larger theme. We untiringly tell ourselves that the principle of equality of opportunity is a generous one. It makes no distinctions of worth among men on any of the factitious grounds, such as race, religion, or nationality, that are usually offered for such distinctions. Nor does it set artificial limits on the individual. On the contrary, it so arranges social conditions that each individual can go as high as his natural abilities will permit. Surely, nothing could be fairer or more generous.

The generosity dissolves under analysis. The doctrine of equal opportunity, followed seriously, removes the question of how men should be treated from the realm of human responsibility and returns it to "nature." What is so generous about telling a man he can go as far as his talents will take him when his talents are meager? Imagine a footrace of one mile in which ten men compete, with the rules being the same for all. Three of the competitors are forty years old, five are overweight, one has weak ankles, and the tenth is Roger Bannister. What sense does it make to say that all ten have an equal opportunity to win the race? The outcome is predetermined by nature, and nine of the competitors will call it a mockery when they are told that all have the same opportunity to win.

The cruelty of the jest, incidentally, is intensified with each increase in our ability to measure traits and talents at an early age. Someday our measuring instruments may be so keen that we will be able to predict, with high accuracy, how well a child of six or eight will do in the social race. Efficiency would dictate that we use these tools to separate the superior from the inferior, assigning the proper kinds and qualities of growth resources, such as education, to each group. The very best training and equipment that society can afford would, of course, go to those in the superior group — in order to assure equality of opportunity for the development of their talents. It would seem more generous for men themselves to take responsibility for the matter, perhaps by devising a system of handicaps to correct for the accidents of birth, or by abandoning the competitive ethic altogether.

Three lines of defense might be raised against these criticisms of the equality of opportunity principle.

It might be replied, first, that I have misstated the principle of equal opportunity. Correctly stated, the principle only guarantees equal opportunity for all to *enter* the race, not to *win* it. That is certainly correct: Whereas the equal opportunity principle lets each individual "go as high as his natural abilities will permit," it does not guarantee that all will reach to the same height. Thus, the metaphor of the footrace twists the case in that it shows fools, presumably deluded by the equal opportunity doctrine, trying to stretch hopelessly beyond their natural reach. But there is no reason to think that fat men who foolishly compete against Roger Bannister are deluded by a doctrine. They are deluded because they are fools.

These reservations are entirely proper. The metaphor of the footrace does misrepresent the case. But it was chosen because it also expresses some features of the case which are often overlooked. The equal opportunity principle probably does excite a great many men to dreams of glory far beyond their real capabilities. Many observers of American life have pointed to the frequency of grand, bold, noble "first acts" in the drama of American life, and the scarcity of any "second acts" at all. The equal opportunity principle, with its emphasis on success, probably does stir many men to excesses of hope for winning and despair at losing. It certainly leaves the losers with no external justification for their failures, and no amount of trying can erase the large element of cruelty from any social doctrine which does that. Cases like that of the footrace, and our growing ability to measure men's abilities, make it clear that the equal opportunity principle really is not very helpful to many men. Under its regime, a man with, say, an Intelligence Quotient of ninety is given equal opportunity to go as far as his native ability will take him. That is to say, it lets him go as far as he could have gone without the aid of the doctrine — to the bottom rung of the social ladder — while it simultaneously stimulates him to want to go farther.

Second, it might be argued that the equality of opportunity principle need not be interpreted and applied, as it has been in this treatment, within a setting and under the assumptions of social competitiveness. The principle could be construed as one that encourages the individual to compete against himself, to compare what he is with what he might become. The contest takes place between one's actual and potential selves rather than between oneself and others.

This is an interesting, and hopeful, revision of the principle. It would shift the locus of judgment from society to the individual, and it would change the criteria of judgment from social utility to personal nobility. This shift is possible, but it would require a revolution in our present ways of thinking about equality, for those ways are in fact socially oriented and utilitarian. Hence, this defense against the criticisms is really no defense at all. It is irrelevant in the strict sense that instead of meeting the specific charges it shifts the question to a different battleground. It is an alternative to the existing, operative theory, not a defense of it. In fact, the operative doctrine, with its stress on overcoming others as the path of self-validation, is one of the toughest obstacles in the way of an ethic of personal validation through self-transcendence. The operative doctrine specifies success as the test of personal worth, and by success is meant victory in the struggle against others for the prizes of wealth and status. The person who enters wholeheartedly into this contest comes to look upon himself as an object or commodity whose value is set not by his own internal standards of worth but by the valuations others place on the position he occupies. Thus, when the dogma of equal opportunity is effectively internalized by the individual members of a society, the result is as humanly disastrous for the winners as for the losers. The winners easily come to think of themselves as beings superior to common humanity, while the losers are almost forced to think of themselves as something less than human.

The third defense is a defense, though not a strong one. It consists in explaining that the metaphor of the footrace oversimplifies the reality that is relevant to an appraisal of the equal opportunity principle. What actually occurs in a society is not just one kind of contest but many kinds, so that those who are not good at one thing need only look around for a different contest where they have a better chance of winning. Furthermore, there is not just one prize in a given contest but several. Indeed, in our complex and affluent society, affairs might even be so arranged that everyone would win something: There need be no losers.

This reply has some strength, but not enough to touch the basic points. Although there are many avenues of opportunity in our society, their number is not unlimited. The theory of equal opportunity must always be implemented within a set of conventions which favors some potentialities and discourages others. Persons who strive to develop potentialities that are not admired in a given society soon find their efforts tagged silly, or wrongheaded, or dangerous, or dysfunctional. This is inherent in any society, and it forms an insurmountable barrier to the full development of the principle of equal opportunity. Every society encourages some talents and contests, and discourages others. Under the equal opportunity doctrine, the only men who can fulfill themselves and develop their abilities to the fullest are those who are able and eager to do what society demands they do.

There is, furthermore, a hierarchy of value even among those talents, virtues, and contests that are encouraged: The winners in some contests are rewarded more handsomely than the winners in other contests. Even in a complex society, where many contests take place, and even in an affluent society, where it might seem that there had to be no losers, we know full well that some awards are only consolation prizes, not the real thing, and a bit demanding to their winners. When the fat boy who finishes last in the footrace gets the prize for "best try," he has lost more than he has won.

The formula of equality of opportunity, then, is by no means the warm generous thing it seems to be on first view. Let us now examine the doctrine from another perspective.

III

The equal opportunity principle is widely praised as an authentic expression of the democratic ideal and temper. I shall argue, to the contrary, that it is a cruel debasement of a genuinely democratic understanding of equality. To argue that is also to imply, of course, that a genuinely democratic conception of equality is not widely held in the United States.

The origins and development of the principle are enough to throw some doubt on its democratic credentials. Plato gave the principle its first great statement, and he was no democrat. Nor was Napoleon, who was the first to understand that the doctrine could be made the animating principle of the power state. In the United States, the Jacksonian demand for equal rights was assimilated by the Whigs and quickly converted into the slogan of equal opportunity. It soon won a secure place in popular political rhetoric. Whig politicians used the slogan to blunt popular demands for equality — interpreted as "leveling equality" — while defending the advantages of the wealthy.

This argument from origins is, of course, merely cautionary, not conclusive, but other, more systematic considerations, lead toward the same conclusion.

The doctrine of equality of opportunity is the product of a competitive and fragmented society, a divided society, a society in which individualism, in Tocqueville's sense of the word,[3] is the reigning ethical principle. It is a precise symbolic expression of the liberal-bourgeois model of society, for it extends the marketplace mentality to all the spheres of life. It views the whole of human relations as a contest in which each man competes with his fellows for scarce goods, a contest in which there is never enough for everybody and where one man's gain is usually another's loss. Resting upon the attractive conviction that all should be allowed to improve their conditions as far as their abilities permit, the equal opportunity principle insists that each individual do this by and for himself. Thus, it is the perfect embodiment of the Liberal conception of reform. It breaks up solidaristic opposition to existing conditions of inequality by holding out to the ablest and most ambitious members of the disadvantaged groups the enticing prospect of rising from their lowly state into a more prosperous condition. The rules of the game remain the same: The fundamental character of the social-economic system is unaltered. All that happens is that individuals are given the chance to struggle up the social ladder, change their position on it, and step on the fingers of those beneath them.

A great many individuals do, in fact, avail themselves of the chance to change sides as offered by the principle of equality of opportunity.[4] More than that, the desire to change sides is probably typical of the lower and middle classes, and is widely accepted as a legitimate ethical outlook. In other words, much of the demand for equality, and virtually all of the demand for the kind of equality expressed in the equal opportunity principle, is really a demand for an equal right and opportunity to become unequal. Very much of what goes by the name of democratic sentiment — as that sentiment is molded within the framework of an individualistic, competitive society and expressed in the vocabulary of such a society — is really envy of those who enjoy superior positions combined with a desire to join them.[5]

This whole way of thinking leads effortlessly to the conclusion that the existence of hierarchy, even of oligarchy, is not the antithesis of democracy but its natural and necessary fulfillment. The idea of equality of opportunity assumes the presence of a mass of men of average talents and attainments. The talents and attainments of the superior few can be measured by comparison with this average, mass background. The best emerge from the democracy, the average, and set themselves over it, resting their position securely on the argument from merit and ability. Those on top are automatically justified because they owe their positions to their natural superiority of merit, not to any artificial claim derived from birth, or wealth, or any other such basis. Hence, the argument concludes, the workings of the equal opportunity principle help the democracy discover its own most capable masters in the fairest and most efficient way. Everybody gains: the average many because they are led by the superior few; the superior few because they can legitimately enjoy rewards commensurate with their abilities and contributions.

So pervasive and habitual is this way of thinking today that it is virtually impossible to criticize it with any hope of persuading others of its weaknesses. One is not dealing with a set of specific propositions logically arrayed, but with an atmospheric condition, a climate of opinion that unconsciously governs articulate thought in a variety of fields. Something like this cluster of opinions and sentiments provides the framework for popular discussion of the origins and legitimacy of economic inequality. We are easily inclined to think that a man gets what he deserves, that rewards are primarily products of one's talents and industry, secondarily the consequences of luck, and only in small part the function of properties of the social-cultural structure. Somewhere around three-fourths of all personal wealth in the United States belongs to the richest fifth of our families.[6] There is no evidence, in the form of major political movements or public policies, that this distribution shocks the American democratic conscience — a fact suggesting that the American conscience on this matter simply is not democratic but is, rather, formed by the rhetoric of equal opportunity. Similarly, the giant public and private bureaucracies of our day could not justify for a minute their powers over the lives of men if the men so used did not themselves believe in the justness of hierarchy based on merit — merit always defined as tested competence in a special subject matter, tested mastery of a special skill or craft. Most modern writers on the theory of democracy accept this argument for elitism and point out happily that no serious moral or political problems arise so long as avenues for the movement of members into and out of the hierarchies are freely provided. The principle of equal opportunity, of course, does just that.

The basic argument is not new. What is new is the failure to appreciate the profoundly antidemocratic spirit of the argument. This failure is the specific novelty of the "democratic" thought and sentiment of our day, and it makes today's democrats as amenable to domination as any men have ever been. It is only necessary to persuade the masses (usually an easy task) that the hierarchs possess superior merit and that anyone (one naturally thinks of himself at this point) with the requisite ability can join them.

All that can be said against this orientation is that a genuinely democratic ethic and vision rejects oligarchy *as such*. The democrat rejects in principle the thesis that oligarchy of merit (special competence) is in some way different in kind from oligarchy of any other sort, and that this difference makes it nobler, more reasonable, more agreeable to democracy, than oligarchies built on other grounds. The democrat who understands his commitment holds oligarchy itself to be obnoxious, not merely oligarchy of this or that kind.

The argument for hierarchy based on merit and accomplished by the method of equal opportunity is so widespread in our culture that there seems no way to find a reasonable alternative to it. We automatically think that the choice is either-or: *either* hierarchy and orderly progress *or* anarchy and disorderly stalemate. But that is not so. It is hardly even relevant. The fact that it is thought to be so is a reflection of the crippling assumptions from which modern thought on these matters proceeds. It is thought that there must be hierarchies and masses, elites and nonelites, and that there can be no more democratic way of selecting elites than by the method of equal opportunity. The complexity of affairs demands elites, and democracy and justice require selection of those elites by merit and equal opportunity.

Of course there must be hierarchy, but that does not imply a hierarchical and bureaucratic mode of thinking and acting. It need imply no more than specialization of function. Similarly, the fact that complexity demands specialization of function does not imply the unique merit and authority of those who perform the special functions. On the contrary: A full appreciation of complexity implies the need for the widest possible diffusion of knowledge, sharing of views, and mutual acceptance of responsibility by all members of the affected community.

Of course there must be organization, and organization implies hierarchy. Selection of the hierarchs by the criterion of merit and the mechanism of equal opportunity seems to reassure the worried democrat that his values are not being violated. But hierarchy may or may not be consonant with the democratic spirit. Most of today's democratic thinkers soothe themselves on this question of democracy and organization with the assertion that everything that can be done is being done when organizations permit factions, provide channels of consultation, and protect individual rights by establishing quasi-judicial bodies for hearing and arbitrating disputes. Certainly these guarantees are valuable, but they have little to do with making organizations democratic. They are constitutionalist devices, not democratic ones.

Before there can be a democratic organization there must first be a democratic mentality — a way of thinking about the relations among men which stresses equality of being and which strives incessantly toward the widest possible sharing of responsibility and participation in the common life. A democratic orientation does not grow from and cannot coexist with the present bureaucratic and "meritorian" ethic. It is an alternative to the present ethic, not an expansion or outgrowth of it. When the democratic mentality prevails, it will not be too hard to find the mechanisms for implementing it.

IV

I hope my argument will not be interpreted as some sort of mindless demand for the abolition of distinctions or as a defense of the ethic of mutual aid against the ethic of competition. The argument was mainly negative in intention, attempting to show that the idea of equality of opportunity is a poor tool for understanding even those sectors of life to which the notion of equality is applicable. It is a poor tool in that, whereas it seems to defend equality, it really only defends the equal right to become unequal by competing against one's fellows. Hence, far from bringing men together, the equal opportunity doctrine sets them against each other. The doctrine rests on a narrow theory of motivation and a meager conception of man and society. It reduces man to a bundle of abilities, an instrument valued according to its capacity for performing socially valued functions with more or less efficiency. Also, the doctrine leads inevitably to hierarchy and oligarchy, and tries to soften that hard outcome by a new form of the ancient argument that the best should rule. In all these ways, the idea of equality of opportunity constitutes a thorough misunderstanding of a democratic conception of equality.

It is not the primary task of this essay to set forth a genuinely democratic conception of equality: that is a work for another time. Still, enough should be done in the second part of this essay to arrest the most obvious and most likely objections to the first part.

The equal opportunity principle is certainly not without value. Stripped of its antagonistic and inequalitarian overtones, the formula can be used to express the fundamental proposition that no member of the community should be denied the basic conditions necessary for the fullest possible participation in the common life, insofar as those conditions can be provided for by public action and through the use of public resources. This formulation will take one some distance toward a democratic conception of equality, but it must be interpreted carefully, for it can easily turn into just another defense of the equal right to become unequal.

Still, the formulation does provide some useful guidelines. It obviously implies equality in and before the law. It also implies a far greater measure of economic equality than is the case today. The issue here is not material comfort. Nor does it have anything to do with the notion that justice is served when economic goods are allocated according to the actual work (in the customary definition) each man does. That is impossible. We may urge that each should contribute according to his ability; we must surely insist that each be provided for according to his need.

What the criterion of a substantial degree of economic equalization requires is the establishment of the material conditions necessary for a generous measure of freedom of choice for all members of the community and the establishment of the conditions necessary for relations of mutual respect and honesty among the various economic and social groups within a society. This is not some kind of leveling demand for equality of condition. It is no more than a recognition of the obvious fact that the great material inequality that prevails in America today produces too much brutishness, impotence, and rage among the lower classes and too much nervous vulgarity among the middle classes. There is no assertion here that economic equalization is the sufficient condition for the democratic New Jerusalem. Rather, the assertion is negative. As Arnold put it, "equality will never of itself alone give us a perfect civilization. But, with such inequality as ours, a perfect civilization is impossible."[7]

The equality of opportunity principle, as formulated above, also implies the equal right of each member to share in the political life of the community to the fullest extent of his interest and ability. But this is the point at which the principle, no matter how carefully formulated, easily leads one away from a democratic view. The equal opportunity principle as employed today in, for example, discussions of representation and voting rights, really does nothing more than fortify the prevailing conception of political action as just another of the various steps individuals and groups take to secure and advance their own interests and advantages. In this view, politics is but another aspect of the struggle for competitive advantage, and men need political power in order to protect and advance their private powers. This conception of politics is drawn from the economic sphere and never rises above the ethical and psychological possibilities of that sphere.

When it is understood that the principle of equal opportunity is in our time an expression of the competitive, capitalistic spirit, and not of the democratic spirit, then the boundaries of its applicability begin to emerge. To the extent that competition is inescapable, or socially useful, all competitors should have the same advantages, and this the equal opportunity principle guarantees. In any competitive situation, some will do better than others, and it seems just that those who do well should be rewarded more generously than those who do poorly. This too the principle guarantees.

The basic question, however, is not whether competition should be praised or condemned, but where and under what conditions competition is a desirable principle of action and judgment and where and under what conditions it is not. Some kinds of competition actually draw men more closely together whereas others produce antagonism and isolation. The problem is to distinguish between these kinds, encouraging the former and discouraging the latter. Peace is but a euphemism for slavery unless men's competitive energies are given adequate outlet. Most people probably have some need for both inward and outward striving. Perhaps the struggles against other people and the struggles within the self can be brought to some kind of balance in each individual and in society as a whole. Ideally, we might strive toward a truly pluralistic society in which nearly everybody could find a specialty he could do fairly well and where he would enjoy friendly competition with others. Judged by this imaginative possibility, our present social order is a mean thing. It is a kind of institutionalized war game, or sporting contest, in which the prizes are far too limited in kind, the referees and timekeepers far too numerous, and the number of reluctant and ill-adjusted players far too high. We need a social order that permits a much greater variety of games. Such a social order could, I think, be based on an effort to find a place for the greatest possible range of natural abilities among men. The variety of available natural abilities is enormous and worth much more exploration than any of the currently dominant conceptions of social order are willing to undertake. In the United States today, the fundamental justification of the equal opportunity principle is that it is an efficient means for achieving an indefinite expansion of wealth and power. Many men are unsuited by nature for that competition, so that nature herself comes to seem unjust. But many of the injustices we regard nature as having perpetrated on individuals are actually no more than artifacts of the narrow we take of nature's possibilities and a consequent distortion of the methods and ideals by which we attempt to transcend nature. For example, in defining intelligence as what I.Q. tests measure, we constrict the meanings of intelligence, for there are many modes of intelligence that the tests do not capture — nature is more protean than man's conception of her. Furthermore, having defined intelligence in a certain way, we then proceed to reward the people who have just that kind of intelligence and encourage them to use it in the pursuit of knowledge, which they are likely to do by building computers, which in turn give only certain kinds of knowledge. Thus our constricted definition of nature is confirmed by the methods we use to study nature. In this special sense, there might still be something to say for the eighteenth-century idea that society should imitate nature.

We must learn to ask questions like these about the method of competition and the principle of equal opportunity. The task is to define their proper spheres of action, not to treat them as blocks to be totally accepted or rejected. At the outer limit, it seems clear that whereas every society is to some extent competitive and competition in some spheres is socially and individually valuable, no society ought to exalt the competitive spirit as such, and the equal opportunity principle that implements it. Both conceptions tend naturally toward selfishness unless carefully controlled.

V

In addition to equality of opportunity, there is another kind of equality that is blind to all questions of success or failure. This is the equality that obtains in the relations among the members of any genuine community. It is the feeling held by each member that all other members, regardless of their many differences of function and rank, belong to the community "as fully as he does himself."[8] Equal opportunity, far from strengthening this kind of equality, weakens it.

When this point is reached, when the discussion turns to the meanings of equality involved in a democratic conception of membership and a democratic conception of ruling and being ruled, the equal opportunity principle — no matter how carefully formulated — begins to mislead. A fuller conception of equality is needed, one stripped of the antagonistic and privatistic overtones of the equal opportunity principle. That fuller conception, in turn, requires a broader view of politics than is afforded by the "who gets what, when, how" perspective.

Political life occupies a middle ground between the sheer givens of nature and society on the one side and the transcendental "kingdom of ends" on the other. Through political action men publicly strive to order and transform the givens of nature and society by the light of values drawn from a realm above or outside the order of the givens. Men, acting together, define the ideal aims of the common life and try to bend realities toward them. Through acting with others to define and achieve what can be called good for all, each realizes part of his own meaning and destiny. Insofar as man is a being that wants not merely to live but to live well, he is a political being. And insofar as any man does not participate in forming the common definition of the good life, to that degree he falls short of the fullest possibilities of the human vocation. No man can assign to another dominion over how he shall live his life without becoming something less than a man. This way of thinking about political action leads to an idea of equality whose tone and implications are very different from those of the equal opportunity formulation.

Other features of political action lead in the same direction, and, specifically, require a rejection of all claims to rulership based on the ancient analogies between the art of ruling and other arts. When one contracts with a carpenter to build a house, he may assume that the carpenter's skills are sufficient to the work that is to be done. But when citizens elevate some among them to places of political authority the case is different. Politics has so few givens and so many contingencies and complexities, contains so many dangerous possibilities and so few perfect solutions, and is such a baffling mixture of empirical, prudential, and ethical considerations that no man or group of men has knowledge and skill sufficient for all situations. As John Winthrop said, no man can "profess nor undertake to have sufficient skill for that office."[9]

Winthrop's comment, grounded as it is on a solid understanding of the political vocation, is a just rebuke to all claims for political authority based on technical competence. Relations between politician and citizen are very different from those between craftsman and employer. Politicians cannot be said to serve or to execute the will of citizens in the way that craftsmen can be said to serve their employers. Nor can politicians claim authority over their work and over other persons engaged in that work on the grounds of technical competence. The relations between politicians and citizens, in sum, are relations among equals in a number of important senses. Above all, their relations are built on premises that, when properly understood, encourage genuine conversation among the participants, not merely the transmission of information and commands up and down a line. This way of thinking about the matter presumes equality among citizens in the sense most basic to a democratic understanding of the relations among the members of a political community — in the sense of equality of being — and hence presumes the widest possible participation in and sharing of responsibility for the policies that govern the whole community.

Just as political authorities may not lay claim to superior rights on the ground of special merit, neither may ordinary citizens absolve themselves from partial responsibility for public policies on the ground that their task is done when they have selected those who will take active charge of the affairs of the policy. The democratic idea offers no such easy absolution from shared responsibility and guilt.

This sharing of responsibility and guilt may be one of the reasons why a genuinely democratic conception of equality is not easy to accept even by those who call themselves democrats. It is comforting to men to think that someone else is competently in charge of the large and dangerous affairs of politics: Somebody else rules; I just live here. Hierarchy and oligarchy provide subjects with that comfort and with easy escapes from shared responsibility and guilt. This freedom from political responsibility is very valuable to men who would much rather devote themselves to their private interests anyway, than share the burden of caring for the public good. The doctrine of equality of opportunity, tied as it is to the principle of hierarchy, easily leads to moral arrogance on the part of the winners and to the taking of moral holidays by the losers.

A proper view of equality still leaves wide scope for the existence of necessary and just superiorities and differences, but it brings a different mentality to their appraisal. Certainly, some things *are* better than others, and more to be preferred. Some vocations and talents are more valuable than others, and more to be rewarded. The implication here is only that the more highly skilled, trained, or talented man has no ground either for thinking himself a better *man* than his less-favored fellows, or for regarding his superiorities as providing any but the most temporary and limited justification for authority over others. The paradigmatic case is that of the relation between teacher and student. The teacher's superior knowledge gives him a just claim to authority over his students. But central to the ethic of teaching is the conviction that the teacher must impart to students not only his substantive knowledge but also the critical skills and habits necessary for judging and contributing to that knowledge. The teacher justifies his authority and fulfills his duty by making himself unnecessary to the student.

Perhaps this at least suggests the outlines of a democratic conception of equality and draws the boundaries of its applicability. The heart of such a view of equality is its affirmation of equality of being and belonging. That affirmation helps identify those sectors of life in which we should all be treated in a common or average way, so that the minimal conditions of a common life are made available to all: legal equality, equal rights of participation in political life, equal right to those average material provisions necessary for living together decently at all. It also stresses the greatest possible participation in and sharing of the common life and culture while striving to assure that no man shall determine or define the being of any other man.

This is what equality is all about, and it is a great deal.[10] But it is far from everything. Beyond the realm of the average and the comparable lies another realm of relations among men where notions of equality have no relevance. Hence, a fair understanding of equality requires a sense of the boundaries of that realm in which equalitarian categories do not apply.

Those boundaries begin where we try to define man himself. Every attempted formulation of equality stumbles on the mystery and the indefinability of the creature for and about whom the formulation is made. In the end, it makes no sense to say that all men are equal, or that any two men are, because it is impossible to say what a man is. It is easy to abstract a part from the whole and define that part in terms that make it commensurable with the same parts abstracted from other whole men. Thus, one can define an American citizen in terms that impart perfect sense to the proposition that all American citizens are equal. But when it comes to talking about whole men and about man, the concept of equality is mute. Then there is only the mystery of being, the recognition of self and others. Lawrence has expressed the idea perfectly, and he should be permitted the last word:

> One man is neither equal nor unequal to another man. When I stand in the presence of another man, and I am my own pure self, am I aware of the presence of an equal, or of an inferior, or of a superior? I am not. When I stand with another man, who is himself, and when I am truly myself, then I am only aware of a Presence, and of the strange reality of Otherness. There is me, and there is *another being*.... There is no comparing or estimating.... Comparison enters only when one of us departs from his own integral being, and enters the material mechanical world. Then equality and inequality starts at once.[11]

Notes

1. Michael Young, *The Rise of the Meritocracy* (London: Thames and Hudson, 1958). Young's book imaginatively explores the conditions under which Jefferson's lovely dream of rule by the natural aristocracy turns into a nightmare of banality and outrage. The main condition, of course, is the dedication of virtually all creative energies to the goal of material abundance.
2. Success is a function of both inborn talent and the urge to do well, and it is

often impossible to tell which is the more important in a particular case. It is certain that the urge to do well can be stimulated by social institutions. How else can we account for Athens or Florence, or the United States?

3. *Democracy in America* (New York: Vintage, 1945), Vol. 2, pp. 104–105.

4. Some civil rights leaders are suspicious of open enrollment plans to combat *de facto* segregation for precisely this reason.

5. "The greatest obstacle which equality has to overcome is not the aristocratic pride of the rich, but rather the undisciplined egoism of the poor." Proudhon, as quoted in James Joll, *The Anarchists* (Boston: Little, Brown, 1964), p. 67.

6. Oscar Goss, "The Political Economy of the Great Society," *Commentary* (October 1965), pp. 31–37, at p. 37.

7. Matthew Arnold, essay on "Equality" (1878), in A. L. Bouton, ed., *Matthew Arnold: Prose and Poetry* (New York: Scribner's, 1927), p. 362.

8. John Plamenatz, *Man and Society* (New York: McGraw-Hill), 1963, Vol. II, p. 120.

9. John Winthrop, "Speech to the General Court" (July 3, 1645), in Perry Miller, ed., *The American Puritans: Their Prose and Poetry* (Garden City, N.Y.: Doubleday Anchor, 1956), pp. 91–92.

10. As Paine said, with permissible exaggeration, "inequality of rights has been the cause of all the disturbances, insurrections, and civil wars, that ever happened...." Thomas Paine, *Works*, ed. J. P. Mendum (Boston: 1878), Vol. I, pp. 454–455.

11. D. H. Lawrence, "Democracy," as quoted in Raymond Williams, *Culture and Society, 1780–1950* (New York: Columbia University Press, 1958), p. 211.

8

The Idea of Equality as a Substantive Principle of Society

John Charvet

I AM concerned in this paper with the idea that a principle of equality must constitute the basis of any good, just, or fully human society. A principle of equality as the basis of such a society could, however, be largely formal — it could be the principle which states that equals should be treated equally, and this is formal because it does not of itself tell us how any of the particular members of a society should be treated. We first have to identify in what respects anybody is to be counted as equal to anybody else before we can say anything about how they should be treated. Such a formal, basic principle of society would thus be a relatively trivial and uninteresting affair. What I am interested in here is the possibility that there could be a substantive principle of equality, a principle, that is, which of itself could tell us how the particular members of a society should be treated.

A principle which tells us that all members of a society ought to be treated equally could only arrive at this conclusion if in the premises of the argument there is some statement about the actual equality of these men. In the arguments that I shall consider, however, it is not supposed that men are equal in such matters as their physical and mental qualities. The respect in which men are said to be equal is sometimes put in the form of an assumed actual natural equality, by which is meant that no man can naturally claim any kind of authority over any other man. In respect of authority all men are naturally equal.

The classical argument for this position, as it is found in the works

This article appeared in *Political Studies*, XVII (1969), 1–13.

of modern political philosophers since Hobbes, proceeds by initially removing men hypothetically from all social relations and putting them into the so-called state of nature. These philosophers then assert that men in such a state must be supposed to be free and equal. And this I take to mean the following: if, having put men hypothetically in such a state, one asks "In virtue of what could one man claim to exercise authority over any other man?" the answer must be in virtue of nothing whatever. In such a state nothing could count as a valid ground for one man to claim such authority. Now this is true because the hypothesis has removed the conditions in which the exercise of authority by one man over others makes sense. That is, authority only makes sense in the context of social relations and human practices and activities, where some men on the basis of the possession of attributes or qualities considered relevant to the carrying on of such practices and activities can legitimately claim a superior position over others, so that if one removes this context one necessarily removes the conditions in which one can talk meaningfully about authority. These philosophers conclude, therefore, that all men are naturally in a state of equal authority toward each other, which is to say that no authoritative relations exist naturally between men.

In the beginning this argument was directed toward politically authoritative positions and concluded from its premises that political superiority, since it could not exist naturally, could only exist with the consent of all the members of society. In addition, since each man is naturally his own master — lord of himself and subject to no other — men could only enter society on equal terms. The conditions for membership in the society must be the same for all. Thus, at the basis of society is an initial principle of equality that appears to be of a substantive nature. While this argument was at first directed toward political authority, it naturally led to a more general attitude toward superior positions and the construction of a derivative principle, namely, the principle of equality of opportunity. For if one begins with the premise that no man can naturally claim a superior position over others and yet recognizes both that human abilities vary and that for human activities and practices to be carried on superior positions will be necessary or beneficial, then one will conclude that the opportunity to attain such positions must be open equally to all. That is, the legitimate title to the occupation of such positions must be merit alone — the possession of the natural abilities considered relevant to the carrying on of the required activities. And since possessing a pedigree of a certain kind or money of a certain amount cannot of itself give one these abilities, to admit such criteria as legitimate bases for a claim to exercise authority would be to admit that, independently of any specific activities or relations, some people have a legitimate claim to exercise authority, which would be inconsistent with the premises.

Now the principle of equality of opportunity as derived from an initial principle of equality together with assumptions about the desirability of differentiated positions is also a substantive principle of society, for it specifies in what ways opportunities to attain superior positions are to be allocated among the members of society, namely, equally to all. But there is something wrong with the above argument, and this is due to the initial hypothesis of a state of nature. For it is difficult to see what sense can be attached to talk about individuals in a state of nature as human beings at all, i.e., as beings possessing the attributes of humanity. We are inclined to think of humanity as essentially social, as only developing in a social context; we do not think of it as a characteristic of individuals independently of their having entered into social relations. If this is true, to talk about beings in a nonsocial state could have no relevance at all to a different type of being existing in a social condition.

However, in his article "Justice as Fairness," John Rawls has attempted to reformulate the classical argument while removing the difficulty of the initial hypothesis of a state of nature. (See pp. 192–216 of this volume.) Rawls' argument is the following: instead of postulating a state of nature we begin by assuming a number of mutually self-interested men already engaged in a well-established system of practices. From time to time individuals engaged in the practice may be expected to complain that they are being treated unjustly. We may then suppose that the participants in the practice discuss among themselves on what principles such complaints are to be adjudicated. Rawls asks us to imagine that they adopt the following procedure: each man is asked to propose the principles on which he would like his complaints to be judged. No complaints will be tried until everyone agrees on the principles by which the complaints are to be judged. It is further understood that once they are accepted, these principles will be binding on all future occasions, so that a man will not be inclined to propose principles to his immediate advantage when on future, unknown occasions they may work to his disadvantage. One would expect such men, Rawls says, to agree on certain general principles which each man sees as a guarantee that his present and future interests will be protected. Now Rawls also assumes that (a) participants are roughly equal in power and ability, so that no one can of himself dominate the others, and (b) no one knows what his future position in the practice will be. Given all this, Rawls says, his men will naturally agree on equality as an initial principle — that is, that advantages of the practice be distributed equally. This will be so because each man, wishing to protect his interests and not knowing what his future condition will be, can only acknowledge equality as a principle safeguarding his interests. But equality is only an initial principle, and assuming them to be reasonable men, they will accept departures from such an initial position if the departures can be justified as being beneficial to all. Departures in the direction of unequal positions will then be accepted, provided that all gain from them and that such positions are open to all to attain. On this argument, then, we have as an initial substantive principle of a just practice, or of a just society seen as a system of practices, equality, and equality of opportunity as a secondary derivative principle. Both these principles, however, may be overridden by a superior consideration, which is that departures from them make *everyone* in the practice better off.

Before examining the validity of this reformulation of the classical position, I shall consider the notion of equality of opportunity as a substantive principle, for I think it can easily be seen that this notion ends in absurdity. But since it is logically derived from the initial principle of equality together with an assumption that unequal positions in human practices will be necessary and beneficial, then it would follow that either this assumption is wrong, which seems implausible, or the principle of equality, as we have it in the above arguments, must be false. If one starts by considering the opportunity to attain superior positions in adult practices, one is rapidly led backward into arguing that the opportunity to obtain the education necessary to attain positions should be equal for all. But one cannot stop at schooling, for the development of abilities begins in the family, and it is obvious that families differ in their ability to provide initial opportunities for development. Entrance into more favored families depends, however, not on merit but on mere accident of birth.

This circumstance, it is true, can be remedied by removing children from families altogether and bringing them up in state nurseries. But at this point I can couch the argument in more general terms. The principle of equality of opportunity requires that everyone be in an equal position in regard to those who help and encourage development, i.e., parents, teachers, friends, etc. Having access to those who help rather than hinder, or help more or hinder less, confers an unfair advantage unless the access itself is awarded on merit. But since it is absurd to suppose that access could be adequately controlled in this way, the only two other possibilities are that all those with whom developing individuals associate be equal in their capacities to help such development or that there be no such association at all. And both these are absurd fantasies. What I am saying in this: the principle of equality of opportunity requires that no one be dependent for self-development on any other human being or human practice unless this dependence is equal for all. It is accepted, however, that men's abilities and capacities vary, so that the condition for the satisfaction of this requirement is that no one be dependent on anyone else. But this condition is one of having no society at all, and so no men.

However, it might be said that Rawls' argument does not require that equality of opportunity be realized in all cases, for it may be overruled by a higher consideration, namely, that all gain from not having equality of opportunity in particular cases. But this argument supposes that equality of opportunity is in itself a good, although it may be overruled by a higher good — everybody being better off. And this must be the case if equality of opportunity is to be a principle at all. But what I am saying is that as a principle it cannot be satisfactorily formulated, i.e., formulated without incoherence or contradiction, for a complete formulation renders it incompatible with any form of human society even while it is being put forward as a principle of a good human society. To say "But we can use it without contradiction in specific areas such as entry into the civil service or education" begs the question: use what? For if one uses the principle of equality of opportunity then one is using an incoherent notion. One can talk sensibly and be understood in specific areas only because one need not be said to be using this principle at all, but applying the formal principle of equality — that equals should be treated equally — and providing reasons for thinking that certain distinctions hitherto made, class, money, etc., should not now be taken as constituting inequalities relevant to treating equals equally in such and such an area of human activity.

Now if the idea of equality of opportunity as a substantive principle of the just society is false, and if it is logically derived from the principle of equality together with the reasonable assumption that human practices require superior positions, then there must be something wrong with this principle of equality. The classical argument for equality was wrong in that it purported to be talking significantly about the human condition while removing the context in which any such talk could be meaningful. And in fact these writers only achieve apparent relevance because, while removing man's social context, they leave him with attributes which he could only have developed in such a context.

However, the reformulation of this position by Rawls is in no better state. For although he assumes his men to be engaged in a well-established system of human practices, and thus can legitimately allow them human attributes, his argument requires two further assumptions which are incompatible with his initial assumption — namely, that his men are roughly equal in power and ability and that no one knows what his future position in the practice will be. To make these two further assumptions is merely to reintroduce the state of nature by the back door. For insofar as his men are engaged in a well-established practice they will necessarily be occupying certain positions within the practice and have legitimate expectations as to what their future positions will be. If this were not so, they could hardly be said to be engaging in a practice at all. But if they occupy such positions then some will have more power within the system than others, and indeed have more or less definite expectations of its maintenance or acquisition. Such men cannot then be said to be equal in power, ability, and expectations. If they are then asked to debate on what general principles claims of injustice within the system are to be adjudicated, there is no reason to suppose that they would all agree on an initial principle of equality. For at least some, those who possess the necessary attributes, occupy established positions of authority whose legitimacy derives from the accepted purposes and standards of the practice. For these men to agree to accept equality as an initial principle would mean agreement to a principle that has no conceivable relevance to their position. Rawls wants to say that all will accept equality as a guarantee against being done down by the others became no one knows what his future position will be. But since this cannot be true, equality cannot serve as a guarantee to those with established positions and expectations. Rawls' argument would only be true if the men engaged in the practice do not have established positions in the practice and so consequently are not engaged in the practice at all. It follows therefore that equality could only make sense as a principle to those in inferior positions who want to destroy the superior positions of others, and if this is all that is going on, it deserves not the slightest attention.

So Rawls' argument is merely a restatement of the classical position and rests on the validity of its starting point — a state of nature in which, it is claimed, something significant is being said about men who have no social relations of any kind. And if the derivative principle of equality of opportunity is self-contradictory, it is because the initial principle of equality from which it is derived is self-contradictory also. For it asserts as a basic principle to govern men's social relations a principle which only makes sense in a condition in which men have no social relations. The contradiction within the notion of equality and its related principle, equality of opportunity, can be further brought out by considering the egalitarian argument in the more complex formulation of Jean-Jacques Rousseau.

Rousseau starts off with the traditional rigmarole about the state of nature in which individuals possessing human attributes pursue their lives independently of each other, and so independently of all social relations. These men, Rousseau argues, cannot be supposed to be corrupt or vicious, for corruption and viciousness between men can only exist in a social context. He then provides an argument to show how corruption accompanies the emergence of social relations. The argument is this: in a state of nature men are conscious only of themselves and not of other human beings; consequently, they cannot compare themselves with others to see whether they are more beautiful, stronger, more able, etc., than others. Once social relations develop, however, men become conscious of others as well as of themselves; at the same time, social relations only develop once men start carrying on common activities together. But carrying on common activities — hunting, dancing, or whatever — involves standards of performance in terms of which some people can be judged superior to others. Now since men have become conscious of others, they have become conscious of themselves as occupying certain positions in relation to others through the activities they carry on together. Some men are respected more than others, and positions of superiority become desired for the respect they command from others. Men come to be concerned with the opinions that others have of them and wish to elicit from others those opinions that most flatter them. Thus they learn to appear what they are not; deceit and lying emerge together with pride, vanity, contempt, vengeance, etc. Men have become corrupt and are henceforth involved in a struggle for power or superiority.

Now the essence of what has gone wrong is that men have become dependent on each other by becoming dependent for their own self-respect on the opinions that others have of them. They cannot do without others, for only others can make the judgments which will provide them with the self-respect they need. At the same time, however, others constitute threats to them because others can withhold the judgments they look for or give judgments that cannot possibly satisfy. In these circumstances individuals are left in a perpetual state of unease and restlessness, out of harmony with themselves and others, alienated; they have no chance of achieving happiness. If, however, this condition of humanity is to be altered, the remedy must strike at the roots of the evil; namely, at the very dependence of men on each other. One must create a form of society in which no one is dependent on any other man.

The concern to win the respect of others Rousseau calls amour-propre; as we have seen, it only emerges in a social condition. However, the amour-propre of a man, Rousseau says, leads him to desire first place for himself — to be superior to others. But since all men desire this, and since by definition not all can be satisfied, it results in perpetual struggle and conflict between men. In these circumstances, Rousseau says, the condition of a good society is that the amour-propre of men be destroyed or at least suppressed, and this can be done if they substitute a demand for equality in the place of the demand for superiority. Now this is fair because equality acts as a guarantee that no one will suffer from its realization, i.e., no one will be made inferior to anyone else. This equality resolves at the same time the problem of the dependence of men on each other, or the living in the opinions of others, which is the root of the problem. For equality necessarily destroys the condition, i.e., inequality, in which the amour-propre of a man can be influential in his relations to others. Amour-propre can only begin to emerge and wreak its havoc if the conditions exist in which some people can achieve superiority over others. And if amour-propre cannot get a grip on a man's activities, then there is no scope for him to be concerned with the opinions or judgments of others, and so no possibility of his achieving or not achieving the respect of others. Thus equality, in constituting the condition which suppresses amour-propre, constitutes also the condition which destroys the dependence of men on each other, and thus all the evils of the human situation. Man ceases to be corrupt, alienated, unhappy.

However, all this is of course an absurdity, for it involves as the condition of the good, just, or fully human society the suppression of that element in man, namely his amour-propre or desire for the respect of others and of himself, which constitutes his specifically human characteristic, and requires as the condition for the overcoming of man's alienation the total alienation of his humanity. For, as Rousseau has shown, human society only emerges with the development of activities that men carry on together, activities which involve standards of performance and so inequalities of performance. Thus given that men are conscious of both themselves and others, and thus of themselves in relation to others, the condition of a human society is also the condition for the existence of amour-propre or the concern for the respect of others and of oneself in relation to others. So, insofar as they are human, men are necessarily dependent on each other in the manner described, and Rousseau's argument involves the establishment as a principle of a human society the very principle which makes human society impossible.

But having argued for equality as the solution to all human problems, Rousseau then admits that distinctions within society are both necessary and permissible, provided that in attaining differentiated positions individuals do not owe their positions, either superior or inferior, to the will of any other men. That is, if inequalities are to be permitted, they must not contradict the basic principle of society, namely, the nondependence of men on each other, and this can only be so if a man is not dependent for the position he occupies on the wills of other men. And this, as we have seen, is the essential implication of the principle of equality of opportunity: in occupying a position of a certain sort, I must not owe it to the relations I may have had with any other man, i.e., the relations must be either equal for all or nonexistent. But this, as we have also seen, is a fantasy. Thus, if distinctions are admitted into society, it will necessarily be the case that interdependence of men will have been recreated. Consequently, the admission of distinctions and of equality of opportunity as a derivative principle must necessarily contradict the basic principle from which it is derived — equality as a condition of nondependence. And this is possible because the basic principle is itself self-contradictory.

The Rousseauian argument introduced the notion of respect, and since then people have argued from a notion of equality of respect which is owed to all men in an egalitarian society. I shall now consider this argument, first in relation to the form it has in an article by Bernard Williams called "The Idea of Equality."[1] Williams' argument is as follows: Men are being with purposes and intentions, who are also conscious of these. In judging a man, one may do so solely in terms of his public achievements, whether he is a good administrator or academic or whatever. But clearly one can also enter into a man's own attitude or consciousness of his life, i.e., see him not only from the external point of view but also from the point of view of how he himself sees his efforts and understands his activities and performances. To treat a man in a fully human way and with respect, Williams says, is to adopt this internal point of view, and all men deserve equally this effort of identification. But while at first sight nothing much seems to follow from this, i.e., it would appear compatible with an hierarchical society based on birth, Williams wants to say that in following out its implications, one is led in the direction of an egalitarian society. A man's consciousness of his role in society, Williams argues, is the product of that society itself, and can be increased or diminished by social action. Now what keeps stable hierarchies together is a belief in the necessity of the social orders of the society. But this will involve false consciousness, for people will not be fully conscious of the roles they actually occupy in society, but see them in a false light. Now suppose that while the lower orders retain their false consciousness, some members of the upper orders come to a clearer and truer view of their roles, i.e., they no longer see them as necessary. Then, in order to preserve the society, it will be necessary to prevent the lower orders from developing the awareness of their roles that would undermine the stability of the system. Consequently an element of conscious deceit enters the system, as well as an element of contempt, as the upper orders will necessarily see the lower orders as self-deceived. These elements destroy the equality of respect that is required for a just society, and so the argument leads to a demand for a socially egalitarian society.

This argument, however, rests on two notions — seeing one's role as necessary and being conscious of one's role; these aspects are insufficiently explored by Williams. With regard to the former notion of seeing the structure of one's society as necessary, which involves false consciousness, it has to be the case that the members of that society perceive their social structure as what must be. But suppose they are not aware of any other possible social structure. Now the idea of their accepting the social structure as what must be or as necessary becomes problematical. For it is not clear what could be meant by this, other than merely repeating that they accept their social structure with no questions asked. But merely accepting something with no questions asked or doubts raised is different from believing it to be necessary, for the latter supposes that one raises the question of alternatives and finds no answer. But then those who merely accept something cannot be said to possess false consciousness with regard to what they accept, because there cannot be anything false in merely accepting something. One is accepting it for what it is, not for what it is not. Furthermore, the notion of necessity is relative. Nothing is necessary in itself, but always in relation to something else. So that being aware of alternative forms of society and still asserting that one's own form is necessary would only involve falseness if what one was asserting was that of all the possible forms of society, this one is the only possible one, i.e., necessary for human beings, which would be like pointing to a tree and saying that this is the only possible tree. One could, however, be asserting or believing that one's own society is the only possible good, just, or fully human one, or necessary for human beings. This may, of course, involve false consciousness, but all I want to say is that the notion of necessity will not do the work and that there could be hierarchical societies based on birth and accepted by all, as either necessary or not, without false consciousness, and so without inequality of respect.

To get from false consciousness to egalitarianism one needs a much stronger notion of false consciousness. Now false consciousness is concerned with the way in which one identifies oneself in relation to other people, and self-identification here means identifying the capacity in which one wishes to be recognized and respected by others. I now propose to consider three general ways in which a man might identify himself and see how these might be related to the notion of false consciousness.

The first case is that of a man who does not identify himself as an individual at all, but as a mere cog in a machine or a member of an organic body apart from which he has no existence. As it stands, this is incoherent, because such a man could not be said to identify himself in any way whatsoever — identifying oneself involves identifying oneself as an individual. So if this is to be a possible case, one has to say that while he is capable of seeing himself as an individual he persists in talking and acting as though he were not. Now this would be a clear case of false consciousness because one is saying both that he has the consciousness and that he refuses to recognize it.

The second case is that of a man who identifies himself satisfactorily as an individual, but as an individual who occupies a certain role in society. He is an individual peasant who never thinks of himself outside his role of peasant.

The third case is that of a man who stands back from his role and thinks of himself as someone, as an individual who could be or could have been any number of things, and who merely happens to be a peasant. He doesn't identify himself with any particular role, but thinks of himself as a man apart from any role.

Now if the third case is to be taken as the standard of true consciousness, then the second case will have to be considered a case of false consciousness. For the peasant in the second case clearly could see himself in the manner of the third case but refuses to do so. It would follow from this that a social structure which prevented or discouraged individuals from identifying themselves properly as men would thereby be deficient. If we take hierarchical societies as typically producing men of the second type of consciousness, this will constitute an argument against hierarchical societies and for egalitarian ones. So what we have to consider is whether case three can meaningfully be taken as the standard of true consciousness.

To decide this one may consider a fourth case, that of a man who occupies a certain role but realizes that he has abilities which his role cannot satisfy, and consequently feels frustrated. Such a man would, of course, no longer be a clear case of the second type, for he would no longer identify himself straight off with his role of peasant, but would view himself as someone with abilities and ambitions to occupy another role. To a certain extent he stands back from his role and considers himself apart from it. Nevertheless, he is not a case of the third type, for it would not follow if this man's consciousness of himself is taken as the standard that the man in the second case is suffering from false consciousness. Case four differs from case two in that the man in the former case has good grounds for thinking he has abilities that could be better realized in another role, while the man in case two entertains no such thought. So that unless one were to say a priori that everyone has good grounds for thinking that, the man in the second case cannot be represented as suffering from false consciousness in relation to the man in the fourth case. And no such assertion could be made.

So what one needs to arrive at case three is the notion of a man who identifies himself as a man apart from any role or any particular abilities he may have to occupy a role. Insofar as self-identification is identifying the capacity in which one wishes to be recognized and respected by others, this man then desires to be identified and respected as a man and not as a role occupier. But what would it involve to be identified and respected as a man? In the first place, this would clearly involve being recognized as a member of the species man, one who possesses the attributes of humanity, is a language speaker, is conscious of himself, and is a free agent.

Now being a free agent is what one is potentially in being a member of the species man, but not what one is necessarily, for one may refuse to recognize or identify oneself in this respect, and this would be a variant of the first above — a case of false consciousness. Being a free agent, then, or being a man or human being in the sense of realizing or actualizing in oneself the attributes of humanity, can be seen as achieving a certain performance, which indeed all men are capable of and which most men achieve to some degree. To be identified and respected as a man is to be identified and respected in one's capacity as an individual free agent. But what is it to respect a man in this capacity? The answer to this lies in the notion of self-respect. For self-respect is that without which a man has no chance of performing anything adequately except evil, for its loss or absence involves the loss or absence of the belief that one has the potential for a certain performance; in the extreme case, where it is lost in relation to everything, it is the abandonment of one's humanity, one's capacity for action. To respect a man, then, in this fundamental way of respecting him in his capacity as free agent, is to behave toward him so as to help him maintain his self-respect, while not to respect him can be either to behave toward him in such a way as to try to destroy his self-respect — to beat him down, make him feel nothing, a mere worm — or, what is the more dominant mode, blandly to ignore the demands of his self-respect, as though there were none, which is to ignore his humanity. But not all men can be given this respect equally, only all men insofar as they possess self-respect to some degree. For to him who possesses none, none can be given — it would be a meaningless gesture. If there is nothing in a man to maintain respect, one would be respecting him for something that he is not. One cannot respect a child of a certain age.

Even if being identified and respected as a man is being identified and respected as a free agent, free agency is not an activity on its own, separable from other activities such as being an engineer, civil servant, citizen, or husband, for it clearly enters into one's performance of these roles and could only be exercised in some such specific context. Nor could one be said to be performing such roles or carrying out such activities without functioning as a free agent. And even if one were to say that free agency is primarily connected with morality or being a good man or achieving the virtues of humanity, it is not the case either that being a good man is a condition separate from and of the same nature as the specific roles mentioned above. For just as free agency enters into one's specific activities, so that condition of being a good man consists in the manner in which one carries on one's specific roles. It has to do with the relations one achieves — relations of justice, generosity, magnanimity, etc. — with those with whom one is connected through the specific roles one occupies. Thus roles and the performance of roles are a fundamental part of the human and moral world, for it is only through specific activities and relations that the condition of being a man and of being a good man can be realized at all, and thus that the respect of others and of oneself can be acquired.

But then the condition of being a man or free agent and the condition of being a role occupier of a certain sort, while different, are nevertheless necessarily related, so that being identified and respected as a man is not something that can be categorically opposed to being identified and respected as a role occupier of a certain sort. One does not have to stand back from one's role and identify oneself as a man apart from one's role, for all one need do is identify oneself as a man *in* one's role or roles. But then case two above, the man who identifies himself as a peasant and does not think of himself outside his role, cannot be represented as a case of false consciousness, for identifying himself as a man *in* his role is what he is perfectly capable of doing. To be a free agent is not to choose in conditions where no restrictions or dependencies exist; it is merely to act and have the courage of acting, i.e., accepting responsibility for what one is doing. But action always takes place in a specific context, and a specific context is always full of limitations and dependencies. To see roles as restrictions on our humanity is to see that which is a necessary condition of our humanity as an impediment to it. To assert case three above as the standard of true consciousness that a man may have of himself is to be involved in such an incoherence. For the condition of its being realized is that one does not identify with any role. Now one may still have a role, but not identifying with the role means not accepting the standards and purposes of the role as relevant criteria for judging one's life activity, one's performances, one's being anything at all. And this means that insofar as one carries on the role, one carries it on without reference to those aspects of it which alone can make the activity meaningful — its standards, purposes, etc. That is to say, while carrying on the role in some individual sense, one is thoroughly alienated from it. But to lose the meaningfulness of roles is to lose the foundations of the human and moral world. Now if this is the standard of true consciousness, those poor unfortunate persons who still identify with their roles will appear as retarded in their degree of self-conscious humanity. To raise them to the highest standards of humanity, equality might be seen as a necessary condition. For equality as a basic and substantive principle of society destroys all traditional roles and alienates everyone equally. But now we have as the condition in which everyone can be equally respected — without arrest or restriction — a condition in which all are equally alienated from the circumstances in which anyone can be respected. Once again, as a principle to govern a truly human society we have a principle which makes human society impossible.

As with the other attempts to make equality a substantive principle of society, equality of respect as a condition of the good, just, or fully human society is incoherent and self-contradictory, for it is only through the existence of common activities and practices, and so of roles, that a human society comes into being at all and the species man acquires the attributes of humanity. It should not be surprising that the various forms of egalitarianism I have considered throughout this argument have turned out to be self-contradictory. For the whole direction of egalitarianism's effort, as is clear from its origin in those totally alienated men who are the free and equal men of the state of nature, has been to attempt to conceive of man's existence apart from his existing under the necessary restrictions, limitations, and dependencies involved in being a member of a human society, and consequently in being a member of the human race.

Note

1. Bernard Williams, "The Idea of Equality," in Peter Laslett and W. G. Runciman, eds., *Philosophy*, *Politics and Society*, Second Series (Oxford: Basil Blackwell, 1962).

Select Bibliography

BENN, S. I., and PETERS, R. S. *The Principles of Political Thought.* New York: Macmillan, 1964. Chapters 5–7.

BLACKSTONE, W. T. "On the Meaning and Justification of the Equality Principle," *Ethics,* LXXVII (1967), 39–53.

BRYSON, L., ed. *Aspects of Human Equality,* New York: Harper, 1956.

DAHRENDORF, R. "On the Origin of Social Inequality," in Peter Laslett and W. G. Runciman, eds., *Philosophy, Politics and Society,* Second Series. Oxford: Basil Blackwell, 1962.

LAKOFF, SANFORD. *Equality in Political Philosophy.* Cambridge, Mass.: Harvard University Press, 1964.

LUCAS, J. R. "Against Equality," *Philosophy,* XL (1965), 296–307.

MARGOLIS, J. "That All Men Are Created Equal," *Journal of Philosophy,* LII (1955), 337–346.

NEWFIELD, J. G. H. "Equality in Society," *Proceedings of the Aristotelian Society,* LXVI (1965–1966), 193–210.

PENNOCK, J. ROLAND, and CHAPMAN, J. W., eds. *Equality: Nomos IX.* New York: Atherton Press, 1967.

SPIEGELBERG, HERBERT. "A Defense of Human Equality," *Philosophical Review,* LIII (1944), 101–124.

TAWNEY, R. H. *Equality.* New York: Harcourt, Brace, 1931.

THOMPSON, DAVID. *Equality.* Cambridge: Cambridge University Press, 1949.

VON LEYDEN, W. "On Justifying Inequality," *Political Studies,* XI (1963), 56–70.

WILLIAMS, BERNARD. "The Idea of Equality," in Peter Laslett and W. G. Runciman, eds., *Philosophy, Politics and Society,* Second Series. Oxford: Basil Blackwell, 1962.

WILSON, JOHN. *Equality.* New York: Harcourt, Brace, 1966.

WOLLHEIM, R., and BERLIN, I. "Symposium: Equality," in F. A. Olafson, ed., *Justice and Social Policy.* Englewood Cliffs, N.J.: Prentice-Hall, 1961.

JUSTICE

THE ARTICLES in this book focus on particular concepts or problems without fitting into any over-all pattern. Hence there is often little connection between the articles in the different sections. But this is quite untrue of the articles by D. D. Raphael and John Rawls in this section; these two articles provide the reader with several bases for relating justice to other concepts and problems. John Schaar's article is particularly relevant to Raphael's discussion of the relation between social utility and justice, and Charvet criticizes Rawls directly. Rawls' analysis of justice is relevant to several concepts. "Justice as Fairness" sketches a theory of political obligation and can be used to analyze the importance of certain liberties, equalities, and rights. This interrelatedness with other topics is partly accidental in that it is peculiar to the chosen articles, yet it is also characteristic of the concept of justice, which seems to be more inclusive and wide-ranging than other social values. This is not to suggest that justice is all-inclusive or synonymous with the "good society," nor that injustices are never defensible. We may want to defend certain freedoms which enable men to act unjustly. But it does suggest that justice is probably a more inclusive concept than freedom, equality, or rights.

Some early liberal political philosophers employed the social contract model to emphasize certain features of political life that other theories had ignored. But contract theories had their own difficulties, which the utilitarians set out to correct. Unlike the contract theorists, the utilitarians based moral principles on the effects of any practice or decision on human happiness. Justice came to mean the greatest happiness for the greatest number. While Raphael and Rawls are equally critical of the utilitarian concept of justice, they develop quite different accounts of justice. Raphael links justice with human needs, whereas Rawls finds the contract theory useful in emphasizing that fairness or reciprocity is fundamental. While the distinction between justice and utility is crucial to both arguments, the differences between Rawls and Raphael are no less significant.

Raphael distinguishes conservative justice, which aims at preserving traditional ideas and social relations, from prosthetic justice, which aims at modifying and adding to those ideas in order to enlarge the realm of justice. One hundred years ago justice did not require the government to provide for the needs of the unemployed, whereas it is now considered just to do so. When human needs are recognized as "moral claims" and charity becomes justice, ideas of prosthetic justice have been at work. Conservative justice is reflected in penal and remedial concepts, which serve to maintain the existing value system. But distributive

173

justice aims at "modifying the status quo," and may be considered a type of prosthetic justice.

It is not unusual to distribute rewards to men on the basis of merit. But is that justice? Raphael answers that question by considering merit under three headings: industry, talent, and virtue. In each case, he suggests that we reward only socially useful practices. Industriousness in carpentry or science may be rewarded, but not in cracking safes. We reward industry not because it is just to do so, but because we find it socially useful to encourage it. So with reward for talent. But here Raphael finds another element: what of those talents which are neither useful nor harmful? Raphael suggests that we may recognize a man's right to opportunities for self-development as a "claim of justice." When the rewards based on utility are extracted from rewards for talent, we are left with a "residual" which is the claim of justice. A similar residual remains with respect to rewards for virtue.

In rejecting distributions based on merit as fundamental to justice, Raphael turns to distributions based on equality or need. He finds that distributions based on need actually imply a belief in a type of equality; that is, such distributions are "fundamentally a respect for individual persons." Raphael argues that this is only a restatement of Kant's categorical imperative, which is a fundamental principle of justice. The residual elements from reward for talent and virtue are elements of justice because they express "the basic notion of the value of persons." And so, according to Raphael, justice is intimately related to provisions for human needs. Raphael concludes that the distinction he draws between conservative and prosthetic justice is not nearly as significant as the distinction between utility and justice.

Rawls would agree that the latter distinction is most crucial, although he would not accept all of Raphael's analysis. While abstract and complex, "Justice as Fairness" has sparked important philosophical debates about justice and utilitarianism. It is fair to say that Rawls' article has become a "classic." But we can here provide only the barest sketch of Rawls' argument, leaving the reader to tackle its many complexities and evaluate its basic propositions and assumptions.

Rawls begins by limiting the scope of his analysis and then states his conception of justice in terms of two fundamental principles. After asking us to grant him several assumptions about men and society, he argues that men will always settle upon these two principles when questions of justice arise. After a detailed discussion of fairness, Rawls directs his analysis to the utilitarians. The concept of fairness, he argues, can account for certain moral positions for which the utilitarian concept of justice cannot. It is essential to note and remember that Rawls' analysis of justice is restricted to social institutions or practices. He does not analyze justice in terms of individual men or particular acts or decisions. Rawls develops a very general concept which is applicable to all societies. But he is quick to point out that these principles need not be the only principles of justice. Since these principles are the center of his argument, it seems best to quote Rawls:

> First, each person participating in a practice, or affected by it, has an equal right to the most extensive liberty compatible with a like liberty for all; and second, inequalities are arbitrary unless it is reasonable to expect that they will work for everyone's advantage, and provided the positions and offices to which they attach, or from which they may be gained, are open to all.

The first principle states the beginning assumptions of considerations of justice, whereas the second principle (in part) specifies how the first principle can be breached. It is important to note that inequalities are unjust unless they work for *everyone's* advantage and that all must have equal access to positions. The distinction between justice and fairness lies in the distinction between voluntary and involuntary institutions. An institution or practice is fair or unfair if it is voluntary (e.g., the rules of baseball), but is just or unjust if it is compulsory or authoritative. Rawls asks us to assume a society with an established set of practices and with persons who are "mutually self-interested," "rational," and have roughly similar needs. When these persons discuss and evaluate their practices, they will recognize that the practices they adopt may apply to them in the future and that they will be bound by them. Therefore it would be unreasonable to adopt a practice merely because it operates in one's present interest, since this may not hold in the future. When these persons acknowledge the principles by which their practices are to be evaluated, "they will settle on these two principles as restrictions governing the assignment of rights and duties...." Unlike the social contract, this analysis is not fictitious. Men need not come together in a primitive setting. In any society "where people reflect on their institutions they will have an idea of what principles of justice would be acknowledged... and there will be occasions when questions of justice are actually discussed in this way...."

As he develops the notion of fair play, Rawls sketches a theory of political obligation. If the participants in a practice accept its rules as fair or just, and accept the benefits of the practice when others abide by the rules, "there arises a prima facie duty" to abide by the rules when it comes to one's own turn. This principle of obligation does not require voluntary participation in a practice, a promise, or a contract. The reader may find it useful to compare Rawls' theory of obligation with that of Michael Walzer in the last section.

Rawls criticizes the utilitarian account of justice by arguing that it cannot account for the moral position that slavery is always unjust. The utilitarian must argue that slavery is unjust because its disadvantages outweigh its advantages. This opens the door to the charge that if the advantages should outweigh the disadvantages, the utilitarian must hold that slavery is just. Rawls contends that the utilitarians erred by ignoring the principle of fairness.

Neither Rawls nor Raphael, despite their criticisms, would want to argue that considerations of utility are irrelevant to morality. Their attack on utilitarianism is restricted to their discussion of justice. Those who would contend that utilitarianism is an important and at least a partially valid ethical theory should not misdirect their criticisms when considering these articles.

9

Conservative
and Prosthetic Justice

D. D. Raphael

THE adjectives in my title are deliberately intended to recall dental as well as political connotations. Traditionalists may think of prosthetic justice as a mere artificial substitute for the genuine natural product, while radicals may think of conservative justice as hidebound.

Law and Morals

The term "justice" is used both of law and of morals. In the law, justice covers the whole field of the principles laid down, the decisions reached in accordance with them, and the procedures whereby the principles are applied to individual cases. The system of law *is* justice in the legal sense of the term. In morals, justice covers only part of the field of judgment and action; justice is contrasted with generosity or charity, this being moral action that goes beyond mere justice. Since the law does not try to, and indeed logically could not, enforce the higher morality of generosity, but confines itself within the domain of moral justice (which is not to say that it necessarily reaches the limits of that domain), it is intelligible that the law should use the term "justice" to describe the whole of its own operations.

Two processes, of conservation and reformation, can be seen clearly enough in the field of law. The first task of a system of law is to preserve an existing order of rights and duties. Like other preservatives, an established system of law tends to produce rigidity. The rights and

From *Political Studies*, XII (1964), 149–162.

duties that it protects and requires are those of a past morality. Changes in moral notions, or in the conditions to which moral notions are applied, lead to a demand that the law be changed in the name of (new notions of) justice or fairness. Thus the Common Law of England, which began as official declaration and enforcement of common practice and common belief about rights and duties, became in time a backward-looking system of precedents, and had to be modified by the application of rules of Equity, that is to say, principles of current thought about justice. In due course, the courts administering Equity became themselves equally stiff with precedent, so that now Common Law includes their findings as well, and the whole system of case law has to be modified by Statute. Broadly speaking, Common Law conserves the moral ideas of the past, while Statute reforms and adds to Common Law in the light of the moral ideas of the present.

If what I have said of law is true, it will follow that moral notions themselves are subject to a similar process of modification, and no one will be surprised at the suggestion that, within the sphere of morals also, the concept of justice is used to cover both the conservation of traditional ideas and the modification of these by new ideas. What I want to argue is that this process of development includes a gradual clarification of the concept of justice and enables us to sift the elements of justice proper from elements of utility.

But before I can proceed to my main problem, I must justify the assumption I have made that one can compare a discussion of the moral notion of justice with a discussion of law. Some people will deny this, saying that law is "objective" while justice is "subjective"; you and I are not free to decide what is the law, but we are free to decide what we shall count as just; judges decide the law, but in the sphere of morality every man may be his own judge.

In fact it is not true that only judges decide the law. When judges decide what the law is, they are often determining what it shall be, and this function is of course not exclusively theirs. Legislatures decide what a part of the law shall be, and insofar as you and I can influence the legislature, we can help, in a small way, to determine what the law shall be. Still, the point remains that once legislatures and judges have decided, their decisions are authoritative. In the sphere of morals, it is said, no one can assert that your views or mine shall not be followed. Can we then speak of any firm concept of justice?

Every Man His Own Judge?

"In those days," concludes the Book of Judges sorrowfully, "there was no king in Israel: every man did that which was right in his own eyes." It may seem strange that the last sentence should count as a reproach. That a man should follow the judgment of his own conscience seems essential to morality, though we may well be troubled when his conscience is so perverted as to deny to other people rights which are almost universally acknowledged. My own view[1] is that in *such* circumstances a man's duty is *not* what his conscience says; for A's duty to B corresponds to B's right against A, and I should not allow that the rights of B always depend on the thought of those against whom he claims a right. Some will disagree, if we are seeking only to determine what is A's *duty*, and will deny that A's duty corresponds to B's right. But if we shift the discussion to the determination of rights, that is to say, of justice,[2] the position implied by the Biblical quotation may receive wider acceptance. It is not open to any individual to decide for himself what are the rights of others, i.e., whether his action toward them is just.

Some will still disagree. As an example, let me cite Hans Kelsen. I cite him *honoris causa*, for I regard his theory of law and the state as the most important contribution of the twentieth century to political theory. We may ask what is law, says Kelsen, but we may not ask what is justice, for justice is a subjective notion; different individuals and groups all have their own ideas of justice, and there is no way of deciding between them. This view of Kelsen's about justice depends partly on a similar account of all value judgments, an account which is less likely to find credence today than in the 1920s and 1930s. It no doubt also depends partly on the fact that there *are* different ideas of justice. If we begin with Aristotle, for example, as so many theorists have done, we find that he distinguishes three or four different concepts. In the first place, Aristotle says, the term "justice" may be applied to the whole of a universe of discourse about right and wrong, or to only part of such a universe. This is more or less the same as the contrast I have already noted between legal and moral justice. Then again, Aristotle distinguishes between distributive, remedial, and commutative (or "reciprocal") justice. And then, as regards distributive justice itself, he distinguishes between a principle of distribution on the basis of merit (aristocratic justice) and a principle of distribution on the basis of equality (democratic justice). Other theorists seem to make a rather different distinction between two principles of distributive justice, distribution according to merit and distribution according to need. Then again, Marx, following some of the French Socialists, narrows down or alters the concept of merit to that of work, and distinguishes the two principles of distribution as: "to each according to his work" and "to each according to his needs." All these different ideas are said to be ideas of justice. How then can we speak of *one* concept? My contention will be that these different notions are not the unrelated ideas of different groups, but fit together so as to manifest the evolution of a single concept.

Plato's Concept of Justice

I propose now to spend a little time on a side issue, which, I think, corroborates my contention although at first sight it appears not to do so. In addition to the two causal factors which I have already mentioned, Kelsen's conclusion about justice owes something, I believe, to the influence of Plato. Plato's concept of justice seems quite remote from familiar uses of the term. Yet it is presented in the *Republic* as being so readily acceptable to Socrates' audience that one is apt to suppose it must be in line with at any rate one main strand of Greek thought. In a sense this is true, in another sense not. If Plato's concept of justice be treated as a version of "aristocratic justice," it is indeed consonant with a strand not only of Greek thought but of the thought of other civilizations. If, however, we take his actual definition of justice literally, it is peculiar to Plato.

Yet does not he himself tell us that it is shared by others? The definition is given in Book IV (433b): justice is doing one's own job. In the text as we have it, Socrates is made to say: "That justice is doing one's own job and not being a busybody, we have heard from many others and have often said ourselves." Then, after receiving ready agreement to this statement, Socrates continues: "Well, it somehow happens to have turned out that doing one's own job is justice" — a rather odd way, when you come to think about it, of putting an apparently unnecessary repetition.

Commentators have asked, *where* has it previously been said, by Plato or by others, in the literature which has come down to us, that justice is doing one's own job and not being a busybody. James Adam, in the commentary of his edition of the *Republic*, gives us the answer: nowhere. It is not said earlier in the *Republic* nor in any previous dialogue of Plato. (This definition of justice is given in one other dialogue attributed to Plato, *Alcibiades I*, at 127c. But *Alcibiades I* is almost certainly not a genuine work of Plato himself. It is evidently a late work, written by a disciple of Plato, and its definition of justice is simply following the doctrine of the *Republic*.) Nor does anyone else, including Aristotle, report that this is a common definition of justice.

Most people who have raised the question have been a little puzzled but have left it at that, assuming that the idea must have been common, though we have no record of it. Adam, however, refuses to be so easily put off. He notes that in the *Charmides*, 161b ff., "doing one's own job" is given as the definition of *sophrosyne* (which we tend to translate as "self-control" or "temperance" or, in a social context, "discipline"). There is also a passage in the *Timaeus* which suggests the same thing. Adam, therefore, conjectures that the word "justice" (*dikaiosyne*) in *Republic* 433a9 is a scribe's error for an original reading of *sophrosyne*. The error, if it is one, is explained easily enough. The scribe would not remember the passage in the *Charmides*; he would simply know that "doing one's own job" is the emphatic definition of justice in the *Republic*, and so he would think that *sophrosyne* was a previous scribe's error for *dikaiosyne*. Adam then points out that if we restore *sophrosyne* as the true reading, the whole passage makes better sense. For now this is how the conversation goes:

> It seems to me that justice is what we spoke of earlier, or something like it. We frequently said, if you remember, that each man should do one job, the job to which he is naturally suited.
> "Yes, we did say that."
> "*And yet* (the Greek is καὶ μὴν . . . γε) we have heard from many others and we ourselves have often said that doing one's own job and not being over-busy is *self-control* (or discipline)."
> "True enough."
> "Well, my friend, it somehow happens to have turned out that this business of doing one's own job is *justice*."

This makes better sense, but there is more to it than Adam's concern simply with the sense of the passage. In the *Charmides*, the definition of *sophrosyne*, as minding your own business and not meddling in other people's affairs, is attributed to Critias. Charmides and Critias were both aristocratic relations of Plato on his mother's side, who became members of the oligarchic government called the Thirty Tyrants and who tried to persuade Plato to join them. It is natural enough for a person of aristocratic or oligarchic tendencies to define *sophrosyne* (self-control or temperance), when turned into a social virtue, as minding your own business and not being a busybody. Being a busybody (*polypragmosyne*), poking your nose into other people's business, was a common charge leveled against the Athenian democrat by his oligarchic critics. The oligarch or aristocrat wants everyone to keep to his proper station, thereby producing a well-ordered or disciplined state akin to the disciplined nature of a self-controlled or temperate man. What Plato does is to take over this aristocratic sentiment and make it seem more palatable by labeling it "justice" instead of "discipline" or "order," for the virtue of justice had come to have the highest rank in the scale of social values, a rank formerly occupied, in the days of heroic society, by the virtue of courage. It is a commonplace that the *Republic* makes justice and temperance almost indistinguishable. This is why Plato's concept of justice is peculiar to himself. Yet in a sense he is following a traditional strand of thought, the aristocratic concept of justice as depending on merit. That men's status in society should depend on their qualities, the best men being at the top and the worst at the bottom, is familiar aristocratic doctrine.

I am not implying that the novelty of Plato's doctrine of justice is wholly determined by a political motive. When he speaks of "justice" in the individual, he wants to deepen the common conception of morality so as to make it include the spirit in which an action is done as well as the external character of the act itself. This also means that the concept of justice is widened to extend over the whole field of morality instead of being confined to one class of moral actions. The practice of extending a concept beyond its normal connotations is both common and proper in philosophy. I have therefore no complaint to make of Plato on that score. All I contend at the moment is that Plato's peculiar use of the term "justice" should not be taken to be that of the ancient Greeks, any more than Berkeley's peculiar use of the term "existence" should be taken to be that of eighteenth-century Irishmen.

Conservative and Prosthetic Justice

If we want to know what were the common conceptions of justice among the Greeks, we should go to Aristotle rather than Plato for our evidence. And when we do look at Aristotle's account of different conceptions of justice, we find that they are not far removed from those of our own civilization. That is why so many theorists find it convenient to make Aristotle's distinctions their starting point for the analysis of justice.

Let us look first at Aristotle's distinction between distributive, remedial, and commutative justice. The last two can, I think, be called conservative. Their object is to preserve an existing order of rights and possessions or to restore it when any breaches have been made. We may add, though Aristotle does not, that penal justice likewise aims at conserving the general social order as remedial and commutative justice aim at conserving the position of individuals within that order.

It is worth noting that while penal and remedial justice describe the work of the law, commutative justice goes beyond what the law requires and enforces. The remedial justice of law will rectify breaches of contract but says nothing about the fairness of contracts themselves. Now a contract is fair when there is an exchange of equal value on each side. The law does not enforce this principle of fairness in the making of contracts. It allows, within pretty wide limits, free play to the self-interested forces of the market, and tells the buyer that he must look out for himself, as the vendor does. Many an unfair contract is made in which there is not an equal exchange of value, but the law will not declare it invalid on that account. In the conditions of a free market, there is no protection of the existing position of individuals, in terms of the value of their possessions, by enforcing the rule of justice, except insofar as there is some restriction of unfair practices, and that implies some restriction of a free market.

It may be said that although conservative justice has little place in the market, where fortunes can be made and lost quickly, the forces of the market nevertheless give effect to the principle of merit. Luck comes in, of course, but to a large extent the man who makes a fortune does so by his ability and consequently "deserves" his fortune. This is true enough. In conditions of competition, ability tends to succeed. Whether this should be called just is another question. For the moment let us suppose that it should.

Penal, remedial, and commutative justice, then, are all conservative. It seems reasonable to say that distributive justice aims at modifying the status quo, and so may be called prosthetic justice. The modification may be made on the basis of merit, or of need, or of equality.

Merit

If the reward of merit is a form of prosthetic justice, must not we say the same of penalties for demerit? This would imply that punishment, like other penalties, is a form of prosthetic justice. Reward and punishment seem to be opposite sides of the same coin, and if so, what goes for the one must go for the other. Yet surely punishment is a device for conserving an existing order of rules conferring duties and rights. This is true whether we think of punishment as deterrence or as retribution. (I ignore the reformative theory of punishment as based on confusion.)

Professor Ralf Dahrendorf, in his inaugural lecture "On the Origin of Social Inequality" (printed as Essay 5 in *Philosophy, Politics and Society, Second Series*, edited by Peter Laslett and W. G. Runciman), sets out a thesis which is of relevance here. Every society, he says, must have a set of norms backed by sanctions which reward those who conform to the norms and penalize those who deviate. The purpose of the sanctions is to preserve the set of norms or values by which that society stands. This thesis couples reward with punishment and would assign both to what I am calling conservative justice. Of course the rewarding of merit alters the existing rights or status of individuals, but it conserves the existing system of social values, as does the punishment of crime.

I thing we can bring out this point more clearly by considering the extent to which the rewarding of merit can be justified by utility. When we say that something is useful, we may mean that it prevents a loss of existing value, in which case it is plainly conservative. Alternatively, we may mean that it leads to an addition to the stock of value. In one sense this is prosthetic, for, as I have said, it is *adding* to what exists. In another sense it is conservative, in that the *kind* of value which is added is the same as that which already exists and is esteemed as an established value of the society concerned.

When we say that it is just to reward merit, what sort of merit do we have in mind? There are three possibilities. We may mean moral merit, or natural talent, or the exercise of industry. Marx's "socialist" principle of distribution according to "work" confines merit to the last of the three. I shall now take these three kinds of merit in the reverse order.

First, we often say it is just to reward industry and to penalize laziness. This principle plainly can, and indeed must, be justified on grounds of utility. Suppose a man were busily industrious at a useless task, like counting the number of grains in every heap of sand he could lay his hands on. Or suppose his industry were always directed to socially harmful tasks, like breaking up all the gas and water supply pipes he could get at. Should we think he deserved any reward? Industry is approved and rewarded only when, and because, it is socially useful. The reward itself, and similarly the penalizing of idleness, are also instruments of utility in encouraging the industrious to continue and the idle to follow their example.

Second, what of the reward of talent? Why is it just to benefit those who are already blessed by nature and not those whom nature has left in the lurch? "To him that hath shall be given." This is what happens, but is it fair? Here again, surely, it may be useful, but it is not just. And here again, it is the useful talents that most obviously call for "reward." If a man has a talent for surgery, we think he should be given opportunity to develop it, and then be paid well for exercising it. But we shall not think the same of a talent for cracking safes.

Utility is not, however, the only reason for giving a man opportunity to develop and exercise his natural talents. We should wish to deny the opportunity to the cracksman, because the exercise of his talent is positively harmful. But suppose a talent is more or less neutral in its effect on others, e.g., a talent for chess playing or for mountaineering (if we exclude supposed effects on national prestige). We are likely to spend money on training schools for surgeons before spending it on training schools for chess players, because the surgeons will be useful to us. But if we can afford both, we shall think that the socially useless (though not the socially harmful) talent should be given training, simply because the individual who has the talent will be happier, will feel that he has realized himself, when he can exercise his talent to the full. We should say, I think, that we owe it to him as an individual and that he has a moral right to such self-development. This is to say that it is a claim of justice.

What then of the *ranking* of talents? Why do we say that the man with a talent for surgery is blessed by nature, while the man who can find self-development in fretwork is less blessed? We have seen that the former talent is rewarded over the latter because of its greater utility. Must not we say the same of the initial ranking of the talents themselves? The potential surgeon is called blessed by nature because he can benefit his fellows and because he will in consequence be well rewarded and highly regarded. But then what of the talent of an artist? His abilities are not so obviously *useful* as is the talent of a surgeon, nor can he usually expect high rewards. Well, I think that here too the rating does lie in utility of a kind. What we call great art is art that we think will give lasting pleasure to many over a long period of time, though it is true that the artist often cannot expect much material reward or even much recognition in his own lifetime. One is tempted to say that he himself will have great happiness or a greater sense of self-fulfillment than will the fretworker, quite apart from the pleasure that his work can give to others. Are we justified in saying this? I do not know. At any rate, it seems to me that at least *part* of the differential rating accorded to talent depends on utility and that the residual claim of justice, the claim of the individual to self-development, *may* not admit of being rated higher or lower than the like claim of another. It is at least possible, then, that the residual claim of justice is an equal one for all human beings.

Third, moral merit. What justifies the rewarding of virtue? Do not we say that virtue is its own reward? We judge nevertheless that virtue ought to be rewarded, but we should hesitate to put this judgment in the form that the virtuous man has a right to be rewarded, for to think of the reward as a right tarnishes the merit of the virtue. All this suggests that the rewarding of virtue is not called for as a matter of justice. On the other hand it is certainly called for as a matter of utility. Morally virtuous actions are those intended to benefit others, while morally vicious actions are those intended to harm others; and since the intentions of action are, more often than not, given effect by the actions they direct, virtuous actions tend to be useful and vicious actions tend to be harmful. Reward of the one, and punishment of the other, are themselves useful in encouraging people to follow the example of the virtuous and avoid that of the vicious.

I have argued here that the rewarding of virtue is justified by utility. While I have referred also to the utility of punishment, I should enter the caveat that in the case of punishment I think utility alone is insufficient justification. Punishment and reward, despite initial appearances, are not on all fours. Although we say that virtue is in a sense its own reward, we do not say that vice is similarly its own punishment. And while most of us would hesitate to speak of a right of the vicious to be punished, this is not for a reason parallel to that which inhibits us from speaking of a right of the virtuous to be rewarded. Indeed, some people (including some wrongdoers) think it is eminently proper to speak of a right to be punished. Two further differences may be mentioned. Everyone, I imagine, whatever his opinion about a right to be punished, would be ready to say that punishment is designed to meet the right of victims to be protected. Justice comes in again in upholding the right of the innocent not to be subjected to the pains imposed as punishment on the guilty. Neither this right nor that of victims has a correlate when rewards are considered.

A further caveat is that, though I have spoken of the utility of virtue as well as of the utility of reward, I do not imply that utility constitutes the whole value of virtue itself. The value of moral action, like the value of the exercise of talent, lies not only in utility but also in the direct realization of human worth. In the case of virtue, however, this means the realization of fellowship, and not, as with the exercise of talent, self-realization, unless we follow the Idealists in making the "real self" go beyond the individual agent.

So far as the rewarding of merit is concerned, my conclusion about all three types of merit is that the ground of differential reward is utility. I have said that utility alone is not enough to justify punishment, but I have also noted that the complications which arise in the theory of punishment do not imply that there are correlative nonutilitarian factors affecting the reward of virtue.

Equality and Need

I turn now to the alternative claimants to the title of distributive justice, equal distribution and distribution according to need.[3] At first sight, these seem to be distinct. Distribution according to need, like distribution according to merit, is a differential distribution. The man with the greater need is given more benefits and fewer burdens than the man with less need.

In fact, however, differential distribution according to need implies a belief in a right to a certain kind of equality. The man who is said to be in need falls below a level of benefits which is taken to be the right of all. When special provision is made for him, this is an attempt to bring him, so far as possible, up to the level of what is due equally to all. Insofar as the initial lack is the result of natural causes (e.g., physical handicap), the principle of justice which attempts to remove it goes against nature. Insofar as the lack is the result of established social conditions, the principle of justice goes against tradition. This principle of justice therefore may certainly be called prosthetic.

The belief in a right to equality, of which the principle of distribution according to need is one manifestation, seems to me to be fundamentally a respect for individual persons — in Kantian language, a respect for ends-in-themselves. When individuals are regarded as having a right to equality, or as being of equal worth, this does not imply an overlooking of the ways in which they are clearly of unequal worth. What I have said about merit shows that the rating of individuals on a scale of worth refers almost wholly to their utility. The Kantian principle, that we should treat all human beings as ends-in-themselves and not *merely* as means, does not say that we may not treat them as means at all. We continually treat men as means without necessarily being immoral. It is when regarded as means that men can be counted better or worse, more or less useful. But means to what? Means to the ends of others, of society, or of humanity at large. The ends to which they are a means are themselves the ends or purposes of human beings. And when it is said that men should be treated as ends-in-themselves, the meaning is that the ends of men are that by reference to which means are counted as means. Now means to an end, or a set of ends, can be rated on a scale as more or less useful for securing the end or ends. But the ends for which these means are useful cannot be placed on the same scale, precisely because they are not means but the ends themselves which provide the point of reference for rating means. The *equality* of men as ends is therefore the absence of that inequality which is correctly attached to them when they are considered as means.

Justice and Utility

I am saying that the principle of egalitarian justice is at root the same as Kant's categorical imperative, i.e., the basic principle of morality. Now utility is not justice; utility is a means to the end of morality. The classical utilitarians said that this end was happiness, but I think they did not go far enough. Happiness is valued because it is an end of persons; it depends on the Kantian principle.

It will be recalled that there were residual elements in the idea of merit that did not seem to be matters of utility. The development of talent and the exercise of virtue are valued not only for utility but also because they express the realization of persons both as individuals and as forming a human community. These residual elements I should count as elements of justice, and I should say that they, like the principle of equality, express the basic notion of the value of persons.

The same goes for conservative justice. The conservation of an established system of rights has a similar twofold value. Insofar as it prevents the breakdown of society, it is useful. Insofar as it respects rights, as being ends of persons, it is just. The initial distinction between conservative and prosthetic justice is less fundamental than a distinction between justice proper and utility.

We may now dispose of a puzzle I raised earlier, whether reward and punishment should be assigned to conservative justice, as is implied by Professor Dahrendorf for instance, or whether they should be assigned to prosthetic justice because they modify the existing order of benefits and burdens. If the distinction between justice and utility is more fundamental than that between conservative and prosthetic justice, it is better to ask whether reward and punishment are entirely a matter of utility (as they obviously are to a large extent anyway) or whether they also involve a residual element of justice.

I have already given my own answer to this question, and I do not expect everyone to agree with it. Whatever answer one gives, however, it is notorious that, in the early days of a society, the utilitarian aspect of punishment goes relatively unnoticed, and punishment is taken to be wholly or largely a matter of retributive justice; but in the course of time, when men reflect upon the moral basis of their institutions, the idea of retribution proper recedes and tends to be replaced by that of utility. I think the same sort of development affects the idea of the justice of reward and the principle of merit in general. It also applies to the concept of conservative justice. Primitive societies think of the established social order as fixed by nature or by supernatural beings. They think that it needs to be protected as representing a fixed order of justice and that inroads upon that order are unjust in themselves. Later reflection leads to the view that the existing order may not be the most just but that the conservation of its main fabric is useful simply because it is *an* order, better than the disorder which would follow a wholesale departure from it. Nevertheless piecemeal revision is approved in the name of justice proper.

Here I revert again to Professor Dahrendorf. He assumes, in Marxian fashion, that the revision of an existing system of social rules is always due to the revolt of an oppressed group who suffer from the sanctions of the existing order. He presumably thinks (or so it appears) that all groups act from motives of self-interest, the upper classes wishing to conserve the present order because it favors them, and the lower wishing to revise it because it oppresses them. This explains many (perhaps not all) revolutions, but fails to explain those reforms which come about from the moral sensitivity of some of the fortunate toward the distress of the unfortunate.

I find it curious that recent accounts of justice should so often rely upon a Hobbesian scheme of self-interest. Professor Dahrendorf is not the only contributor to *Philosophy, Politics and Society, Second Series*, to take this line. It is also taken by Professor John Rawls in his article "Justice as Fairness." Professor Rawls makes it clear that he is not presupposing, like the usual stereotype of Hobbes, that men's *only* motive is self-interest. But his account of justice as fairness relies upon a notion of quasi-contract which comes about from thoughts of "mutual self-interest." Most oddly of all, Mr. A. M. Honoré, in a recent article on "Social Justice" (*McGill Law Journal*, vol. 8, no. 2, February 1962), again uses a Hobbesian hypothesis to account for the notion of justice. I say most oddly of all because Mr. Honoré, like myself, interprets the concept of social justice as basically egalitarian. In order to account for this egalitarianism, he refers to Hobbes's view of men as roughly equal in power and therefore in fear of each other. I have the greatest respect for Hobbes, and it would be absurd to deny the force of what he says about human equality. Nevertheless it simply will not do to base egalitarian *justice* on men's natural powers and fear of each other. These Hobbesian facts imply that one may risk exerting one's power against another where one sees that the other is abnormally weak. So indeed one may. But the sentiment of justice urges precisely the opposite course of action. It urges us to give special consideration to the weak or the needy, from whom we have little to fear. If the fortunate fear the *numbers* of the needy, and meet their demands on that account, they have not been motivated to do so by thoughts of *justice*.

Hobbesian facts account well enough for conservative justice and for the so-called justice, but really utility, of distribution according to merit. Prosthetic justice proper, which asserts a universal right to equality especially manifest in the claims of need, must depend on nonegoistic sentiments.

Someone may say this is all very well, but I am obscuring the distinction between justice and generosity or charity. In fact, it may be said, the whole business of altruistic provision for need, which I have stressed, is a matter of generosity or charity, not of justice at all. It is indeed moral action at its best, but that is not justice. In identifying the basic principle of justice with Kant's categorical imperative, am I not making justice the whole of morality, including generosity?

I think not. My view is that charity turns into justice when the needs of the beneficiaries are widely recognized in a society as moral *claims*. No one has a right to charity, but once the benefit which the needy lack is regarded as something due to all, as something to which all have a right, it passes out of the domain of charity into that of justice. Would anyone say that the Welfare State is a *charity* organization, or deny that it is a more *just* (whether or not it be judged a better) society than one in which the relief of basic needs is left to private generosity? Would anyone say that the provision of uneconomic transport services to remote, sparsely populated areas of Britain is charitable rather than fair?

Conservative justice preserves established rights. Prosthetic justice adds further rights, rights to benefits which were not formerly counted due as a matter of right. In this way, with the development of the social conscience (and of the economic capacity of a society), the field of justice gradually takes in more from the field of charity. The character of the order of rights to be protected by conservative justice accordingly changes, the society becomes a more just society, and the nature of justice itself, both conservative and prosthetic, becomes clearer.

Notes

1. Elaborated in *Moral Judgement*, Chap. VII, Sec. 6.
2. I have been asked whether the scope of justice is not narrower than that of rights in general, for we should not say that, e.g., the right to be told the truth is a part of justice. I think (and here I am indebted to discussion with my colleague, Mr. J. G. Dawson) the answer is that justice is coextensive with rights, and that the supposed counterexample induces doubts simply because of the misleading form in which it is phrased. A man does not have a right to be told all the truths that his companions know; he might rather claim a right to be spared the boredom of such revelations. Nor does he have a right to be given a truthful answer to all his questions, for some of the questions might be unwarranted intrusion into the private affairs of other people. He has a right not to be deliberately deceived, and this is what is properly meant when we speak of a right to be told the truth. When a man is deliberately deceived, it would be apt for him to say to the deceiver: "You have not dealt fairly with me." That is, a breach of the right in question is a breach of fairness or justice.
3. This short section contains the kernel of my view of justice. It is short because it simply summarizes an account which I have already given elsewhere (*Moral Judgement*, Chap. V, Sec. 4, and Chap. VII, Sec. 5).

10

Justice as Fairness

John Rawls

IT might seem at first sight that the concepts of justice and fairness are the same and that there is no reason to distinguish them or to say that one is more fundamental than the other. I think that this impression is mistaken. In this paper I wish to show that the fundamental idea in the concept of justice is fairness, and I wish to offer an anlysis of the concept of justice from this point of view. To bring out the force of this claim, and the analysis based upon it, I shall then argue that it is this aspect of justice for which utilitarianism, in its classical form, is unable to account, but which is expressed, even if misleadingly, by the idea of the social contract.

I

To start with I shall develop a particular conception of justice by stating and commenting upon two principles which specify it and by considering the circumstances and conditions under which they may be thought to arise. The principles defining this conception, and the conception itself, are, of course, familiar. It may be possible, however, by using the notion of fairness as a framework, to assemble and to look at them in a new way. Before stating this conception, however, the following preliminary matters should be kept in mind.

From *Philosophy, Politics and Society*, Second Series, ed. Peter Laslett and W. G. Runciman (Oxford: Basil Blackwell, 1962), pp. 132–157. This article was originally published in *The Philosophical Review*, LXVII (1958), 164–194.

Throughout I consider justice only as a virtue of social institutions, or what I shall call practices.[1] The principles of justice are regarded as formulating restrictions as to how practices may define positions and offices, and assign thereto powers and liabilities, rights and duties. Justice as a virtue of particular actions or of persons I do not take up at all. It is important to distinguish these various subjects of justice since the meaning of the concept varies according to whether it is applied to practices, particular actions, or persons. These meanings are, indeed, connected, but they are not identical. I shall confine my discussion to the sense of justice as applied to practices, since this sense is the basic one. Once it is understood, the other senses should go quite easily.

Justice is to be understood in its customary sense as representing but *one* of the many virtues of social institutions, for these may be antiquated, inefficient, degrading, or any number of other things, without being unjust. Justice is not to be confused with an all-inclusive vision of a good society; it is only one part of any such conception. It is important, for example, to distinguish that sense of equality which is an aspect of the concept of justice from that sense of equality which belongs to a more comprehensive social ideal. There may well be inequalities which one concedes are just, or at least not unjust, but which, nevertheless, one wishes, on other grounds, to do away with. I shall focus attention, then, on the usual sense of justice in which it is essentially the elimination of arbitrary distinctions and the establishment, within the structure of a practice, of a proper balance between competing claims.

Finally, there is no need to consider the principles discussed below as *the* principles of justice. For the moment it is sufficient that they are typical of a family of principles normally associated with the concept of justice. The way in which the principles of this family resemble one another, as shown by the background against which they may be thought to arise, will be made clear by the whole of the subsequent argument.

II

The conception of justice which I want to develop may be stated in the form of two principles as follows: first, each person participating in a practice, or affected by it, has an equal right to the most extensive liberty compatible with a like liberty for all; and second, inequalities are arbitrary unless it is reasonable to expect that they will work out for everyone's advantage and provided the positions and offices to which they attach, or from which they may be gained, are open to all. These principles express justice as a complex of three ideas: liberty, equality, and reward for services contributing to the common good.[2]

The term "person" is to be construed variously depending on the circumstances. On some occasions it will mean human individuals, but in others it may refer to nations, provinces, business firms, churches, teams, and so on. The principles of justice apply in all these instances, although there is a certain logical priority to the case of human individuals. As I shall use the term "person," it will be ambiguous in the manner indicated.

The first principle holds, of course, only if other things are equal: that is, while there must always be a justification for departing from the initial position of equal liberty (which is defined by the pattern of rights and duties, powers and liabilities, established by a practice), and the burden of proof is placed on him who would depart from it, nevertheless, there can be, and often there is, a justification for doing so. Now, that similar particular cases, as defined by practice, should be treated similarly as they arise is part of the very concept of a practice; it is involved in the notion of an activity in accordance with rules. The first principle expresses an analogous conception, but as applied to the structure of practices themselves. It holds, for example, that there is a presumption against the distinctions and classifications made by legal systems and other practices to the extent that they infringe on the original and equal liberty of the persons participating in them. The second principle defines how this presumption may be rebutted.

It might be argued at this point that justice requires only an equal liberty. If, however, a greater liberty were possible for all without loss or conflict, then it would be irrational to settle on a lesser liberty. There is no reason for circumscribing rights unless their exercise would be incompatible, or would render the practice defining them less effective. Therefore no serious distortion of the concept of justice is likely to follow from including within it the concept of the greatest equal liberty.

The second principle defines what sorts of inequalities are permissible; it specifies how the presumption laid down by the first principle may be put aside. Now by inequalities it is best to understand not *any* differences between offices and positions, but differences in the benefits and burdens attached to them either directly or indirectly, such as prestige and wealth, or liability to taxation and compulsory services. Players in a game do not protest against there being different positions, such as batter, pitcher, catcher, and the like, nor to there being various privileges and powers as specified by the rules; nor do the citizens of a country object to there being the different offices of government such as president, senator, governor, judge, and so on, each with their special rights and duties. It is not differences of this kind that are normally thought of as inequalities, but differences in the resulting distribution established by a practice or made possible by it, of the things men strive to attain or avoid. Thus they may complain about the pattern of honors and rewards set up by a practice (e.g., the privileges and salaries of government officials) or they may object to the distribution of power and wealth which results from the various ways in which men avail themselves of the opportunities allowed by it (e.g., the concentration of wealth which may develop in a free price system allowing large entrepreneurial or speculative gains).

It should be noted that the second principle holds that an inequality is allowed only if there is reason to believe that the practice with the inequality, or resulting in it, will work for the advantage of *every* party engaging in it. Here it is important to stress that *every* party must gain from the inequality. Since the principle applies to practices, it implies that the representative man in every office or position defined by a practice, when he views it as a going concern, must find it reasonable to prefer his condition and prospects with the inequality to what they would be under the practice without it. The principle excludes, therefore, the justification of inequalities on the grounds that the disadvantages of those in one position are outweighed by the greater advantages of those in another position. This rather simple restriction is the main modification I wish to make in the utilitarian principle as usually understood. When coupled with the notion of a practice, it is a restriction of consequence, and one which some utilitarians, e.g., Hume and Mill, have used in their discussions of justice without realizing apparently its significance, or at least without calling attention to it. Why it is a significant modification of principle, changing one's conception of justice entirely, the whole of my argument will show.

Further, it is also necessary that the various offices to which special benefits or burdens attach are open to all. It may be, for example, to the common advantage, as just defined, to attach special benefits to certain offices. Perhaps by doing so the requisite talent can be attracted to them and encouraged to give its best efforts. But any offices having special benefits must be won in a fair competition in which contestants are judged on their merits. If some offices were not open, those excluded would normally be justified in feeling unjustly treated, even if they benefited from the greater efforts of those who were allowed to compete for them. Now if one can assume that offices are open, it is necessary only to consider the design of practices themselves and how they jointly, as a system, work together. It will be a mistake to focus attention on the varying relative positions of particular persons, who may be known to us by their proper names, and to require that each such change, as a once for all transaction viewed in isolation, must be in itself just. It is the system of practices which is to be judged, and judged from a general point of view: unless one is prepared to criticize it from the standpoint of a representative man holding some particular office, one has no complaint against it.

III

Given these principles one might try to derive them from a priori principles of reason, or claim that they were known by intuition. These are familiar enough steps and, at least in the case of the first principle, might be made with some success. Usually, however, such arguments made at this point are unconvincing. They are not likely to lead to an understanding of the basis of the principles of justice, not at least as principles of justice. I wish, therefore, to look at the principles in a different way.

Imagine a society of persons among whom a certain system of practices is *already* well established. Now suppose that by and large they are mutually self-interested; their allegiance to their established practices is normally founded on the prospect of self-advantage. One need not assume that, in all senses of the term "person," the persons in this society are mutually self-interested. If the characterization as mutually self-interested applies when the line of division is the family, it may still be true that members of families are bound by ties of sentiment and affection and willingly acknowledge duties in contradiction to self-interest. Mutual self-interestedness in the relations between families, nations, churches, and the like is commonly associated with intense loyalty and devotion on the part of individual members. Therefore, one can form a more realistic conception of this society if one thinks of it as consisting of mutually self-interested families, or some other association. Further, it is not necessary to suppose that these persons are mutually self-interested under all circumstances, but only in the usual situations in which they participate in their common practices.

Now suppose also that these persons are rational: they know their own interests more or less accurately; they are capable of tracing out the likely consequences of adopting one practice rather than another;

they are capable of adhering to a course of action once they have decided upon it; they can resist present temptations and the enticements of immediate gain; and the bare knowledge or perception of the difference between their condition and that of others is not, within certain limits and in itself, a source of great dissatisfaction. Only the last point adds anything to the usual definition of rationality. This definition should allow, I think, for the idea that a rational man would not be greatly downcast from knowing, or seeing, that others are in a better position than himself unless he thought their being so was the result of injustice, or the consequence of letting chance work itself out for no useful common purpose, and so on. So if these persons strike us as unpleasantly egoistic, they are at least free in some degree from the fault of envy.[3]

Finally, assume that these persons have roughly similar needs and interests, or needs and interests in various ways complementary, so that fruitful cooperation among them is possible; and suppose that they are sufficiently equal in power and ability to guarantee that in normal circumstances none is able to dominate the others. This condition (as well as the others) may seem excessively vague, but in view of the conception of justice to which the argument leads, there seems no reason for making it more exact here.

Since these persons are conceived as engaging in their common practices, which are already established, there is no question of our supposing them to come together to deliberate as to how they will set these practices up for the first time. Yet we can imagine that from time to time they discuss with one another whether any of them has a legitimate complaint against their established institutions. Such discussions are perfectly natural in any normal society. Now suppose that they have settled on doing this in the following way. They first try to arrive at the principles by which complaints, and so practices themselves, are to be judged. Their procedure for this is to let each person propose the principles upon which he wishes his complaints to be tried with the understanding that, if acknowledged, the complaints of others will be similarly tried, and that no complaints will be heard at all until everyone is roughly of one mind as to how complaints are to be judged. They each understand further that the principles proposed and acknowledged on this occasion are binding on future occasions. Thus each will be wary of proposing a principle which would give him a peculiar advantage, in his present circumstances, supposing it to be accepted. Each person knows that he will be bound by it in future circumstances the peculiarities of which cannot be known, and which might well be such that the principle is then to his disadvantage. The idea is that everyone should be required to make *in advance* a firm commitment, which others also may reasonably be expected to make, and that no one be given the opportunity to tailor the canons of a legitimate complaint to fit his own special condition and then to discard them when they no longer suit his purpose. Hence each person will propose principles of a general kind which will, to a large degree, gain their sense from the various applications to be made of them, the particular circumstances of which being as yet unknown. These principles will express the conditions in accordance with which each is the least unwilling to have his interests limited in the design of practices, given the competing interests of the others, on the supposition that the interests of others will be limited likewise. The restrictions which would so arise might be thought of as those a person would keep in mind if he were designing a practice in which his enemy were to assign him his place.

The two main parts of this conjectural account have a definite significance. The character and respective situations of the parties reflect the typical circumstances in which questions of justice arise. The procedure whereby principles are proposed and acknowledged represents constraints, analogous to those of having a morality, whereby rational and mutually self-interested persons are brought to act reasonably. Thus the first part reflects the fact that questions of justice arise when conflicting claims are made upon the design of a practice and where it is taken for granted that each person will insist, as far as possible, on what he considers his rights. It is typical of cases of justice to involve persons who are pressing on one another their claims, between which a fair balance or equilibrium must be found. On the other hand, as expressed by the second part, having a morality must at least imply the acknowledgment of principles as impartially applying to one's own conduct as well as to another's, and moreover principles which may constitute a constraint, or limitation, upon the pursuit of one's own interests. There are, of course, other aspects of having a morality: the acknowledgment of moral principles must show itself in accepting a reference to them as reasons for limiting one's claims, in acknowledging the burden of providing a special explanation, or excuse, when one acts contrary to them, or else in showing shame and remorse and a desire to make amends, and so on. It is sufficient to remark here that having a morality is analogous to having made a firm commitment in advance, for one must acknowledge the principles of morality even when they work to one's disadvantage. A man whose moral judgments always coincided with his interests could be suspected of having no morality at all.

Thus the two parts of the foregoing account are intended to mirror the kinds of circumstances in which questions of justice arise and the constraints which having a morality would impose upon persons so situated. In this way one can see how the acceptance of the principles of justice might come about, for given all these conditions as described, it would be natural if the two principles of justice were to be acknowledged. Since there is no way for anyone to win special advantages for himself, each might consider it reasonable to acknowledge equality as an initial principle. There is, however, no reason why they should regard this position as final, for if there are inequalities which satisfy the second principle, the immediate gain which equality would allow can be considered as intelligently invested in view of its future return. If, as is quite likely, these inequalities work as incentives to draw out better efforts, the members of this society may look upon them as concessions to human nature: they, like us, may think that people ideally should want to serve one another. But as they are mutually self-interested, their acceptance of these inequalities is merely the acceptance of the relations in which they actually stand and a recognition of the motives which lead them to engage in their common practices. *They* have no title to complain of one another. And so, provided that the conditions of the principle are met, there is no reason why they should not allow such inequalities. Indeed, it would be short-sighted of them to do so, and could result, in most cases, only from their being dejected by the bare knowledge, or perception, that others are better situated. Each person will, however, insist on an advantage to himself, and so on a common advantage, for none is willing to sacrifice anything for the others.

These remarks are not offered as a rigorous proof that persons conceived and situated as the conjectural account supposes, and required to adopt the procedure described, would settle on the two principles of justice. For such a proof a more elaborate and formal argument would have to be given: there remain certain details to be filled in and various alternatives to be ruled out. The argument should, however, be taken as a proof, or a sketch of a proof, for the proposition I seek to establish is a necessary one, that is, it is intended as a theorem: namely, that when mutually self-interested and rational persons confront one another in typical circumstances of justice, and when they are required by a procedure expressing the constraints of having a morality to jointly acknowledge principles by which their claims on the design of their common practices are to be judged, they will settle on these two principles as restrictions governing the assignment of rights and duties, and thereby accept them as limiting their rights against one another. It is this theorem which accounts for these principles as principles of justice and explains how they come to be associated with this moral concept. Moreover, this theorem is analogous to those about human conduct in others branches of social thought. That is, a simplified situation is described in which rational persons pursuing certain ends and related to one another in a definite way are required to act subject to certain limitations; then, given this situation, it is shown that they will act in a certain manner. Failure so to act would imply that one or more of the assumptions does not obtain. The foregoing account aims to establish, or to sketch, a theorem in this sense; the aim of the argument is to show the basis for saying that the principles of justice may be regarded as those principles which arise when the constraints of having a morality are imposed upon rational persons in typical circumstances of justice.

IV

These ideas are, of course, connected with a familiar way of thinking about justice which goes back at least to the Greek Sophists and which regards the acceptance of the principles of justice as a compromise between persons of roughly equal power who would enforce their will on each other if they could, but who, in view of the equality of forces among them and for the sake of their own peace and security, acknowledge certain forms of conduct insofar as prudence seems to require. Justice is thought of as a pact between rational egoists the stability of which is dependent on a balance of power and a similarity of circumstances. While the previous account is connected with this tradition, and with its most recent variant, the theory of games, it differs from it in several important respects which, to forestall misinterpretations, I will set out here.

First, I wish to use the previous conjectural account of the background of justice as a way of analyzing the concept. I do not want, therefore, to be interpreted as assuming a general theory of human motivation: when I suppose that the parties are mutually self-interested and are not willing to have their (substantial) interests sacrificed to others, I am referring to their conduct and motives as they are taken for granted in cases where questions of justice ordinarily arise. Justice is the virtue of practices where there are assumed to be competing interests and conflicting claims and where it is supposed that persons will press their rights on each other. That persons are mutually self-interested in certain situations and for certain purposes is what gives rise to the question of justice in practices covering those circumstances. Among an association of saints, if such a community could really exist, the disputes about justice could hardly occur, for they would all work selflessly together for one end, the glory of God as defined by their common religion, and reference to this end would settle every question of right. The justice of practices does not come up until there are several different parties (whether we think of these as individuals, associations, or nations and so on, is irrelevant) who do press their claims on one another, and who do regard themselves as representatives of interests which deserve to be considered. Thus the previous account involves no general theory of human motivation. Its intent is simply to incorporate into the conception of justice the relations of men to one another which set the stage for questions of justice. It makes no difference how wide or general these relations are, as this matter does not bear on the analysis of the concept.

Again, in contrast to the various conceptions of the social contract, the several parties do not establish any particular society or practice; they do not covenant to obey a particular sovereign body or to accept a given constitution. Nor do they, as in the theory of games (in certain respects a marvelously sophisticated development of this tradition), decide on individual strategies adjusted to their respective circumstances in the game. What the parties do is to *jointly* acknowledge certain *principles* of appraisal relating to their common *practices* either as already established or merely proposed. They accede to standards of judgment, not to a given practice; they do not make any specific agreement, or bargain, or adopt a particular strategy. The subject of their acknowledgment is, therefore, very general indeed; it is simply the acknowledgment of certain principles of judgment, fulfilling certain general conditions, to be used in criticizing the arrangement of their common affairs. The relations of mutual self-interest between the parties who are similarly circumstanced mirror the conditions under which questions of justice arise, and the procedure by which the principles of judgment are proposed and acknowledged reflects the constraints of having a morality. Each aspect, then, of the preceding hypothetical account serves the purpose of bringing out a feature of the notion of justice. One could, if one liked, view the principles of justice as the "solution" of this highest order "game" of adopting, subject to the procedure described, principles of argument for all coming particular "games" whose peculiarities one can in no way foresee. But this comparison, while no doubt helpful, must not obscure the fact that this highest order "game" is of a special sort.[4] Its significance is that its various pieces represent aspects of the concept of justice.

Finally, I do not, of course, conceive the several parties as necessarily coming together to establish their common practices for the first time. Some institutions may, indeed, be set up *de novo*, but I have framed the preceding account so that it will apply when the full complement of social institutions already exists and represents the result of a long period of development. Nor is the account in any way fictitious. In any society where people reflect on their institutions they will have an idea of what principles of justice would be acknowledged under the conditions described, and there will be occasions when questions of justice are actually discussed in this way. Therefore, if their practices do not accord with these principles, this will affect the quality of their social relations. For in this case there will be some recognized situations wherein the parties are mutually aware that one of them is being forced to accept what the other would concede is unjust. The foregoing analysis may then be thought of as representing the actual quality of relations between persons as defined by practices accepted as just. In such practices the parties will acknowledge the principles on which it is constructed, and the general recognition of this fact shows itself in the absence of resentment and in the sense of being justly treated. Thus one common objection to the theory of the social contract, its apparently historical and fictitious character, is avoided.

V

That the principles of justice may be regarded as arising in the manner described illustrates an important fact about them. Not only does it bring out the idea that justice is a primitive moral notion in that it arises once the concept of morality is imposed on mutually self-interested agents similarly circumstanced, but it emphasizes that fundamental to justice is the concept of fairness which relates to right dealing between persons who are cooperating with or competing against one another, as when one speaks of fair games, fair competition, and fair bargains. The question of fairness arises when free persons, who have no authority over one another, are engaging in a joint activity and among themselves settling or acknowledging the rules which define it and which determine the respective shares in its benefits and burdens. A practice will strike the parties as fair if none feels that, by participating in it, they or any of the others are taken advantage of, or forced to give in to claims which they do not regard as legitimate. This implies that each has a conception of legitimate claims which

203 JUSTICE AS FAIRNESS | 203

he thinks it reasonable for others as well as himself to acknowledge. If one thinks of the principles of justice as arising in the manner described, then they do define this sort of conception. A practice is just or fair, then, when it satisfies the principles which those who participate in it could propose to one another for mutual acceptance under the aforementioned circumstances. Persons engaged in a just, or fair, practice can face one another openly and support their respective positions, should they appear questionable, by reference to principles which it is reasonable to expect each to accept.

It is this notion of the possibility of mutual acknowledgment of principles by free persons who have no authority over one another which makes the concept of fairness fundamental to justice. Only if such acknowledgment is possible can there be true community between persons in their common practices; otherwise their relations will appear to them as founded to some extent on force. If, in ordinary speech, fairness applies more particularly to practices in which there is a choice whether to engage or not (e.g., in games, business competition), and justice to practices in which there is no choice (e.g., in slavery), the element of necessity does not render the conception of mutual acknowledgment inapplicable, although it may make it much more urgent to change unjust than unfair institutions. For one activity in which one can always engage is that of proposing and acknowledging principles to one another supposing each to be similarly circumstanced, and to judge practices by the principles so arrived at is to apply the standard of fairness to them.

Now if the participants in a practice accept its rules as fair, and so have no complaint to lodge against it, there arises a prima facie duty (and a corresponding prima facie right) of the parties to each other to act in accordance with the practice when it falls upon them to comply. When any number of persons engage in a practice, or conduct a joint undertaking according to rules, and thus restrict their liberty, those who have submitted to these restrictions when required have the right to a similar acquiescence on the part of those who have benefited by their submission. These conditions will obtain if a practice is correctly acknowledged to be fair, for in this case all who participate in it will benefit from it. The rights and duties so arising are special rights and duties in that they depend on previous actions voluntarily undertaken, in this case on the parties having engaged in a common practice and knowingly accepted its benefits.[5] It is not, however, an obligation which presupposes a deliberate performative act in the sense of a promise, or contract, and the like. An unfortunate mistake of proponents of the idea of the social contract was to suppose that political obligation does require some such act, or at least to use language which suggests it. It is sufficient that one has knowingly participated in and accepted the benefits of a practice acknowledged to be fair. This prima facie obligation may, of course, be overridden: it may happen, when it comes one's turn to follow a rule, that other considerations will justify not doing so. But one cannot, in general, be released from this obligation by denying the justice of the practice only when it falls on one to obey. If a person rejects a practice, he should, so far as possible, declare his intention in advance, and avoid participating in it or enjoying its benefits.

This duty I have called that of fair play, but it should be admitted that to refer to it in this way is, perhaps, to extend the ordinary notion of fairness. Usually, acting unfairly is not so much the breaking of any particular rule, even if the infraction is difficult to detect (cheating), but taking advantage of loopholes or ambiguities in rules, availing oneself of unexpected or special circumstances which make it impossible to enforce them, insisting that rules be enforced to one's advantage when they should be suspended, and more generally, acting contrary to the intention of a practice. It is for this reason that one speaks of the sense of fair play: acting fairly requires more than simply being able to follow rules; what is fair must often be felt, or perceived, one wants to say. It is not, however, an unnatural extension of the duty of fair play to have it include the obligation which participants who have knowingly accepted the benefits of their common practice owe to each other to act in accordance with it when their performance falls due, for it is usually considered unfair if someone accepts the benefits of a practice but refuses to do his part in maintaining it. Thus one might say of the tax-dodger that he violates the duty of fair play: he accepts the benefits of government but will not do his part in releasing resources to it; and members of labor unions often say that fellow workers who refuse to join are being unfair: they refer to them as "free riders," as persons who enjoy what are the supposed benefits of unionism, higher wages, shorter hours, job security, and the like, but who refuse to share in its burdens in the form of paying dues, and so on.

The duty of fair play stands beside other prima facie duties such as fidelity and gratitude as a basic moral notion, yet it is not to be confused with them. These duties are all clearly distinct, as would be obvious from their definitions. As with any moral duty, that of fair play implies a constraint on self-interest in particular cases; on occasion it enjoins conduct which a rational egoist strictly defined would not decide upon. So while justice does not require of anyone that he sacrifice his interests in that *general position* and procedure whereby the principles of justice are proposed and acknowledged, it may happen that in particular situations, arising in the context of engaging in a practice, the duty of fair play will often cross his interests in the sense that he will be required to forgo particular advantages which the peculiarities of his circumstances might permit him to take. There is, of course, nothing surprising in this. It is simply the consequence of the firm commitment which the parties may be supposed to have made, or which they would make, in the general position, together with the fact that they have participated in and accepted the benefits of a practice which they regard as fair.

Now the acknowledgment of this constraint in particular cases, which is manifested in acting fairly or wishing to make amends, feeling ashamed, and the like, when one has evaded it, is one of the forms of conduct by which participants in a common practice exhibit their recognition of each other as persons with similar interests and capacities. In the same way that, failing a special explanation, the criterion for the recognition of suffering is helping one who suffers, acknowledging the duty of fair play is a necessary part of the criterion for recognizing another as a person with similar interests and feelings as oneself.[6] A person who never under any circumstances showed a wish to help others in pain would show, at the same time, that he did not recognize that they were in pain; nor could he have any feelings of affection or friendship for anyone; for having these feelings implies, failing special circumstances, that he comes to their aid when they are suffering. Recognition that another is a person in pain shows itself in sympathetic action; this primitive natural response of compassion is one of those responses upon which the various forms of moral conduct are built.

Similarly, the acceptance of the duty of fair play by participants in a common practice is a reflection in each person of the recognition of the aspirations and interests of the others to be realized by their joint activity. Failing a special explanation, their acceptance of it is a necessary part of the criterion for their recognizing one another as persons with similar interests and capacities, as the conception of their relations in the general position supposes them to be. Otherwise they would show no recognition of one another as persons with similar capacities and interests, and indeed, in some cases perhaps hypothetical, they would not recognize one another as persons at all, but as complicated objects involved in a complicated activity. To recognize another as a person one must respond to him and act toward him in certain ways, and these ways are intimately connected with the various prima facie duties. Acknowledging these duties in *some* degree, and so having the elements of morality, is not a matter of choice, or of intuiting moral qualities, or a matter of the expression of feelings or attitudes (the three interpretations between which philosophical opinion frequently oscillates); it is simply the possession of one of the forms of conduct in which the recognition of others as persons is manifested.

These remarks are unhappily obscure. Their main purpose here, however, is to forestall, together with the remarks in Section IV, the misinterpretation that, on the view presented, the acceptance of justice and the acknowledgment of the duty of fair play depends in everyday life solely on there being a *de facto* balance of forces between the parties. It would indeed be foolish to underestimate the importance of such a balance in securing justice, but it is not the only basis thereof. The recognition of one another as persons with similar interests and capacities engaged in a common practice must, failing a special explanation, show itself in the acceptance of the principles of justice and the acknowledgment of the duty of fair play.

The conception at which we have arrived, then, is that the principles of justice may be thought of as arising once the constraints of having a morality are imposed upon rational and mutually self-interested parties who are related and situated in a special way. A practice is just if it is in accordance with the principles which all who participate in it might reasonably be expected to propose or to acknowledge before one another when they are similarly circumstanced and required to make a firm commitment in advance without knowledge of what will be their peculiar condition, and thus when it meets standards which the parties could accept as fair should occasion arise for them to debate its merits. Regarding the participants themselves, once persons knowingly engage in a practice which they acknowledge to be fair and accept the benefits of doing so, they are bound by the duty of fair play to follow the rules when it comes their turn to do so, and this implies a limitation on their pursuit of self-interest in particular cases.

Now one consequence of this conception is that, where it applies, there is no moral value in the satisfaction of a claim incompatible with it. Such a claim violates the conditions of reciprocity and community among persons, and he who presses it, not being willing to acknowledge it when pressed by another, has no grounds for complaint when it is denied; whereas he against whom it is pressed can complain. As it cannot be mutually acknowledged it is a resort to coercion; granting the claim is possible only if one party can compel acceptance of what the other will not admit. But it makes no sense to concede claims the denial of which cannot he complained of in preference to claims the denial of which can be objected to. Thus, in deciding on the justice of a practice it is not enough to ascertain that it answers to wants and interests in the fullest and most effective manner. For if any of these conflict with justice, they should not be counted, as their satisfaction is no reason at all for having a practice. It would be irrelevant to say, even if true, that it resulted in the greatest satisfaction of desire. In tallying up the merits of a practice one must toss out the satisfaction of interests the claims of which are incompatible with the principles of justice.

VI

The discussion so far has been excessively abstract. While this is perhaps unavoidable, I should now like to bring out some of the features of the conception of justice as fairness by comparing it with the conception of justice in classical utilitarianism as represented by Bentham and Sidgwick, and its counterpart in welfare economics. This conception assimilates justice to benevolence and the latter in turn to the most efficient design of institutions to promote the general welfare. Justice is a kind of efficiency.

Now it is said occasionally that this form of utilitarianism puts no restrictions on what might be a just assignment of rights and duties in that there might be circumstances which, on utilitarian grounds, would justify institutions highly offensive to our ordinary sense of justice. But the classical utilitarian conception is not totally unprepared for this objection. Beginning with the notion that the general happiness can be represented by a social utility function consisting of a sum of individual utility functions with identical weights (this being the meaning of the maxim that each counts for one and no more than one), it is commonly assumed that the utility functions of individuals are similar in all essential respects. Differences between individuals are ascribed to accidents of education and upbringing, and they should not be taken into account. This assumption, coupled with that of diminishing marginal utility, results in a prima facie case for equality, e.g., of equality in the distribution of income during any given period of time, laying aside indirect effects on the future. But even if utilitarianism is interpreted as having such restrictions built into the utility function, and even if it is supposed that these restrictions have in practice much the same result as the application of the principles of justice (and appear, perhaps, to be ways of expressing these principles in the language of mathematics and psychology), the fundamental idea is very different from the conception of justice as fairness. For one thing, that the principles of justice should be accepted is interpreted as the contingent result of a higher order administrative decision. The form of this decision is regarded as being similar to that of an entrepreneur deciding how much to produce of this or that commodity in view of its marginal revenue, or to that of someone distributing goods to needy persons according to the relative urgency of their wants. The choice between practices is thought of as being made on the basis of the allocation of benefits and burdens to individuals (these being measured by the present capitalized value of their utility over the full period of the practice's existence), which results from the distribution of rights and duties established by a practice.

Moreover, the individuals receiving these benefits are not conceived as being related in any way: they represent so many different directions in which limited resources may be allocated. The value of assigning resources to one direction rather than another depends solely on the preferences and interests of individuals as individuals. The satisfaction of desire has its value irrespective of the moral relations between persons, say as members of a joint undertaking, and of the claims which, in the name of these interests, they are prepared to make on one another;[7] and it is this value which is to be taken into account by the (ideal) legislator who is conceived as adjusting the rules of the system from the center so as to maximize the value of the social utility function.

It is thought that the principles of justice will not be violated by a legal system so conceived provided these executive decisions are correctly made. In this fact the principles of justice are said to have their derivation and explanation; they simply express the most important general features of social institutions in which the administrative problem is solved in the best way. These principles have, indeed, a special urgency because, given the facts of human nature, so much depends on them, and this explains the peculiar quality of the moral feelings associated with justice. This assimilation of justice to a higher order executive decision, certainly a striking conception, is central to classical utilitarianism, and it also brings out its profound individualism, in one sense of this ambiguous word. It regards persons as so many *separate* directions in which benefits and burdens may be assigned, and the value of the satisfaction or dissatisfaction of desire is not thought to depend in any way on the moral relations in which individuals stand, or on the kinds of claims which they are willing, in the pursuit of their interests, to press on each other.

VII

Many social decisions are, of course, of an administrative nature. Certainly this is so when it is a matter of social utility in what one may call its ordinary sense: that is, when it is a question of the efficient design of social institutions for the use of common means to achieve common ends. In this case either the benefits and burdens may be assumed to be impartially distributed, or the question of distribution is misplaced, as in the instance of maintaining public order and security or national defense. But as an interpretation of the basis of the principles of justice, classical utilitarianism is mistaken. It *permits* one to argue, for example, that slavery is unjust on the grounds that the advantages to the slaveholder as slaveholder do not counterbalance the disadvantages to the slave and to society at large burdened by a comparatively inefficient system of labor. Now the conception of justice as fairness, when applied to the practice of slavery with its offices of slaveholder and slave, would not allow one to consider the advantages of the slaveholder in the first place. As that office is not is accordance with principles which could be mutually acknowledged, the gains accruing to the slaveholder, assuming them to exist, cannot be counted as in *any* way mitigating the injustice of the practice. The question whether these gains outweigh the disadvantages to the slave and to society cannot arise, since in considering the justice of slavery these gains have no weight at all which requires that they be overridden. Where the conception of justice as fairness applies, slavery is *always unjust*.

I am not, of course, suggesting the absurdity that the classical utilitarians approved of slavery. I am only rejecting a type of argument which their view allows them to use in support of their disapproval of it. The conception of justice as derivative from efficiency implies that judging the justice of a practice is always, in principle at least, a matter of weighing up advantages and disadvantages, each having an intrinsic value or disvalue as the satisfaction of interests, irrespective of whether or not these interests necessarily involve acquiescence in principles which could not be mutually acknowledged. Utilitarianism cannot account for the fact that slavery is always unjust, nor for the fact that it would be recognized as irrelevant in defeating the accusation of injustice for one person to say to another, engaged with him in a common practice and debating its merits, that nevertheless it allowed of the greatest satisfaction of desire. The charge of injustice cannot be rebutted in this way. If justice were derivative from a higher order executive efficiency, this would not be so.

But now, even if it is taken as established that, so far as the ordinary conception of justice goes, slavery is always unjust (that is, slavery by definition violates commonly recognized principles of justice), the classical utilitarian would surely reply that these principles, as other moral principles subordinate to that of utility, are only generally correct. It is simply for the most part true that slavery is less efficient than other institutions, and while common sense may define the concept of justice so that slavery is unjust, nevertheless, where slavery would lead to the greatest satisfaction of desire, it is not wrong. Indeed, it is then right, and for the very same reason that justice, as ordinarily understood, is usually right. If, as ordinarily understood, slavery is always unjust, to this extent the utilitarian conception of justice might be admitted to differ from that of common moral opinion. Still the utilitarian would want to hold that, as a matter of moral principle, his view is correct in giving no special weight to considerations of justice beyond that allowed for by the general presumption of effectiveness. And this, he claims, is as it should be. The everyday opinion is morally in error, although, indeed, it is a useful error, since it protects rules of generally high utility.

The question, then, relates not simply to the analysis of the concept of justice as common sense defines it, but the analysis of it in the wider sense as to how much weight considerations of justice, as defined, are to have when laid against other kinds of moral considerations. Here again I wish to argue that reasons of justice have a *special* weight for which only the conception of justice as fairness can account. Moreover, it belongs to the concept of justice that they do have this special weight. While Mill recognized that this was so, he thought that it could be accounted for by the special urgency of the moral feelings which naturally support principles of such high utility. But it is a mistake to resort to the urgency of feeling; as with the appeal to intuition, it manifests a failure to pursue the question far enough. The special weight of considerations of justice can be explained from the conception of justice as fairness. It is only necessary to elaborate a bit what has already been said as follows.

If one examines the circumstances in which a certain tolerance of slavery is justified, or perhaps better, excused, it turns out that these are of a rather special sort. Perhaps slavery exists as an inheritance from the past and it proves necessary to dismantle it piece by piece; at times slavery may conceivably be an advance on previous institutions. Now while there may be some excuse for slavery in special conditions, it is never an excuse for it that it is sufficiently advantageous to the slaveholder to outweigh the disadvantages to the slave and to society. A person who argues in this way is not perhaps making a wildly irrelevant remark, but he is guilty of a moral fallacy. There is disorder in his conception of the ranking of moral principles. For the slaveholder, by his own admission, has no moral title to the advantages which he receives as a slaveholder. He is no more prepared than the slave to acknowledge the principle upon which is founded the respective positions in which they both stand. Since slavery does not accord with principles which they could mutually acknowledge, they each may be supposed to agree that it is unjust: it grants claims which it ought not to grant and in doing so denies claims which it ought not to deny. Among persons in a general position who are debating the form of their common practices, it cannot, therefore, be offered as a reason for a practice that, in conceding these very claims that ought to be denied, it nevertheless meets existing interests more effectively. By their very nature the satisfaction of these claims is without weight and cannot enter into any tabulation of advantages and disadvantages.

Furthermore, it follows from the concept of morality that, to the extent that the slaveholder recognizes his position *vis-à-vis* the slave to be unjust, he would not choose to press his claims. His not wanting to receive his special advantages is one of the ways in which he shows that he thinks slavery is unjust. It would be fallacious for the legislator to suppose, then, that it is a ground for having a practice that it brings advantages greater than disadvantages, if those for whom the practice is designed, and to whom the advantages flow, acknowledge that they have no moral title to them and do not wish to receive them.

For these reasons the principles of justice have a special weight, and with respect to the principle of the greatest satisfaction of desire, as cited in the general position, among those discussing the merits of their common practices, the principles of justice have an absolute weight. In this sense they are not contingent, and this is why their force is greater than can be accounted for by the general presumption (assuming that there is one) of the effectiveness, in the utilitarian sense, of practices which in fact satisfy them.

If one wants to continue using the concepts of classical utilitarianism, one will have to say, to meet this criticism, that at least the individual or social utility functions must be so defined that no value is given to the satisfaction of interests the representative claims of which violate the principles of justice. In this way it is no doubt possible to include these principles within the form of the utilitarian conception, but to do so is, of course, to change its inspiration altogether as a moral conception. For it is to incorporate within it principles which cannot be understood on the basis of a higher order executive decision aiming at the greatest satisfaction of desire.

It is worth remarking, perhaps, that this criticism of utilitarianism does not depend on whether or not the two assumptions, that of individuals having similar utility functions and that of diminishing marginal utility, are interpreted as psychological propositions to be supported or refuted by experience, or as moral and political principles expressed in a somewhat technical language. There are, certainly, several advantages in taking them in the latter fashion. For one thing, one might say that this is what Bentham and others really meant by them, as least as shown by how they were used in arguments for social reform. More importantly, one could hold that the best way to defend the classical utilitarian view is to interpret these assumptions as moral and political principles. It is doubtful whether, taken as psychological propositions, they are true of men in general as we know them under normal conditions. On the other hand, utilitarians would not have wanted to propose them merely as practical working principles of legislation or as expedient maxims to guide reform, given the egalitarian sentiments of modern society. When pressed they might well have invoked the idea of a more or less equal capacity of men in relevant respects if given an equal chance in a just society. But if the argument above regarding slavery is correct, then granting these assumptions as moral and political principles makes no difference. To view individuals as equally fruitful lines for the allocation of benefits, even as a matter of moral principle, still leaves the mistaken notion that the satisfaction of desire has value in itself irrespective of the relations between persons as members of a common practice and irrespective of the claims upon one another which the satisfaction of interests represents. To see the error of this idea one must give up the conception of justice as an executive decision altogether and refer to the notion of justice as fairness: that participants in a common practice be regarded as having an original and equal liberty and that their common practices be considered unjust unless they accord with principles which persons so circumstanced and related could freely acknowledge before one another, and so could accept as fair. Once the emphasis is put upon the concept of the mutual recognition of principles by participants in a common practice the rules of which are to define their several relations and give form to their claims on one another, then it is clear that the granting of a claim the principle of which could not be acknowledged by each in the general position (that is, in the position in which the parties propose and acknowledge principles before one another) is not a reason for adopting a practice. Viewed in this way, the background of the claim is seen to exclude if from consideration; that it can represent a value in itself arises from the conception of individuals as separate lines for the assignment of benefits, as isolated persons who stand as claimants on an administrative or benevolent largesse. Occasionally persons do so stand to one another, but this is not the general case, nor, more importantly, is it the case when it is a matter of the justice of practices themselves in which participants stand in various relations to be appraised in accordance with standards which they may be expected to acknowledge before one another. Thus, however mistaken the notion of the social contract may be as history, and however far it may overreach itself as a general theory of social and political obligation, it does express, suitably interpreted, an essential part of the concept of justice.

VIII

By way of conclusion I should like to make two remarks: first, the original modification of the utilitarian principle (that it require of practices that the offices and positions defined by them be equal unless it is reasonable to suppose that the representative man in *every* office would find the inequality to his advantage), slight as it may appear at first sight, actually has a different conception of justice standing behind it. I have tried to show how this is so by developing the concept of justice as fairness and by indicating how this notion involves the mutual acceptance, from a general position, of the principles on which a practice is founded, and how this in turn requires the exclusion from consideration of claims violating the principles of justice. Thus the slight alteration of principle reveals another family of notions, another way of looking at the concept of justice.

Second, I should like to remark also that I have been dealing with the *concept* of justice. I have tried to set out the kinds of principles upon which judgments concerning the justice of practices may be said to stand. The analysis will be successful to the degree that it expresses the principles involved in these judgments when made by competent persons upon deliberation and reflection.[8] Now every people may be supposed to have the concept of justice, since in the life of every society there must be at least some relations in which the parties consider themselves to be circumstanced and related as the concept of justice as fairness requires. Societies will differ from one another not in having or in failing to have this notion but in the range of cases to which they apply it and in the emphasis which they give to it as compared with other moral concepts.

A firm grasp of the concept of justice itself is necessary if these variations, and the reasons for them, are to be understood. No study of the development of moral ideas and of the differences between them is more sound than the analysis of the fundamental moral concepts upon which it must depend. I have tried, therefore, to give an analysis of the concept of justice which should apply generally, however large a part the concept may have in a given morality, and which can be used in explaining the course of men's thoughts about justice and its relations to other moral concepts. How it is to be used for this purpose is a large topic which I cannot, of course, take up here. I mention it only to emphasize that I have been dealing with the concept of justice itself and to indicate what use I consider such an analysis to have.

Notes

1. I use the word "practice" throughout as a sort of technical term meaning any form of activity specified by a system of rules which defines offices, roles, moves, penalties, defenses, and so on, and which gives the activity its structure. As examples one may think of games and rituals, trials and parliaments, markets and systems of property. I have attempted a partial analysis of the notion of a practice in a paper, "Two Concepts of Rules," *Philosophical Review*, LXIV (1955), 3–32.

2. These principles are, of course, well known in one form or another and appear in many analyses of justice even where the writers differ widely on other matters. Thus if the principle of equal liberty is commonly associated with Kant (see *The Philosophy of Law*, trans. W. Hastie, Edinburgh, 1887, pp. 56–57), it may be claimed that it can also be found in J. S. Mill's *On Liberty* and elsewhere, and in many other liberal writers. Recently H. L. A. Hart has argued for something like it in his paper, "Are There Any Natural Rights?" *Philosophical Review*, LXIV (1955), 175–191. The injustice of inequalities which are not won in return for a contribution to the common advantage is, of course, widespread in political writings of all sorts. The conception of justice here discussed is distinctive, if at all, only in selecting these two principles in this form, but for another similar analysis, see the discussion by W. D. Lamont, *The Principles of Moral Judgment* (Oxford, 1946), Chap. V.

3. It is not possible to discuss here this addition to the usual conception of rationality If it seems peculiar, it may be worth remarking that it is analogous to the modification of the utilitarian principle which the argument as a whole

is designed to explain and justify. In the same way that the satisfaction of interests, the representative claims of which violate the principles of justice, is not a reason for having a practice (see Section VII), unfounded envy, within limits, need not to be taken into account.

4. The difficulty one gets into by a mechanical application of the theory of games to moral philosophy can be brought out by considering, among several possible examples, R. B. Braithwaite's study *Theory of Games as a Tool for the Moral Philosopher* (Cambridge, 1955). What is lacking is the concept of morality, and it must be brought into the conjectural account in some way or other. In the text this is done by the form of the procedure whereby principles are proposed and acknowledged (Section III). If one starts directly with the particular case as known, and if one accepts as given and definitive the preferences and relative positions of the parties, whatever they are, it is impossible to give an analysis of the moral concept of fairness.

5. For the definition of this prima facie duty, and the idea that it is a special duty, I am indebted to H. L. A. Hart. See his "Are There Any Natural Rights?" pp. 185–186.

6. I am using the concept of criterion here in what I take to be Wittgenstein's sense. That the response of compassion, under appropriate circumstances, is part of the criterion for whether or not a person understands what "pain" means, is, I think, in the *Philosophical Investigations*. The view in the text is simply an extension of this idea. I cannot, however, attempt to justify it here.

7. An idea essential to the classical utilitarian conception of justice. Bentham is firm in his statement of it. (*The Principles of Morals and Legislation*, chap. II, sec. iv. See also chap. X, sec. x, note 1.) The same point is made in *The Limits of Jurisprudence Defined*, pp. 115–116. Although much recent welfare economics, as found in such important works as I. M. D. Little, *A Critique of Welfare Economics*, 2d ed. (Oxford, 1957) and K. J. Arrow, *Social Choice and Individual Values* (New York, 1951), dispenses with the idea of cardinal utility and uses instead the theory of ordinal utility as stated by J. R. Hicks, *Value and Capital*, 2d ed. (Oxford, 1946), Pt. I, it assumes with utilitarianism that individual preferences have value as such, and so accepts the idea being criticized here. I hasten to add, however, that this is no objection to it as a means of analyzing economic policy, and for that purpose it may, indeed, be a necessary simplifying assumption. Nevertheless it is an assumption which cannot be made insofar as one is trying to analyze moral concepts, expecially the concept of justice, as economists would, I think, agree. Justice is usually regarded as a separate and distinct part of any comprehensive criterion of economic policy. See, for example, Tibor Scitovsky, *Welfare and Competition* (London, 1952), pp. 59–69, and Little, *Critique of Welfare Economics*, chap. VII.

8. For a further discussion of the idea expressed here, see my paper "Outline of a Decision Procedure for Ethics," *Philosophical Review*, LX (1951),

177–197. For an analysis similar in many respects but using the notion of the ideal observer instead of that of the considered judgment of a competent person, see Roderick Firth, "Ethical Absolutism and the Ideal Observer," *Philosophy and Phenomenological Research*, XII (1952), 317–345. While the similarities between these two discussions are more important than the differences, an analysis based on the notion of a considered judgment of a competent person, as it is based on a kind of judgment, may prove more helpful in understanding the features of moral judgment than an analysis based on the notion of an ideal observer, although this remains to be shown. A man who rejects the conditions imposed on a considered judgment of a competent person could no longer profess to *judge* at all. This seems more fundamental than his rejecting the conditions of observation, for these do not seem to apply, in an ordinary sense, to making a moral judgment.

Select Bibliography

BENN, S. I., and PETERS, R. S. *Principles of Political Thought.* New York: Macmillan, 1964. Chapters 5 and 6.

BRANDT, R. B., ed. *Social Justice.* Englewood Cliffs, N.J.: Prentice-Hall, 1962.

FRIEDRICH, C. J., and CHAPMAN, J. W., eds. *Justice: Nomos VI.* New York: Atherton Press, 1963.

GINSBERG, M. "The Concept of Justice," *Philosophy,* XXXVIII (1963), 99–116.

GINSBERG, M. *On Justice in Society.* Baltimore: Penguin, 1965.

HARRISON, JONATHAN. "Utilitarianism, Universalization and Our Duty to Be Just," *Proceedings of the Aristotelian Society,* LIII (1952–1953), 105–134.

HOBBHOUSE, L.T. *The Elements of Social Justice.* London: Allen & Unwin, 1922.

KELSEN, HANS. *What Is Justice?* Berkeley: University of California Press, 1957.

LEYS, W. A. R. "Justice and Equality," *Ethics,* LXVII (1956), 17–24.

OLAFSON, F. A., ed. *Justice and Social Policy.* Englewood Cliffs, N.J.: Prentice-Hall, 1961.

RAPHAEL, D. D. "Justice and Liberty," *Proceedings of the Aristotelian Society,* LI (1950–1951), 167–196.

RAWLS, JOHN. "Distributive Justice: Some Addenda," *Natural Law Forum,* XIII (1968), 51–71.

ROSS, ALF. *On Law and Justice.* Berkeley: University of California Press, 1959.

WOLFF, R. P. A. "A Refutation of Rawls' Theorem on Justice," *Journal of Philosophy,* LXIII (1966), 179–190.

RIGHTS

J EREMY BENTHAM once referred to
the claim to natural rights as "nonsense upon stilts," and many later
philosophers have shared his very critical opinion of the doctrine that
is the focus of this section. Like the social contract theory, it is almost
impossible to give historical or empirical support to the doctrine of
natural rights, and almost as difficult to provide a sound philosophical
defense. The articles by Margaret Macdonald and Stuart Brown are
excellent examples of constructive political philosophy. While accepting
the validity of many of the criticisms of the doctrine, both feel that
it contains some important truths which warrant a further attempt
to "make sense" of it before deciding whether or not to discard it.

The reader will not find a detailed discussion of the meaning of
rights in this section, as he did in the section on liberty. Rather, both
articles focus on the doctrine of natural rights or inalienable rights
(these terms are used interchangeably). The basic characteristic of
such rights, says Brown, is that they cannot "morally or logically be
waived, conveyed, and voided." It is logically impossible because if an
inalienable right is asserted it cannot be denied for any reason; it is
morally impossible because its denial is "the most intolerable and
inexcusable injustice against a man."

The purpose of Margaret Macdonald's article is to "understand
what can be meant by the assertion that there are some rights to which
human beings are entitled independently of their varying social relationships." She offers a plausible and intelligible interpretation of the
doctrine by focusing on what the idea *can* mean, not on what it *has
meant* to its several proponents. Stuart Brown goes further in suggesting
that earlier philosophers "were correct in holding that there is an
inalienable right to *protection*," although they were incorrect on other
grounds. In addition to interpreting the doctrine, Brown attempts to
defend it. Note that Macdonald discusses natural rights in the plural,
while Brown defends only one inalienable right. Unlike Macdonald,
Brown is quite clear about the right that he is discussing.

Margaret Macdonald's article might serve as an interesting case
for a study in the sociology of knowledge. That the article was written
shortly after the end of World War II and contains numerous references
to Nazi Germany suggests that the social and political environment
was not irrelevant to the motives of the author. The actions of the Third
Reich, which seemed to deny any basic human rights, may have
focused her attention on the importance of the doctrine. Further,
her association of Goebbels with the view that moral values are capable
of scientific proof (in the last paragraph) may supply us with a psycho-

logical explanation for her rejection of certain ethical theories. Needless to say, the nature of any writer's motives is irrelevant to the validity of an argument.

Macdonald's article is not only an analysis and interpretation of natural rights but also an explication of ethical theory. A brief outline of the article will show why this discussion of ethics is crucial to her argument. She begins by distinguishing three types of propositions: one, tautological or analytic propositions, which state "rules for the use of symbols"; two, empirical propositions, which "state matter of fact and existence"; and three, assertions or expressions of values. Next she considers several traditional interpretations of the natural rights doctrine including natural law, the social contract, and teleology. All these approaches commit an error in interpreting the doctrine as a "curious hybrid" of tautological and empirical propositions. The only satisfactory interpretation is to understand the natural rights doctrine as an expression of values, an assertion about what society ought to be like. It is here that the discussion of ethical theory becomes crucial.

Ethical utterances are not subject to scientific or empirical proof. But this does not mean that they are merely "sophisticated ways of cheering and cursing," as the emotivists would argue. Ethical assertions can be supported by reasons, principles, and facts. They can be defended with reasons, and one can try to persuade others that one's moral decision is right. Macdonald has adopted an existentialist position in arguing that the conditions of a good society, or the nature of natural rights (they are equivalent), are "not given by nature or mystically bound up with the essence of man and his inevitable goal, but [are] determined by human decisions." One important question remains: even granting the validity of the argument, it can still be asked whether the idea of natural rights is necessary in order to make these ethical assertions.

In approaching Stuart Brown's article, the reader should attempt to keep his general argument in focus lest he become too involved in the more intricate arguments. The general argument consists of three stages: a statement of the inalienable right which is to be explicated and defended, a discussion of the characteristics of inalienable rights, and the presentation of two major objections to the doctrine together with an attempt to meet those objections.

Brown makes an important distinction between the protection of private goods (e.g., life, happiness) and the goods themselves. Persons have an inalienable right to institutions which provide protection of such private goods but not to the goods themselves. Inalienable rights,

as they have traditionally been understood, have four major characteristics. They are moral as opposed to institutional; that is men may
have an inalienable right which institutions or laws may not provide.
Second, such rights are politically basic since they are a condition of
an individual's moral consent to government. Third, inalienable rights
are "natural" if that term is understood as a "moral commitment
based in part on scientific studies about the differences between men...."
Fourth, inalienable rights are "self-evident."

The two major objections to the doctrine, together with Brown's
answers, are the most important parts of his article. The first objection
rests on the fact of "cultural diversity." Some suggest that because
inalienable rights are neither asserted nor recognized in many cultures,
the proposition that all men have such rights is false. Brown replies
that men may have rights that they do not recognize. One obvious
example is that we speak of the rights of children which they certainly
do not recognize or assert. To meet the objection fully, he suggests
that two conditions must be fulfilled: the existence of private moral
interests and the possibility of creating or modifying institutions. If
the latter were impossible, it would seem nonsensical to claim an
inalienable right to institutions where such institutions could not be
created. And the former, if fulfilled, would insure the diversity of the
private goods for which men may claim a right to protection. Since
both conditions are fulfilled, the "undeniable fact of cultural diversity
in no way disconfirms the inalienable rights of men."

The second major objection is based on the philosophical premise
that "all significant moral assertions must be subject to denial." It is
often argued that any assertion about what a person ought to do can
be successfully denied if it can be shown that such action is impossible.
If A ought to perform X but does not do so, a sufficient defense would
be to demonstrate that A could not perform X. If this premise were
accepted, any claim to an inalienable right could be successfully denied
by demonstrating that the right cannot be fulfilled. But then the
right would not be inalienable or unconditional. Brown does not
meet this objection by arguing that an inalienable right is subject to
denial, for that would involve a contradiction. Rather, he holds that
the premise is mistaken and that it begs the question. A different but
similar objection is based on the premise that there are inalienable
rights which can be waived — therefore, that they are not inalienable.
For example, if there is an inalienable right to life (as many philosophers
have claimed), it can be shown that this right is not inalienable by
pointing to circumstances in which this right cannot or ought not to
be claimed or recognized. Brown would accept the premise that a right

to life is not inalienable. But Brown is not defending an inalienable right to life, or any other "high order good." He is defending a right to institutions which provide protection of these goods. This argument seems much more difficult to dispute even if its claims are somewhat narrower.

The articles in this section should cause even the most skeptical reader to consider seriously the doctrine of natural rights.

11

Natural Rights

Margaret Macdonald

DOCTRINES of natural law and natural rights have a long and impressive history from the Stoics and Roman jurists to the Atlantic Charter and Roosevelt's Four Freedoms.[1] That men are entitled to make certain claims by virtue simply of their common humanity has been equally passionately defended and vehemently denied. Punctured by the cool skepticism of Hume, routed by the contempt of Bentham for "nonsense upon stilts," submerged by idealist and Marxist philosophers in the destiny of the totalitarian state, the claim to "natural rights" has never been quite defeated. It tends in some form to be renewed in every crisis in human affairs, when the plain citizen tries to make, or expects his leaders to make, articulate his obscure, but firmly held, conviction that he is not a mere pawn in any political game, nor the property of any government or ruler, but the living and protesting individual for whose sake all political games are played and all governments instituted. As one of Cromwell's soldiers expressed it to that dictator: "Really, sir, I think that the poorest he that is in England hath a life to live as the greatest he."[2]

It could, perhaps, be proved hedonistically that life for most ordinary citizens is more *comfortable* in a democratic than a totalitarian state. But would an appeal for effort, on this ground, have been sanctioned between 1939 and 1945? However true, it would have been rejected as inefficient because *uninspired*. Who could be moved to endure

From *Proceedings of the Aristotelian Society*, XLVII (1946–1947), 225–250. Copyright 1947 by The Aristotelian Society.

"blood and toil, tears and sweat" for the sake of a little extra comfort? What, then, supplied the required inspiration? An appeal to the instinct of national self-preservation? But societies have been known to collapse inexplicably almost without waiting to be physically defeated. No doubt there are several answers, but at least one, I suggest, was an appeal to the values of freedom and equality among men. An appeal to safeguard and restore, where necessary, the Rights of Man, those ultimate points at which authority and social differences vanish, leaving the solitary individual with his essential human nature, according to one political theory, or a mere social fiction, according to another.

All this sounds very obscure. And the doctrine of natural law and of the natural rights of men is very obscure, which justifies the impatience of its opponents. It seems a strange law which is unwritten, has never been enacted, and may be unobserved without penalty, and peculiar rights which are possessed antecedently to all specific claims within an organized society. Surely, it will be said, the whole story now has only historical interest as an example of social mythology? Nothing is so dead as dead ideology. All this may be true,[3] but nevertheless the doctrine is puzzling. For if it is sheer nonsense why did it have psychological, political, and legal effects? Men do not reflect and act upon collections of meaningless symbols or nonsense rhymes.

There seems no doubt that the assertions of certain Greek philosophers about the "natural" equality of men and their consequent right to freedom caused intelligent contemporaries to become uneasy about the institution of slavery,[4] that doctrines of the primal Rights of Man were significantly connected with the French and American Revolutions. It even seems probable that the Communist Manifesto owed much of its success not to its "scientific" analysis of capitalist society but to its denouncement of a wage slavery degrading to human nature and its appeal to all workers to assert their equal brotherhood. A major crime of capitalist society for Marx was that it had destroyed all ties between men other than naked self-interest and had "resolved personal worth into exchange value." Only after the proletarian revolution would *human* history begin and men treat each other as equal human beings, not as exploiter and exploited. The object of the transfer of class power is to end class power and to reveal or restore some essential human nature at present disguised by distorting social relationships.

So even if the theory were dead, the puzzle of its effects would remain and suggest that it had been introduced to solve a genuine problem of political and social philosophy. And it is interesting, therefore, to inquire what the problem was, whether it has found an alternative solution or is bogus and insoluble.

Why should people have supposed, and, as I believe, continue to suppose, in obscure fashion, that they have "natural" rights, or rights as human beings, independently of the laws and governments of any existing society? It is surely, partly at least, because no existing social compulsion or relationship is self-justifying. Men may always ask why they should or should not endure it and expect a convincing answer. And, ultimately, it would seem, they may challenge the dictates of all existing governments and the pressures of every society if they find them equally oppressive, i.e., if they deny what the individual considers his fundamental "right." But since, *ex hypothesi*, this "right" is denied by every existing law and authority, it must be a right possessed independently of them and derived from another source. If, e.g., the laws of every existing society condemn a human being to be a slave, he, or another on his behalf, may yet hold that he has a "right" to be free. What sort of proposition is this and how is such a claim to be justified? This seems to be one most important problem which the doctrine of natural rights tried to solve.

Natural Law, Natural Laws, and Natural Rights

There are an indefinite number of different types of propositions and other forms of human utterance. I will, for my present purpose, notice three: (1) tautological or analytic propositions which state rules for the uses of symbols or which follow from such rules within a linguistic or logical system, (2) empirical or contingent propositions which state matter of fact and existence (propositions which describe what does or may occur in the world and not the symbolic techniques employed in such description), (3) assertions or expressions of value. With the help of this classification it may be possible to show that some of the difficulties of the doctrine of natural rights have been due to an attempt to interpret propositions about natural rights as a curious hybrid of types (1) and (2) of the above classification.

For in the theory which conceived of natural rights as guaranteed by a "natural" law, the position seems to have been considered in the following terms. The "rights" of a slave, e.g., derive from the laws in any society which govern his artificial status as a slave. Yet he has a right to be free. But in virtue of what status and law? Only, it seems, by his status of being a man like other men. This, however, is a natural status as opposed to one determined by social convention. Every man is human "by nature"; no human being is "by nature" a slave of another human being. There must then be an essential human nature which determines this status and a law governing the relations of human beings as such, independently of the laws of all particular societies concerning their artificial relationships. But essential human nature or human "essence" is constituted by those properties expressed in the definition of "human being." And what is expressed or entailed by a definition is a necessary or analytic proposition. Thus by a logical fusion of the characteristics of two different types of proposition, statements about natural rights tended in this theory to be represented as statements of a necessary natural fact.

But not even statements of actual fact, necessary or contingent. For another element intervened. Though the slave had an actual "right" to be free, he was not free, because no existing law admitted his right. Because laws were imperfect, he was not free though he "ought" to be. And this introduces into the situation a further complication. By nature a man must be that which yet he is not. Or, it follows from the definition of "human being" that every human being is, or must be, free — or possess any other "natural" right — though his freedom is ideal and not real. But the ideal as well as the actual is natural fact.

Thus the Roman lawyers who gave the earliest authoritative statements of the doctrine of natural law conceived of natural law as an ideal or standard not yet completely exemplified in any existing legal code but as a standard fixed by nature to be discovered and gradually applied by men. And the good lawyer kept his eye on this standard as the good gardener keeps his eye fixed on the prize rose which he is hoping to reproduce among his own blooms next summer. For the lawyer, said Ulpian, is not merely the interpreter of existing laws but also the priest or guardian of justice, which is the "fixed and abiding disposition to give every man his right."[5] This standard was not determined by men, but by nature, or, sometimes, by God. It was fact and not fancy.

The institution of slavery showed that no existing code was perfectly just. Thus natural *law* is only imperfectly realized in positive *laws*. And it is significant that the lawyers and later political theorists who adopted this distinction talked only of natural *law* and *the* Law of Nature, never of natural laws and laws of nature. But what is most characteristic of legal codes and systems is that they consist of many laws regulating the different relations of men as debtor and creditor, property owner and thief, employer and employee, husband and wife, etc. But natural law was not conceived of as consisting of ideal regulations corresponding to all positive laws. Indeed, if completely realized, some positive laws would be abolished, e.g., those relating to slave owner and slave. Natural law was not formulated in natural *laws*. It was neither written nor customary and might even be unknown. But it applies, nevertheless, to all men everywhere whether they are debtors or creditors, masters or servants, bond or free. But how is it discovered?

It seems probable that the concept of natural law influenced the later conception of natural or scientific laws obtained by the observation of natural events. For natural law applies impartially to all men in all circumstances, as the law of gravitation applies to all bodies. But the law of gravitation is obtained by deduction from the observation of bodies in sense perception. Are the Law of Nature and the Rights which it implies known by similar observation of the nature of man? The law of gravitation, like all other laws of nature, states a uniformity exemplified in the actual movements of natural bodies. But no existing society may observe the Law of Nature or guarantee natural rights. These cannot, therefore, have been learned from observation of the actual practice of existing societies.

"Man is born free," said Rousseau, "and everywhere he is in chains." What sort of proposition is this? Did Rousseau observe ten or ten million babies immediately after birth and record when the infant limbs were manacled? The law of nature applies to all men equally, said Cicero. For if we had not been corrupted by bad habits and customs "no one would be so like his own self as all men would be like others."[6] But since everyone everywhere has been subjected to customs and laws of varying degrees of imperfection where and when did Cicero observe our uncorrupted nature? How can facts about nature be discovered which have never been observed or confirmed by observation?

The answer lies in the peculiar status given to reason in the theory. Propositions about natural law and natural rights are not generalizations from experience nor deductions from observed facts subsequently confirmed by experience. Yet they are not totally disconnected from natural fact. For they are known as entailed by the intrinsic or essential nature of man. Thus they are known by reason. But they are entailed by the proposition that an essential property of men is that they have reason. The standard of natural law is set by reason and is known because men have reason. But that men have reason, i.e., are able to deduce the ideal from the actual, is a natural fact. And it is by having this specific, and natural, characteristic of being rational that men resemble each other and differ from the brutes. Reason is the great leveler or elevator. According to Sir Frederick Pollock, "Natural law was conceived to be an ultimate principle of fitness with regard to the nature of man as a rational and social being which is, or ought to be, the justification of every form of positive law."[7] "There is, in fact," said Cicero, "a true law — namely right reason — which is in accordance with nature, applies to all men, and is unchangeable and eternal."[8] And for Grotius, too, "The law of nature is a dictate of right reason."[9]

Let it be admitted that all or most human beings are intelligent or rational. And that what is known by reason is certainly true. But, also, what can be known by unaided reason is what *must* be true, and perhaps what *ought* to be but never what *is* true of matter of fact. And statements which are logically certain are tautological or analytic and are neither verified nor falsified by what exists. Statements about what ought to be are of a peculiar type which will be discussed later, but it is certain that they say nothing about what *is*. Because it is confused on these distinctions the theory of natural law and natural rights constantly confounds reason with right and both with matter of fact and existence. The fact that men do reason is thought to be somehow a natural or empirical confirmation of what is logically deduced by reason as a standard by which to judge the imperfections of what exists.

The Social Contract

Though the Roman lawyers conceded that a man might be entitled by natural law to that which he was denied by every positive law, they do not seem to have related this to any particular doctrine of legal and political authority. But in the seventeenth century the doctrines of natural law and natural rights were directly connected with the Contract theory of the State. Because he is rational, Locke emphasized, man is subject to the law of nature even before the establishment of civil society. And he never ceases to be so subject. By right of the law of nature men lived in a state of freedom, equality, and the possession of property — "that with which a man hath mixed his labour." True, this picture differs from that of Hobbes, whose "natural man" is constantly at war, possesses only the right to preserve his life, if he can, but usually finds it short and nasty. Nevertheless, even Hobbes' unpleasant savages have sufficient sense, or reason, to enable them to escape their "natural" predicament. Locke's natural individualists are peaceful property owners who nevertheless sometimes dispute and want an impartial arbitrator. Civil society is formed by compact that natural rights may be better preserved. Man did not enter society, said Paine, to become *worse* than he was before by surrendering his natural rights, but only to have them better secured. His natural rights are the foundation of all his civil rights. It was essential for the social contract theorists to deny that all rights are the gift of civil society, since existing societies denied certain rights which they affirmed. In order to claim them, therefore, it was supposed that they had been enjoyed or were such as would be enjoyed by rational creatures in a "natural" as opposed to an established society. The Declaration of the French Revolutionary Assembly enunciated the Rights of Man and of citizens, the two being distinct.

His "natural" rights attach, by virtue of his reason, to every man much as do his arms and legs. He carries them about with him from one society to another. He cannot lose them without losing himself. "Men are born free and equal," said the French Assembly, "in respect of their *natural* and *imprescriptible* rights of liberty, property, security, and resistance of oppression."[10] The framers of the American Declaration of Independence declare as self-evident truths that all men are created equal, that they are endowed by their creator with certain inalienable rights, among which are Life, Liberty, and the Pursuit of Happiness, and that governments are instituted to secure these rights.[11] The free people of Virginia proclaimed that the rights with which men enter society they cannot by any compact deprive themselves or their posterity.[12]

These were self-evident truths about a state which men might have left or not yet attained but which was "natural" to them as opposed to accidental or conventional. A person is accidentally a native of England, France, America; a Red Indian, Negro, or Jew. His social environment is determined by accident of birth. He may change his family by adoption and his citizenship by naturalization. And he is accidentally, or conventionally, a doctor, soldier, employer, etc. These conventionalities determine his civic and legal rights in a particular society. But he is not accidentally human. Humanity is his essence or nature. There is no essence of "being Greek" or "being English," of "being a creditor" or "being an old age pensioner," all of which properties, however, might be the basis of civil rights. The nature of man determines his "natural" rights. And since, though not accidental, it also seemed to be a matter of fact that men exist and are rational, rights claimed on account of this fact seemed also to be natural and to follow from the essence of man, even though they might be denied. But the essence of man is expressed in the definition of the word "man." So that the statement "Men have natural rights" is equivalent to the prepositional function "x is human entails x has natural rights" which is a tautology. Again the ambiguity inherent in the theory between what is necessary and what is natural is revealed. It is hard to believe that a barren tautology generated the ardors of that time in which it was good to be alive and to be young was "very heaven."[13] But what is meant by the nature or essence of man by "being rational" or "having reason"?

Rights and Reason

"Man" equals "rational animal" (definition) is the fossil preserved in logic textbooks since Aristotle. It was never accompanied by any adequate account of the meaning of "rational," which was, however, generally assumed to include the capacity to abstract and generalize by the use of symbols in speech and writing, to formulate and understand general propositions and laws, and to perceive necessary or logical connections between propositions. It is true that Aristotle himself used the term "reason" more widely to include the practical intelligence manifested in various skills and the appropriate behavior of the well-trained character in various moral situations. But reason is usually conceived to be the capacity by which men understand abstractions. This was certainly Kant's view. To be rational is to be able to think abstractly. And the most characteristic activities of men, including living in societies, are due to this capacity to use reason. It is peculiar to men and shared by no other animal. Hence the basis of the equality of men for the exponents of natural law, and of their intrinsic worth for Kant, is the fact that they all have reason. Men share all other characteristics with the brutes and might themselves have them in varying degrees, but reason was alike in all men, it was man's defining characteristic. Hence it is the foundation, too, of his natural rights as a human being.

It is probable that other animals do not abstract and generalize, for they do not use symbols. But neither is it true that all men do this with equal skill. Reason, in this sense, is no less or no more invariable among human beings than sense perception, and the rights of man might as well depend upon eyesight as upon rationality. But if the term reason is to be used more widely to include nonverbal manifestations of intelligence, knowing-how as well as knowing-that,[14] then intelligence does not set an unbridgeable gulf between men and other living creatures. For in many activities, those, e.g., of hunting, building, fighting, and even social organization, other creatures display skill, adaptability of means to ends, and other characteristics which are evidence of intelligence in men. And as for social life, ants use tools, domesticate other insects, and live a highly organized social life. Bees and wasps manage their affairs by a complicated system of government. Moreover, many of the most characteristic human activities depend very little on abstract thought or use of symbols, e.g., cooking, sewing, knitting, carpentry. And at a higher level the excellence of pictures, sculptures, symphonies, is not due to their expression of abstract thought. But where in this variety are we to find the constant factor by which to determine human rights? What passport will admit to the Kingdom of Ends?

What may be agreed is that only at a certain level of intellectual development do men claim natural rights. Savages do not dream of life, liberty, and the pursuit of happiness. For they do not question what is customary. Neither do the very depressed and down-trodden. It was not the slaves who acclaimed their right to be free but the philosophers and lawyers. Marx and Engels were not themselves wage slaves of the industrial system. It is generally agreed that the doctrines of natural rights, natural law, and the social contract are individualistic. To claim rights as an individual independently of society, a man must have reached a level of self-consciousness which enables him to isolate himself in thought from his social environment. This presupposes a considerable capacity for abstraction. To this extent natural rights, or the ability to claim natural rights, depends on reason. But it does not follow from this that reason alone constitutes the specific nature of man or that the worth of human beings is determined solely by their I.Q.s. Reason is only one human excellence.

But the Aristotelian dream of fixed natures pursuing common ends dies hard. It reappears, e.g., in M. Maritain's account of the Rights of Man cited earlier. He says, e.g.:

> There is a human nature and this human nature is the same in all men ... and possessed of a nature, constituted in a given determinate fashion, man obviously possesses ends which correspond to his natural constitution and which are the same for all—as all pianos, for instance, whatever their particular type and in whatever spot they may be, have as their end the production of certain attuned sounds. If they do not produce these sounds, they must be attuned or discarded as worthless ... since man has intelligence and can determine his ends, it is up to him to put himself in tune with the ends necessarily demanded by his nature.[15]

And men's rights depend upon this common nature and end by which they are subject to the natural or "unwritten" law. But this seems to me a complete mistake. Human beings are not like exactly similar bottles of whisky each marked "for export only" or some device indicating a common destination or end. Men do not share a fixed nature, nor, therefore, are there any ends which they must necessarily pursue in fulfillment of such nature. There is no definition of "man." There is a more or less vague set of properties which characterize in varying degrees and proportions those creatures which are called "human." These determine for each individual human being what he *can* do but not what he *must* do. If he has an I.Q. of 85 his intellectual activities will be limited; it he is physically weak he cannot become a heavyweight boxer. If a woman has neither good looks nor acting ability she is unlikely to succeed as a film star. But what people may do with their capacities is extremely varied, and there is no one thing which they must do in order to be human. It would be nonsense to say: "I am not going to be an actress, a school teacher, a postman, a soldier, a taxpayer, but simply a human being." For what is the alternative? A man may choose whether he will become a civil servant or a school-master, a conservative or a socialist, but he cannot choose whether he will be a man or a dog. There is certainly a sense in which it is often said that in the air raid shelter or in the battle people forgot that they were officers or privates, Assistant Secretaries or typists, rich or poor, and remembered only that they were all human beings, i.e., all liable to die without regard to status. But that is always true. They did not remember that they were something *in addition* to being the particular human being they each were and which they might be without being any particular individual. And, as individuals, when the "all clear" sounded, each returned to pursue his or her own ends, not the purpose of the human race. Certainly, many human beings may cooperate in a joint enterprise to achieve a particular end which each chooses. But that cannot be generalized into the spectacle of all human beings pursuing one end. There is no end set for the human race by an abstraction called "human nature." There are only ends which individuals choose, or are forced by circumstances to accept. There are none which they *must* accept. Men are not created for a purpose as a piano is built to produce certain sounds. Or if they are we have no idea of the purpose.

It is the emphasis on the individual sufferer from bad social conditions which constitutes the appeal of the social contract theory and the "natural" origin of human rights. But it does not follow that the theory is true as a statement of verifiable fact about the actual constitution of the world. The statements of the Law of Nature are not statements of the laws of nature, not even of the laws of an "ideal" nature. For nature provides no standards or ideals. All that exists, exists at the same level, or is of the same logical type. There are not, by nature, prize roses, works of art, oppressed or unoppressed citizens. Standards are determined by human choice, not set by nature independently of men. Natural events cannot tell us what we ought to do until we have made certain decisions, when knowledge of natural fact will enable the most efficient means to be chosen to carry out those decisions. Natural events themselves have no value, and human beings as natural existents have no value either, whether on account of possessing intelligence or having two feet.

One of the major criticisms of the doctrine of natural rights is that the list of natural rights varies with each exponent. For Hobbes, man's only natural right is self-preservation. More "liberal" theorists add to life and security; liberty, the pursuit of happiness, and sometimes property. Modern socialists would probably include the right to "work or adequate maintenance." M. Maritain enumerates a list of nine natural rights which includes, besides the rights to life, liberty, and property of the older formulations, the right to pursue a religious vocation, the right to marry and raise a family, and, finally, the right of every human being to be treated as a person and not as a thing.[16] It is evident that these "rights" are of very different types which would need to be distinguished in a complete discussion of the problem. My aim in this paper, however, is only to try to understand what can be meant by the assertion that there are some rights to which human beings are entitled independently of their varying social relationships. And it seems difficult to account for the wide variations in the lists of these "rights" if they have all been deduced from a fixed human nature or essence, subject to an absolutely uniform "natural law." Nor is the disagreement one which can be settled by more careful empirical observation of human beings and their legal systems. The doctrine seems to try to operate by an analogy which it is logically impossible to apply.

The word "right" has a variety of uses in ordinary language, which includes the distinction between "legal right" and "moral right." "A has a legal right against B" entails B has a duty to A which will be enforced by the courts. A has a claim against B recognized by an existing law. No person has a legal right which he cannot claim from some other (legal) person and which the law will not enforce. That A has a moral right against B likewise entails that B has a duty to A. But it is not necessarily a duty which can be legally enforced. A has a right to be told the truth by B and B has a corresponding duty to tell A the truth. But no one, except in special circumstances recognized by law, can force B to tell the truth, or penalize him, except by censure, if he does not. No one can, in general, claim to be told the truth, by right, under penalty. But a creditor can claim repayment of a debt or sue his debtor.

When the lawyers said that a slave had a right in natural law to be free, they thought of a legal right not provided for by any existing statute, enactment, or custom and to whose universal infringement no penalties attached. But this, surely, is the vanishing point of law and of legal right? It indicates that there just wasn't a law or legal right by which a slave might demand his freedom. But perhaps there was a moral right and a moral obligation. The slave ought to be free and maybe it was the duty of every slaveholder to free his slaves and of legislators to enact laws forbidding slavery. But until this happened there was no law which forbade a man to keep slaves. Consequently, there is no point in saying there was "really" a natural law which forbade this. For the natural law was impotent. Statements about natural law were neither statements of natural fact nor legal practice.

So, does it follow that a "natural" right is just a "moral" right? Kant said, in effect, that to treat another human being as a person of intrinsic worth, an end in himself, is just to treat him in accordance with the moral law applicable to all rational beings on account of their having reason. But this is not quite the sense in which the term "natural rights" has been historically used. Declarations of the Rights of Man did not include his right to be told the truth, to have promises kept which had been made to him, to receive gratitude from those he had benefited, etc. The common thread among the variety of natural rights is their *political* character. Despite their rugged individualism, no exponent of the Rights of Man desired to enjoy them in solitude on a desert island. They were among the articles of the original Social Contract, clauses in Constitutions, the inspiration of social and governmental reforms. But "Keep promises," "Tell the truth," "Be grateful" are not inscribed on banners carried by aggrieved demonstrators or circulated among the members of an oppressed party. Whether or not morality can exist without society, it is certain that politics cannot. Why then were "natural rights" conceived to exist independently of organized society and hence of political controversies? I suggest that they were so considered in order to emphasize their basic or fundamental character. For words like freedom, equality, security, represented for the defenders of natural rights what they considered to be the fundamental moral and social values which should be or should continue to be realized in any society fit for intelligent and responsible citizens.

When the contract theorists talked of the rights as human beings which men had enjoyed in the state of nature, they seemed to be asserting unverifiable and nonsensical propositions since there is no evidence of a state of nature in which men lived before the establishment of civil societies. But they were not simply talking nonsense. They were, in effect, saying, "In any society and under every form of government men ought to be able to think and express their thoughts freely, to live their lives without arbitrary molestation with their persons and goods. They ought to be treated as equal in value, though not necessarily of equal capacity or merit. They ought to be assured of the exclusive use of at least some material objects other than their own bodies; they ought not to be governed without some form of consent. And that the application of these rights to the particular conditions of a society, or their suspension, if necessary, should be agreed with them." The exponents of the natural Rights of Man were trying to express what they deemed to be the fundamental conditions of *human* social life and government. And it is by the observance of some such conditions, I suggest, that human societies are distinguished from ant hills and beehives.

This, however, has frequently been denied by utilitarian, idealist, and Marxist philosophers who, though differing in other respects, agree in holding that the rights of an individual must be determined only by the needs and conveniences of society as a whole. Surely, they say, there can be no "natural" right to life in any society when a man may be executed as a criminal or killed as a conscripted soldier. And very little right to liberty exists when external danger threatens the state. "The person with rights and duties," says the evolutionist utilitarian Ritchie, "is the product of society and the rights of the individual must, therefore, be judged from the point of view of society as a whole and not the society from the point of view of the individual."[17] It is the duty of the individual to preserve society for his descendants. For individuals perish but England remains. But the plain man may well ask why he must preserve a society for his descendants if it neither is nor shows any prospect of being worth living in. Will his descendants thank him for this consideration? All that seems to follow from Ritchie's view is that at any time the members of a society may agree to sacrifice some goods in order to achieve a certain result. And the result will include the restoration of basic rights. Does the ordinary citizen consider that he has no right to life and liberty because he agrees to (or does not protest against) the suspension of those rights in an emergency? He would be very unlikely to approve of such suspension if he thought the result would be the massacre or enslavement of himself, his contemporaries, and possibly his children and descendants at the arbitrary will of a ruler or government. To suspend, or even to forfeit rights, as a criminal does, also temporarily, is not to deny rights. Nor is it to deny that such practices must be justified to the individuals required to submit to them. Though it may be much more useful to society that a man should remain a slave and even that he may be happier in that condition, it is not possible to prove to him that he has no right to be free, however much society wants his slavery. In short, "natural rights" are the conditions of a good society. But what those conditions are is not given by nature or mystically bound up with the essence of man and his inevitable goal, but is determined by human decisions.

Propositions and Decisions

Assertions about natural rights, then, are assertions of what ought to be as the result of human choice.[18] They fall within class (3) of the division stated on page 227, as being ethical assertions or expressions of value. And these assertions or expressions include all those which result from human choice and preference, in art and personal relations, e.g., as well as in morals and politics. Such utterances in which human beings express choices determined by evaluation of better and worse have been variously interpreted, and it is, indeed, difficult to introduce a discussion of the topic without assuming an interpretation. I have tried, e.g., to avoid the use of the words "proposition" and "statement" in referring to these utterances since these words emphasize a relation between what is asserted and a fact by which it is verified or falsified. And this leads either to the attempts of the natural law and natural rights theories to find a "natural" fact which justifies these assertions or to a search for non-sensible entities called "Values" as the reference of ethical terms. Yet, of course, it is in some sense true that "No one ought to be ill-treated because he is a Jew, a Negro, or not able to count above ten." Alternatively, to talk of "expressions of value" sounds as though such utterances are sophisticated ways of cheering and cursing. Just as the blow becomes sublimated into the sarcastic retort, so our smiles of delight at unselfish action and howls of woe at parricide become intellectualized into apparent judgments about good and evil, right and wrong, without, however, losing their fundamentally emotive character.[19] On this view, value judgments do not state what is true or false but are expressions of feeling, sometimes combined with commands to do or forbear. But whatever its emotional causes and effects, an articulate utterance does not seem to be simply a substitute for a smile or a tear. It *says* something. But I cannot hope in a necessarily brief discussion to do justice to the enormous variety of value utterances. So I will plunge and say that value utterances are more like records of *decisions* than propositions.[20] To assert that "Freedom is better than slavery" or "All men are of equal worth" is not to state a fact but to *choose a side*. It announces *This is where I stand*.

I mentioned earlier that in the late war propaganda appeals to defend our comforts and privileges would have been rejected as uninspiring but that appeals to defend the rights of all men to freedom and equality obtained the required response, at least in all but the depraved and cynical. I now suggest that they did so because they accorded with our decisions about these ultimate social values. That whether or not we were more or less comfortable as a result, we should not choose to act only upon orders about which we had not in some way been consulted, to suppress the truth, to imprison without trial, or to permit human individuals or classes of individuals to be treated as of no human value.

Two questions suggest themselves on this view. First, if ethical judgments, and particularly the ethical judgments which concern the fundamental structure of society, are value decisions, who makes these decisions and when? Is this not, as much as the natural law theory, the use of an analogy without application? I did safeguard myself to some extent by saying that these assertions are "more like" decisions than they are like propositions. They are unlike propositions because they are neither tautologies nor statements of verifiable fact. But it is also true that if asked when we decided in favor of free speech or democratic government or many of our social values we could not give a date. It is, therefore, suggested that we no more record a decision by a value assertion than we signed a Social Contract. Nevertheless, I think the analogy does emphasize important differences between value and other assertions. For, if intelligent, we do choose our politics as we choose our friends or our favored poems, novels, pictures, symphonies and as we do not choose to accept Pythagoras' theorem or the law of gravitation. And when challenged we affirm our decision or stand by our choice. We say, "I did not realize how much I valued free speech until I went to Germany in 1936," indicating that a choice had been made but so easily that it had seemed scarcely necessary to record its occurrence.

For, indeed, the fundamental values of a society are not always recorded in explicit decisions by its members, even its rulers, but are expressed in the life of the society and constitute its quality. They are conveyed by its "tone" and atmosphere as well as its laws and Statutory Rules and Orders. The members of a society whose values are freedom and equality behave differently, walk, speak, fight differently from the members of a slave society. Plato expressed this nastily in the *Republic*[21] when he said that in a democracy even the horses and asses behaved with a gait expressive of remarkable freedom and dignity, and like everyone else became "gorged with freedom." Suspicion, fear, and servility are absent, or at least inconspicuous in such a society. And no one who visited Germany after 1933 needs to be reminded of the change of atmosphere.

Decisions concerning the worth of societies and social institutions are not made by an *elite*, by rulers or a governing class, but, explicitly or by acceptance, by those who live and work in the society and operate its institutions. But these decisions may be changed by the effective propaganda of a minority who have reached other decisions of whose value they desire to convince the majority. Perhaps, ultimately, men get the societies and governments which they choose, even if not those which they deserve, for they may deserve better than passion, indolence, or ignorance permits them to choose.

This leads to a second question. Upon what grounds or for what reasons are decisions reached? Consider the expression of the doctrine of equality, that all human beings are of equal worth, intrinsic value, or are ends in themselves. Is there an answer to the question, why? On what *evidence* is this assertion based? How can such a decision be maintained despite the obvious differences between human beings? The answer of the natural law theorists and of Kant was that the "natural" fact that all men have reason proves that they are of intrinsic worth, and are thus entitled to the Rights of Man. It is not clear, however, whether imbeciles and lunatics forfeit human rights. No one can deny that they are human beings. A person who becomes insane does not thereby become a mere animal. But if statements about the possession by anything of a natural characteristic is related to a decision of worth as evidence for a conclusion, then it would be illogical to retain the decision when the characteristics were absent or had changed. It is irrational to continue to believe a proposition when evidence shows that it is false. I affirm that no natural characteristic constitutes a *reason* for the assertion that all human beings are of equal worth. Or, alternatively, that *all* the characteristics of *any* human being are equally reasons for this assertion. But this amounts to saying that the decision of equal worth is affirmed of all human beings *whatever their particular characteristics*. It does not follow that they are of equal *merit* and that their treatment should not vary accordingly, in ways compatible with their intrinsic value. But even a criminal, though he has lost merit and may deserve punishment, does not become worthless. He cannot be cast out of humanity.

I am aware that this view needs much more elaboration, and especially illustration, than can be given in very limited space. I can, therefore, indicate only in a general way the type of value assertions and the manner in which they are related to each other and to other assertions. They are not related as evidence strengthening a conclusion. For decisions are not true or false and are not deduced from premises. Do we, then, decide without reason? Are decisions determined by chance or whim? Surely, it will be said, the facts have some relevance to what is decided? To say that decisions are made without reason looks like saying that we choose by tossing a coin, opening the works of Shakespeare or the Bible at random and reading the first sentence, or shutting our eyes and sticking a pin into the list of starters to pick the Derby winner. These seem very irrational methods of choice. Nevertheless, we do sometimes choose by a not very dissimilar procedure. If two candidates for a post are of exactly equal merit, the selectors may well end by plumping for one or the other. This, it may be said, was justified because there was "nothing to choose between them," not that the decision bore no relation to their merits. But there are some choices into which merit hardly enters. Those involving personal relations, for instance. It would seem absurd to try to prove that our affections were not misplaced by listing the characteristics of our friends. To one who asked for such "proof" we should reply, with Montaigne: "If a man urge me to tell him wherefore I loved him, I feel it cannot be expressed but by answering, because it was he, because it was myself.... It is not one especial consideration, nor two, nor three, nor four, nor a thousand. It is I wot not what kind of quintessence of all this commixture which seized my will."[22]

Yet, it is also correct to say that our decisions about worth are not merely arbitrary and intelligent choices are not random. They cannot be proved correct by evidence. Nor, I suggest, do we try to prove them. What we do is to support and defend our decisions. The relation of the record of a decision to the considerations which support it is not that of proof to conclusion. It is much more like the defense of his client by a good counsel.

Consider an analogous situation in art. Suppose one were trying to defend a view that Keats is a greater poet than Crabbe. One would compare passages from each writer, showing the richness and complexity of the imagery and movement of Keats' verse and the monotonous rhythm, moral platitudes, and poverty-stricken images of Crabbe. One would aid the effect by reading passages aloud for their comparable musical effects; one would dwell on single lines and passages which show the differences between the evocative language of Keats and the conventional "poetic diction" of Crabbe — the "Season of mists and mellow fruitfulness" of the one and the "finny tribes" etc., of the other. One might eventually resort to the remarks of the best critics on both writers. In short, one would employ every device to "present" Keats, to build up a convincing advocacy of his poetry. And the resistance of Crabbe's defender might collapse, and he would declare the case won with the verdict "Keats is the better poet." But nothing would have been *proved*. Crabbe's supporter might still disagree. He would dwell on Crabbe's "sincerity," his genuine sympathy with the poor, and excuse his poetic limitations as due to a bad tradition for which he was not responsible. He might add that Crabbe was one of Jane Austen's favorite poets. And if he so persisted he would not be *wrong*, i.e., he would not be believing falsely that Crabbe was a better poet than Keats, but much more persuasion would be needed to induce him to alter his decision.

Compare with this the correct attitude to the proof of a scientific law. If the empirical evidence is conclusive then a person who rejects the conclusion is either stupid or biased. He is certainly believing a false proposition. We do not "defend" the law of gravitation but all instructed persons accept the proof of the law.

On the other hand, we do not refer to Mill's proof but to his "magnificent defense" of civil liberty. For a successful defense involves much more than statement of facts. The facts of the case are known to both the prosecuting and defending counsel. The question is, should the accused be condemned or acquitted? The skillful lawyer uses these facts, but he uses them differently from the scientist. He marshals them so as to emphasize those which favor his client. He interprets those which appear unfavorable in terms of legal decisions in similar cases which would benefit the accused. He chooses language which does not merely state, but impresses, he uses voice, gesture, facial expression, all the devices of eloquence and style in order to influence the decision of the jury in favor of his client. His client may still lose, but he would admit that he has a better chance of winning if he briefs a good counsel.

But, it may be asked, is this a recommendation to take fraudulent advocacy as our model for defending the rights of man? Not at all. Lawyers and art critics are not frauds, but neither are they scientists. They are more like artists who use material with results which impress and convince but do not *prove*. There is no conceivable method of *proving* that Keats is a better poet than Crabbe or that freedom is better than slavery. For assertions of value cannot be subjected to demonstrative or inductive methods. It is for this reason that such assertions have been regarded as simple expressions of feeling or emotion like cries of pain and anger. But we do not defend or support a cry of pain or shout of joy though it may be related to a cause. If our value choices are defensible their defense requires other methods.

The lawyer says: "I agree that my client was on the premises; I deny that his being there in those circumstances constitutes a *trespass*. This may be confirmed from *Gower* v. *Flint* where this ruling was given in similar circumstances." The critic says: "You agree that Keats' imagery is *rich* and *complex*, his language *original* and *powerful*, that Crabbe, on the contrary, is *frigid* and *conventional* in language, *meager* in imagery, etc., etc." The lawyer supports his plea from previous decisions. The critic likewise appeals not to physical or psychological facts about the occurrences of marks on paper, internal pictures, etc., but to previous decisions *evaluating* these and other occurrences. Rich and powerful poetry is good; frigid and meager versifying is bad. If we stand by our previous decisions it does not follow that we *must* on account of them make a further decision now, but they are certainly relevant. Incorporated into a system of skillful advocacy they may win a favorable verdict. But, on the other hand, we may reject our former decisions. Elaborate imagery, lyrical quality, are dismissed as *barbarous* or *sentimental*; our choice is now for the *plain* and *elegant* statement. Such a complete change in systems of evaluation seems to occur in different ages. The eighteenth century listened to Shakespeare but gave the palm to Pope. The Victorians saw Georgian houses but chose sham gothic. So we may present the authoritarian with an attractive picture of a free and democratic society and if he already values independence, experimentation, mutual trust, he may agree that these values are realized in such a society. But he may call independence insolence, experimentation rash meddling, and the picture will fail in its effect.

There are no certainties in the field of values. For there are no true or false beliefs about values, but only better or worse decisions and choices. And to encourage the better decisions we need to employ devices which are artistic rather than scientific. For our aim is not intellectual assent, but practical effects. These are not, of course, absolutely separate, for intellectual assent to a proposition or theory is followed by using it. But values, I think, concern only behavior. They are not known, but accepted and acted upon.

Intellectuals often complain that political propaganda, e.g., is not conducted as if it were scientific argument. But if moral values are not capable of scientific proof it would be irrational to treat them as if they were. The result of a confusion of logical types is to leave the field of nonscientific persuasion and conviction to propagandists of the type of the late Dr. Goebbels.

Notes

1. Freedom of speech and worship, freedom from want and fear for all persons everywhere.
2. *Clarke Papers*, vol. 1, p. 301.
3. It is not quite true, for the doctrines of natural law and consequent natural rights flourish in Catholic social philosophy. See, e.g., *The Rights of Man and Natural Law* by Jacques Maritain (1944).
4. Cf. K. R. Popper, *The Open Society and Its Enemies* (London: Routledge and Kegan Paul, 1945), vol. I, especially pp. 58–59.
5. Cf. George H. Sabine, *A History of Political Theory* (London: George G. Harrap, 1937), p. 170.
6. *Laws*, bk. 1, 10, 28–29 (trans. C. W. Keyes).
7. "The History of the Law of Nature"; *Essays in the Law* (1922).
8. *Republic*, bk. 3, p. 22 (trans. Sabine and Smith).
9. *De jure belli ac pacis*, Bk. 1, Chap. I, sec. X, p. 1.
10. Declaration of the Rights of Man and of Citizens, by the National Assembly of France (1791).
11. Declaration of Independence of the United States of America (July 4, 1776).
12. The Virginia Declaration of Rights (June 12, 1776).
13. Wordsworth in *The French Revolution*.
14. See Presidential Address to the Aristotelian Society by Professor G. Ryle, 1945.
15. *Rights of Man*, p. 35.
16. *Rights of Man*, p. 60.
17. Ritchie, *Natural Rights* (London: Macmillan, 1903), p. 101.
18. I am greatly indebted, especially in this section, to Professor Gilbert Ryle, who discussed with me an earlier version of this paper and made several criticisms and suggestions from which I have tried to benefit. The mistakes which remain are entirely my own.
19. Cf. A. J. Ayer, *Language, Truth and Logic* (London: Victor Gollancz, 1951), chap. 6.
20. Dr. K. R. Popper makes a similar distinction in an interesting discussion of value judgments in *The Open Society*, vol. I, chap. 5.
21. Book 8, 563.
22. "Of Friendship," *Essays*, trans. John Florio (1892–1893).

12

Inalienable Rights

Stuart M. Brown

THE concept of inalienable rights is not like our concept of the right to the fulfillment of promises, to the return of borrowed goods, or to some appropriate payment when we have been damaged in direct consequence of another's carelessness. Rights like the right to the fulfillment of promises can be waived, conveyed, delegated, and voided. Most of the rights which we assert, exercise, and debate are of this sort. But in the seventeenth and eighteenth centuries many philosophers and ordinary people became convinced that rights to the *protection* of life, liberty, and the pursuit of happiness cannot morally or logically be waived, conveyed, and voided. Because the adjective "alienable" means "transferable" or "voidable," these rights were labeled "inalienable" to indicate the moral and logical impossibility of transferring and voiding them. Thus the notions of moral and logical impossibility were from the beginning essential parts of the concept of inalienable rights. The impossibility is logical because, if there are any rights properly called "inalienable," assertions of these rights cannot, for any reason under any circumstances, be denied. It is a moral impossibility, because the refusal to honor an asserted inalienable right is the most intolerable and inexcusable injustice against a man.

We can neither reject nor radically reinterpret this notion of inalienable rights. Each man has an inalienable right to the protection of his moral interests, his person, and estate. The goods for which each man has a right to protection are private rather than public. They are the

From *The Philosophical Review*, LXIV (1955), 192–211.

rights of a man to the protection of what is in *his* interest. The moral interests of one man may differ radically from those of another. Different men may have radically different needs and capacities. And these differences, in conjunction with unavoidable differences in opportunity, produce differences in estate. We cannot, therefore, specify precisely what these interests are. We must use vague and general terms like "life," "liberty," and "happiness," or "moral interests," "persons," and "estates." But despite this vagueness about what is to be protected, each man has a right to the protection of private goods, and this right cannot be transferred, voided, or denied.

In undertaking to show this, I shall first treat inalienable rights in terms appropriate to the seventeenth- and eighteenth-century discussions of them. I shall then state and meet two major philosophical objections to holding that there are such rights. In meeting these objections, I shall show that the seventeenth- and eighteenth-century philosophers were correct in holding that there is an inalienable right to *protection* but incorrect in supposing that this right to *protection* is logically dependent upon inalienable rights to *life*, *liberty*, and *happiness*.

I

In the seventeenth and eighteenth centuries inalienable rights would have been appropriately described as moral rather than institutional or legal; politically basic rather than derived; natural rather than fortuitous, conventional, or supernatural; and self-evident rather than inferred. To assert an inalienable right is to assert a right that has all four of these features.

First, inalienable rights are moral rather than institutional or legal. Regardless of how we wish to interpret the relations between morality and institutions, legal or otherwise, it is essential to interpret them in such a way as to admit the possibility of institutions requiring or permitting what is morally wrong. To admit this is not to deny a general obligation to submit to the control of institutions, even those which are manifestly unjust. It is to recognize, however, that such things as legal statutes, decrees, and decisions may permit acts which ought to be forbidden and require acts which are morally evil and intolerable.

Presupposing this distinction between morality and institutions, inalienable rights are moral, and assertions of inalienable rights subject institutions to moral scrutiny. To say that men have inalienable rights to the protection of their moral interests, persons, and estates is to say that men have an inalienable right to legal and political institutions affording this protection. There are inalienable rights where, apart from institutions, there is no security of private goods and where institutions can provide protection. They are not rights against other private citizens or organizations. They are not rights against murderers, thieves, bigots, demagogues, and fools. They are rights to be protected from murder, theft, tyranny, and injury. And though there may be institutions which do not provide this protection, there is no protection which is not institutional in the sense of being a conventionalized practice. Inalienable rights, therefore, are rights *to* institutions of a specific sort, and where the required institutions are lacking and the rights infringed, they are rights *against* governments to provide the specific legal procedures which constitute the protection. Thus existing institutions, including the law, are always in principle subject to moral scrutiny. Whether or not institutions in fact protect the individual's interest, person, and estate, they morally ought to do so.

For example: A man bitten by a dog has a claim to damages against the dog's owner. Though the claim is not itself a right to damages, it presupposes the right to be protected from bodily injury, inconvenience, and the expense incurred as a result of another's activity. This right to protection can be secured in one or the other of two very different ways. It can be secured in some cases by prohibiting the kind of thing which results in injury. Protection from dog bites might be secured by prohibiting the keeping of dogs or by destroying all of them. But such radical prohibitions are, in some cases, practically impossible and, in others, incompatible with each man's right to other kinds of protection. Thus, on both practical and moral grounds, it is necessary in many circumstances to permit a state of affairs which results in injury. In these circumstances each man's right to protection is secured by institutions which, once an injury has occurred, permit the injured party's claim to damages to be heard, weighed, and decided. Once the claim is heard and decided in favor of the injured party, then he has a legal right to damages, a right which rests upon his inalienable moral right to be protected. Because any man who incurs medical expenses and loss of income after being bitten by a dog may go to court and collect damages from the dog's owner, our right to protection in this kind of case is secure.

But contrast this kind of case with the treatment of witnesses by legislative committees. Loyal American citizens, innocent of any crime, are summoned before these committees, questioned in ways which raise but do not substantiate suspicions of knavery and treason, and forced to incur the terrible liabilities of ruined reputations and careers. Regardless of how great this damage to the witness may be, no institutional protection is provided. Though there could be committee procedures preventing this kind of damage altogether, the committees do not employ them. And though there could, alternatively, be legal procedures enabling a witness, once he has been injured, to present his claim to damages against the committee members and the government, there is now no such recourse to law available. Hence our inalienable right to protection in this important class of cases is infringed. We have an inalienable right *to* this protection *against* a government which has so far failed to provide it. By asserting our right, we subject the existing law of this land to moral criticism.

Second, inalienable rights are politically basic. They are politically basic because the protection of moral interests, persons, and estates is the condition of an individual's moral consent to government. The assertion of a right to any object is incompatible with moral consent to refusals of that object. Part of the evidence that one knows how to use these assertions correctly is furnished by specific kinds of attitudes and acts which occur when rights are asserted. It would be conclusive evidence of a man's failure to understand rights if he went about asserting rights to this, that, and the other thing but never made any efforts to obtain these things and never showed resentment or indignation at his failure to obtain them. The assertion of a right, therefore, is incompatible with the acts, attitudes, and expressions constituting or evidencing moral consent.

But if the assertion of a right is incompatible with moral consent to the right's denial, then statements about consent are always relevant to statements about rights. In the case of some alienable rights, a question as to whether there is a right can be resolved by evidence that a man has failed to assert it in a large number of cases and has thus consented to what would have been infringements had he asserted it. If over a period of time I do not assert or exercise my right to prevent people from using a lane across my property, and if people do in fact use the lane, then my right to prevent this use is void; and there is a *public right* of way across my lands. To maintain my right, I need not, of course, prevent others from using the lane altogether. I need only require people to get my permission to use it. By requiring permission, I refuse consent to any restriction of my option to prevent use of the lane. Failure to refuse consent, in a large number of cases over a considerable period of time, is construed as consent to a waiver of the option.

But an inalienable right cannot be voided or waived. Men have these rights even if they do not understand and assert them. If a man *says* he waives his inalienable rights or if he submits without protest to infringements of them, this is evidence of his failure to understand what he is doing or of his fear of the consequences. A man may, in fear or ignorance, accept or submit to an infringement, but he cannot be understood to morally consent to it. Thus he cannot be understood to morally consent to a government infringing his rights. For this reason inalienable rights are politically basic. Depending upon the particular political circumstances, they justify the defense, modification, subversion, or overthrow of existing institutions.

Third, inalienable rights are natural rather than fortuitous, conventional, or supernatural. To say this is to emphasize that these rights are the rights of each and every man, irrespective of the characteristics which enable us to distinguish one man from another and one group of men from other groups. There are two very different reasons for using the term "natural" in this way.

(1) It has been widely supposed that all men have inalienable rights by reason of certain properties common to all men and to nothing else. On this supposition, the term "natural" is used in reference to the set of unspecified defining properties. But this use of "natural" conceals and perpetuates a basic error. It is the error of supposing that a statement known to be true may be true for reasons which cannot be given or which, if given, would be highly debatable. If I know that all men have inalienable rights, I cannot know this by reason of empirical generalizations about characteristics common to all men and to nothing else. For, on the one hand, I may know that all men have inalienable rights and yet be unable to provide any empirical generalizations which would tend to support this. On the other hand, I can dispute the truth or moral relevance of any empirical generalization, but I cannot, in the same way and for the same kind of reason, dispute the truth and relevance of the statement "All men have inalienable rights." Indeed, if I know that all men have inalienable rights, I will reject, on grounds of truth or relevance, any empirical generalizations which do not support or which seem to count against inalienable rights. Because this use of the term "natural" perpetuates the error of trying to prove statements in ways in which they logically cannot be proved, and because in the history of ethics "natural" has been used primarily in just this way, any undefined use of "natural" in moral philosophy is more misleading than illuminating.

(2) Nonetheless, "natural" has been and can appropriately be used as a moral notion, to express a moral commitment based in part on scientific studies about the differences between men. Because inalienable rights are rights to the protection of interests, persons, and estates, institutional protection for certain groups of people might justifiably

be denied if the characteristics definitive of these groups were correlated strictly with irremediable defects in interest and capacity. Differences in parentage, culture, and race might, that is, be correlated with heritable differences in interest and capacity. If we knew that they were and could discover how they were, we would know that the members of certain groups simply lacked interests of a specified sort and that the members of other groups lacked the capacity to develop some interests they in fact profess. Institutional protections could then be denied to the members of these groups on the ground that there was no interest to protect. But scientific studies, though they provide no morally useful definitions of "man," have shown that there are no reliable correlations of this sort, that interests and capacities are in part the product of institutions and that in the absence of institutions providing individuals an opportunity to profess and develop interest, it is theoretically impossible to determine differences and defects in interest. Thus anyone who asserts his right to institutional protections of a specific sort is committed to providing these institutions for all individuals irrespective of the obvious differences between men. To say that inalienable rights are "natural" is simply to express this commitment. Whether or not the term "natural" is used to express this, the commitment itself is an indispensable condition for securing the rights of man.

Fourth, inalienable rights are self-evident. It is self-evident that, if any man has a right to the protection of his interest, then all men have the same right, and it is self-evident that all men have this right. *That* inalienable rights are thus self-evident can be shown in the following ways:

(1) If any man has a right to the protection of his interest, then each and every man has a right to this protection. People and institutions have rights if there are good and sufficient reasons for providing them with objects, options, and services, or if there are no good and sufficient reasons for denying them these things. From this, it follows that, wherever any given man under given circumstances has a right, any similar man under similar circumstances has the same right. If we decide, for example, that Smith has a right to keep pigs in his patio, but that Brown does not have this right, then there must be some difference between their situations such that no man in Brown's situation has a right to keep pigs though any man in Smith's situation does have this right. But there is no difference between men in respect to the protection of a private interest *as private*. The specific objects, goods, and services for which protection is required can and usually do differ radically from one man to another. But if any man has a right to the protection

of these, simply as being in *his* interest, then every other man has the same right to protection.

(2) That all men have rights to the protection of their interests, persons, and estates cannot be directly proven by any deductive or inductive argument. Any proof would require the premise that men have rights in respect to goods which they may secure and evils which they may avoid. But an inalienable right is simply the right of a man to protection in avoiding the clearest possible cases of preventable evils and in securing the clearest possible cases of obtainable goods. It is the minimum possible right, the right to protection, in respect to a specific class of indubitable goods. Any reason for doubting this right would be a reason for doubting any premise from which the right could be deduced. Thus the statement "All men have inalienable rights" is self-evidently true in the weak sense that, if it is true at all, its truth cannot be demonstrated to anyone who doubts it. But it is also self-evidently true in the strong sense that one cannot deny its truth and admit the validity of moral inference. Moral arguments about the rights and duties of men in particular circumstances presuppose the validity of reasoning from specific instances of good and evil to specific instances of rights and duties. They presuppose, as a principle of moral inference, that statements about goods and evils confirm or disconfirm statements about rights and obligations. But since an inalienable right is the minimum possible right in respect to a class of indubitable goods, this right can be denied only by denying that statements about goods validate statements about rights. To deny this would be to reject the principle of moral inference. Inalienable rights are, therefore, self-evident in the strong sense. It is logically impossible to deny a statment where this requires the denial of the principle of inference presupposed in validating any statement of that kind.

II

Having described, in terms of the traditional vocabulary, what at a minimum we must mean by "inalienable rights," I shall now state and meet two traditional objections to supposing that men have such rights.

The first objection is based upon the undeniable fact of cultural diversity. Using this undeniable fact as its premise, the argument is simple and straightforward. People of different cultures display an almost fantastic diversity of behavior, attitude, and belief. Inalienable rights are neither asserted nor recognized in vast numbers of known cultures. In the languages of some known cultures there are no abstract terms of the sort necessary even for understanding or translating our notion of inalienable rights. By reason of these facts and others of the same order, the statement "All men have inalienable rights" is alleged to be false. And it is then concluded: Because "All men have inalienable rights" is false, "No men have inalienable rights" is true.

This argument, however, will not bear close examination. Its entire force rests upon the supposition that recognizing and asserting inalienable rights is a necessary condition of having them. This supposition is initially plausible because there are rights, like the right to inherit property, which are possessed only within some specific institutional framework. There is a right to inherit property if and only if there is the institution of private property and some institutional procedure for conveying the rights of the deceased. There is no right to inherit where, in the absence of an institution of private property, there is no initial right to convey. Nor is there any right to inherit where there is property right only to the kind of object that, in the event of death, is buried with the man. In any culture where there is no recognition and exercise of these rights, there is no right. And so it is initially plausible to suppose that inalienable rights depend, in a similar way, upon specific institutions, like democratic government, and that, in the absence of these institutions, there are no such rights.

But plausible as it is, this supposition is mistaken. Any man can have rights and yet not know that he has them. A child has rights which it does not understand and has no wish to exercise. Claims which a child could not itself make may be made by others in the child's behalf, and may then be heard, weighed, and decided in the child's favor. It is strictly irrelevant that many of the child's rights are institutional and would not be its rights at all under different institutions. Under the institutions in which the child has the rights, he has them whether or not he or any other child recognizes and asserts them. It is true that in order for there to be rights there must be some conditions under which they can be meaningfully asserted. But it is not necessary that persons who have rights know the conditions of having them and, under appropriate circumstances, actually assert them. Since an inalienable right does not presuppose a specific institution but is a right *to* institutional protections, the question is whether there are specifiable conditions under which men do have them. If we can specify these conditions, then wherever the conditions are fulfilled men have these rights even though they may not themselves recognize and assert them.

It is a general condition of any right that there be objects, services, or options which, under at least some conditions, are in the interest of persons or institutions and which can in principle be secured for them.

The *point* of asserting a right is either to express, under the appropriate conditions, a resolve to secure these objects, services, or options, *by reason of* the interest in them, or to refuse moral consent to a denial of these things. No right would ever be asserted unless one envisaged a risk of losing or failing to secure what is in one's interest and unless one supposed that this loss or failure is preventable. There is no point in trying or resolving to secure some thing or in refusing moral consent to the denial of it unless there is risk of loss and unless the loss can be prevented.

The first of two special conditions of inalienable rights is private moral interest. There must, that is, be objects, services, and options which are goods, because they are in the interests of private persons; and these goods must be moral in the sense that, under some conditions, an individual has a right to them because they are in his interest. Mere interest in something is not a sufficient condition of a right to its protection. If we suppose, for example, that every man has an interest in happiness but that no man, under any circumstances, ever has a right to happiness when it is in jeopardy, then all problems about the preventable loss of happiness may be prudentially resolved. No question about an inalienable right to the protection of happiness can arise. In order for there to be an inalienable right, the happiness of any given man must have a moral value by reason of its being the particular happiness of that particular man. Then questions about the preventable loss of happiness are questions about a possible right to it, and there is an inalienable right to protection. Each man has an inalienable right to protection in the pursuit of happiness, this protection being afforded to all men on the same basis.

The private moral interest of which I am here speaking is even more clearly illustrated by moral obligations. Each man in a community has very specific obligations dependent upon his religion, his parentage, his occupation, his social status, his friends, and so forth. These obligations are primary, not in the sense that they are all equal in importance or all equally reasonable, but in the sense that merely to *state* them honestly is to give a good moral reason why one should not be restrained in the discharge of them. If a man says he has a duty, the burden of moral proof lies with anyone who would deny it and prevent his discharging it. Under these conditions, all men have inalienable rights to the protection of moral interest. There is a right to institutions securing the greatest possible degree of moral liberty for each man and permitting claims based on honor and conscience to be impartially decided on moral grounds.

The second special condition for inalienable rights is the possibility of modifying and creating institutions. If human institutions had a form and structure that could not be changed under any circumstances, by any human agency or effort, inalienable rights could be asserted only in ignorance. For no man can do the impossible, resolve to do what he knows to be impossible, or give or withhold consent in regard to an impossibility. Assertions of inalienable right, expressing the resolve to change defective institutions or the refusal to give moral consent to them, can be made only if institutions are believed to be modifiable. There are inalienable rights only if institutions are in fact modifiable.

All men have inalienable rights whether or not they recognize and assert them because these two special conditions are fulfilled for all men everywhere. The condition that institutions must in principle be modifiable is certainly fulfilled. Despite many practical difficulties, old institutions can be changed in very radical ways within relatively short periods of time. And over the course of a generation or two, effective new institutions can be created. It is an established fact that all this is practically possible. The other condition, private moral interest, is also fulfilled. It is a fact that men do have private interests and do differ from one another in respect to their obligations. Each man has an interest in securing certain great goods for himself and in avoiding evils. And most men are moral in the sense that they act, in certain circumstances, solely by reason of the duty to act. In view of these facts and the fact that institutions are modifiable, it is morally self-evident that men have inalienable rights.

The undeniable fact of cultural diversity in no way disconfirms the inalienable rights of men. Insofar as this fact has any direct bearing upon the moral questions here involved, it is itself the most conclusive evidence of private moral interests and of the practical possibility of modifying institutions. It is conclusive evidence that the factual conditions of inalienable right are fulfilled. And this simply makes it easier to isolate and answer the basic moral question as to whether, in view of these facts, men do have inalienable rights. Even if one fails to understand the moral issues in respect to which it is self-evident that men have these rights, the rights cannot be denied on the grounds that some men do not recognize and assert them. A child's ignorance of property right and its complete indifference to a legacy do not count against its right to inherit under a will. A man's ignorance and indifference do not count against his inalienable right to the protection of his interests, person, and estate.

I do not, however, want to deny in any way the moral and political importance of recognizing and asserting inalienable rights. The indispensable condition for realizing social and political justice is the recognition and assertion of these rights, the resolve of each and every man to secure and preserve the necessary institutions. Today, all of the culturally diverse groups in the world tend more and more to be included within one world-wide community. Under these conditions, the protections to which all men have a right cannot be secured without changing many existing institutions and creating new ones. They will not be secured unless men recognize their rights, assert them for themselves and in behalf of others, and resolve to preserve and establish justice.

III

A second traditional objection to inalienable rights is argued on the premise that all significant moral assertions must be subject to denial in both of two different ways. In two different respects, it is held, the conditions sufficient for the meaningful assertion of a right or a duty are not sufficient for the truth of the assertion. It is a sufficient condition of the meaningful assertion of my right to the fulfillment of a promise that I have, under appropriate circumstances, been promised. But in one class of clear cases, my right to fulfillment can be denied by establishing that the corresponding obligation *cannot* be discharged. "Ought," that is, implies "can." Wherever the alleged duty to keep the promise can be denied *because* it is impossible to keep it, the asserted right must be denied *because* it is impossible to exercise it. In another class of clear cases, there are moral considerations that would make it right to break the promise or wrong to keep it. "Ought" in the primary sense of "ought to do" implies "morally right." Wherever we can deny that it is morally right to keep a promise, we can deny the duty to keep it and the right to its fulfillment. But it is an essential feature of inalienable rights that they cannot be denied in either one of these two different ways. So on the premise that any significant assertion of right must be subject to denial for both of these two kinds of reason, assertions of inalienable right are declared lacking in significance.

Stated thus in skeleton outline, this objection clearly begs all the fundamental questions. Rights and obligations, which are dependent upon a prior moral transaction between two parties, are carefully analyzed and then used as a model of moral significance against which other rights and obligations are to be tested.

In any case of promising, borrowing, and contracting, there must be at least two parties to a transaction occurring at some specific time and place. In the transaction, by using such expressions as "I promise" or "I'll be pleased to let you borrow it," or by signing one's name to various kinds of document, at least one of the two .parties incurs an obligation and conveys a right to the other. To say "I promise" is to incur an obligation to do what is promised. This conveys a right in the sense that solely by reason of my saying "I promise it," you may say "I have a right to it." But in all these cases, what is morally sacred is the transaction itself and not necessarily what is accomplished by means of it on any one occasion. The act which we promise to do may, taken by itself, be utterly trivial. The object which we borrow may be almost valueless, even to its owner. Hence, there are innumerable cases in which, if one had not promised to do something, there would be no reason, moral or other, for doing it at all. And when in these cases, even though one has promised, there are strong reasons, moral and other, for not doing the act, the general moral value of promise-keeping must be weighed against the particular moral and other values which would have to be sacrificed in keeping the particular promise. The obligations incurred in promising, borrowing, and contracting are therefore deniable in principle. The rights conveyed can be waived, modified, or voided. To say that these obligations presuppose the possibility of discharging them is true but misleading. It suggests that, in the absence of strong moral reasons, we can deny these obligations only if it is impossible to discharge them. Yet in fact it is quite sufficient in the case of trivial promises to deny the obligation by reason of inconvenience or practical difficulties.

Now it is a mistake to use the rights and obligations dependent upon conventionalized prior transactions as a model for all rights and obligations. Most of our obligations are not incurred in this way. No man ever contracts his obligations to his parents, his children, his colleagues, his fellow citizens, and the community as a whole. Most of us, at times when we find the discharge of these obligations extremely difficult, protest against the injustice of a world wherein we find ourselves with solemn duties which we never as free agents incurred. In regard to some of these obligations, it is plainly impossible to seek out the person or persons with the corresponding rights and to negotiate a waiver. In regard to others, where we do know who has the right, the man's willingness to waive or void it does not relieve us of our duty. A man in dire need, refusing to exercise his right to help which we can give him, does not thereby waive his right or void it. In being independent of prior transactions between the parties concerned, these rights and obligations are not, in many cases, directly negotiable by the parties. Even where they are negotiable, we do not weigh the general moral value, of parental obligation for example, against the specific moral values at issue in the particular case. On the contrary, we weigh some parent's specific obligation to a child against the other specific values in conflict with it on a given occasion. Once we distinguish the rights and duties dependent upon prior transactions from those independent of it, it is clear that questions about unconditional rights and duties arise largely in regard to the latter. The particular rights and duties independent of prior transactions can be arranged in rough orders of moral precedence. In any particular circumstances where there is a clear duty to act in behalf of the community to avert some terrible disaster, this duty takes precedence over the duty to one's family not to risk one's life and fortune. The man who has been injured in a traffic accident and whose life is in jeopardy has a right to help, exercisable against every passing motorist, the highway police, and the local hospital. This right, under these circumstances, takes precedence over the asserted right of the motorist's wife to have him home in time for an anniversary celebration; it takes precedence over the shopkeeper's asserted right to police protection against an attempted burglary; and it takes precedence over the hospital intern's right to his night off. But if rights and duties can be arranged in such orders of precedence there can be rights or duties which, in all of the particular circumstances where they can be asserted, take precedence over all other asserted rights and duties.

Any such high-order right or duty would be unconditional. It could not be denied on moral grounds because it would take moral precedence over all rights and obligations with which it is in conflict. Having this precedence, it would also be a clear and indisputable case of what we mean by "right" or "duty." Nor could it be denied in any particular case on grounds that it is impossible to secure the good for which there is a right to protection. We may know that it is impossible to save the life of a dying man. On the assumption that we are obliged to secure the good and save the life, philosophers are sometimes tempted to salvage the *"Ought" implies "can"* rule by saying that in such cases we are obliged *to try* to save the life rather than *to save* it. But to know that saving a life is impossible is to know that trying to save it will be ineffectual, and between these two there is no difference whatsoever in respect to what it is our duty to do. The acts performed in genuinely *trying* to save the life are precisely the acts performed in *saving* it. These are the acts which constitute help and which it is our duty to perform. Whether or not these acts will in fact be effectual in the particular case, our duty to perform them cannot be denied so long as it is possible in some cases to act effectively and save life.

In cases where life is in jeopardy, the individual's right to help has a sufficiently high order of moral precedence to illustrate clearly what an unconditional right would be like. I am not arguing that this right to help is unconditional. I am showing how the fact that rights can be ranked in order of moral precedence makes a difference to the logic of moral assertions. This difference can be illustrated by taking any right high in the order of moral precedence and asking how we would justify denying it. Once we do this, we see that there can in principle be rights which are undeniable in any circumstances where they can be asserted. It is wrong, therefore, to insist that all significant moral assertions must be deniable.

The second traditional objection to inalienable rights begs the question and rests upon a demonstrably false thesis.

IV

Although I have interpreted this second traditional objection as an argument denying moral significance to any assertion of inalienable right, there is an alternative interpretation. One can interpret the objection as an argument designed to show that the high-order rights to life, liberty, and happiness are conditional or alienable and that there are, therefore, no inalienable rights.

In the context of the history of philosophy and of inalienable rights theory, this argument, at first glance, appears valid and conclusive. In traditional inalienable rights theory, the moral right of each man to the protection of his moral interests is made logically dependent upon each man's unconditional right to his life, his liberty, the pursuit of his happiness, and his property. The concept of a state of nature is employed to establish a radical distinction between a prepolitical moral community and civil government under civil law. It is then argued that, under civil government, each man has an equal right to the legal protection of his life and liberty and happiness *because* governments are instituted among men in order to secure just these goods and *because* in a state of nature each man has an equal and unconditional right to them. The theory then is that democratic government is necessary because in a state of nature each man has an inalienable right to the high-order goods of life, liberty, and happiness. The objection to the theory is that neither in a state of nature nor in civil society is there any unconditional right to these high-order goods. Since the logic of the theory requires such unconditional rights and calls them "inalienable," to show that there are no such rights is to show that there are no inalienable rights in the traditional sense.

There is an important but limited sense in which this objection to inalienable rights is wholly valid. The traditional theories confuse the high-order moral goods of the individual person with the individual's unconditional rights to these goods. Wherever a man has a right, he has a right to something, which can in fact be refused or lost to him but which, under the circumstances where he has a right, cannot for moral reasons be refused him. If under specific conditions there are conclusive moral reasons for refusing a man some good or service, then there is no right to that good or service under these conditions. The question now is whether there are circumstances where we would be morally justified in refusing to save or spare the life of a man and where in consequence we would have to say there is no right to life. There are, of course, many such circumstances. They occur very frequently when disaster threatens an entire community, and we can imagine their occurring in a purely hypothetical moral community like the state of nature. These occurrences, despite the high courage and nobility often elicited by them, offer no occasion for moral rejoicing. The life, liberty, and happiness of a man are no less goods to him because conditions require their sacrifice. These goods are precious, their sacrifice tragic. But there are conditions where the tragedy is morally inescapable. That it is a tragedy shows that the goods sacrificed have an extremely high order of precedence. That the tragedy is at times morally inescapable shows that no individual has an unconditional right to them. It is therefore a mistake to suppose that each man has an inalienable right to these goods. And if by "inalienable right," we must mean each man's unconditional right to these high-order goods, then there are no inalienable rights.

V

But the exposure of this error does not, in any fundamental way, undermine or invalidate the theory of inalienable rights. In the first place, there is no reason why, if the term "inalienable" is meaningful at all, its use should be arbitrarily restricted to a group of rights which are obviously conditional and alienable. I have shown that the concept of an unconditional right is meaningful. If all the great moral goods could be ranked in an order of precedence, with a single, highest good heading the order, there would be an unconditional right to this highest good in any particular circumstance where it was in jeopardy. There could, of course, be basic and irreconcilable conflicts in respect to the highest good. On certain occasions, for example, there could be two parties for both of whom this highest good was in jeopardy but for only one of whom it could be secured. In any such case, the conflict could be appropriately described in either of two alternative ways. We could say that the irreconcilable conflict is between goods to which neither party has a right, or we could say that it is an irreconcilable conflict of unconditional right. The fact that either of these two descriptions is equally appropriate in this extreme case would in no way make the concept of unconditional right meaningless. An unconditional right would be clearly inalienable in that no man with this right could for any reason waive, convey, or forfeit it. The necessary and sufficient reason for waiving, conveying, or forfeiting a good is the realization of some other, higher good. But since an unconditional right is a right to the highest good, it is self-contradictory to suppose that there can be any such necessary and sufficient reason.

When we closely scrutinize inalienable rights theory, we see that it does not presuppose a single order of precedence among goods with a highest good at the top of the order. On the contrary, it presupposes a number of great goods. It presupposes the good of community welfare, a rough order of *common goods*. It also presupposes the great goods of the individual member of the community: his life, his happiness, his freedom to do what he wants and what in honor and conscience he is obliged to do. In most circumstances, where there is conflict of these individual goods, it is possible to determine which takes precedence over the others. But there is no single, rigid order of precedence valid under all conceivable circumstances and headed by some specific good. Because inalienable rights theory does not presuppose a highest good, there could not on the theory be an unconditional and inalienable right to good.

There can, however, be an unconditional and inalienable right to institutions which provide general protection to all high-order goods and permit each individual member of the community to place the burden of proof upon those who would deny him his good or interfere with his pursuit of it. To put it crudely, different kinds of legal institution can be ranked in order of goodness, dependent upon the extent to which they protect and secure all of the great human goods. If we grant, as we must, a diversity of these goods, the possibility of conflict between them and the reasonableness of ranking them in different ways dependent upon the circumstances, then we must also grant that the highest good in the order of institutions is law which takes cognizance of this diversity and which settles conflict by weighing what any party claims to be his good against the good of other parties and of the community as a whole. In respect to the diversity of great moral goods, there is a substantive highest good in a particular kind of legal institution. To this highest good, each man has an unconditional right. He cannot for any reason waive or convey it. Nor can he, by any act of his, forfeit it.

Because inalienable rights theory is primarily a justification of this unconditional right to protection and because it presents, on the whole, a clear and adequate elucidation of the conditions for asserting this right, it is not seriously damaged by showing that men have no direct and unconditional right to high-order goods. But even if it were damaged by this criticism, it is nonetheless a theory about the rights and the meaningful moral assertions I have here discussed. And democracy can be neither created nor preserved in the absence of the deep moral resolution and indubitable conviction expressed in these assertions.

Select Bibliography

BRAYBROOKE, DAVID. *Three Tests for Democracy*. New York: Random House, 1968.

CRANSTON, MAURICE. *What Are Human Rights?* New York: Basic Books, 1963.

FEINBERG, JOEL. "Duties, Rights, and Claims," *American Philosophical Quarterly*, III (1966), 137–144.

FRANKENA, WILLIAM. "Natural and Inalienable Rights," *Philosophical Review*, LXIV (1955), 212–232.

HART, H. L. A. "The Ascription of Responsibility and Rights," *Proceedings of the Aristotelian Society*, XLIX (1948–1949), 171–194.

HART, H. L. A. "Are There Any Natural Rights?" *Philosophical Review*, LXIV (1955), 175–191.

MARITAIN, JACQUES. *The Rights of Man and Natural Law*, trans. Doris Anson. New York: Scribner's, 1943.

MAYO, B. "Human Rights," *Proceedings of the Aristotelian Society*, XXXIX, suppl. (1965), 219–236.

MELDEN, ABRAHAM. *Rights and Right Conduct*. Oxford: Basil Blackwell, 1959.

PLAMENATZ, J., LAMONT, W. D., and ACTON, H. B. "Symposium: Rights," *Proceedings of the Aristotelian Society*, XXIV, suppl. (1950), 75–110.

RAPHAEL, D. D. "Human Rights," *Proceedings of the Aristotelian Society*, XXXIX, suppl. (1965), 205–218.

RAPHAEL, D. D., ed. *Political Theory and the Rights of Man*. Bloomington: Indiana University Press, 1967.

RITCHIE, D. G. *Natural Rights*. London: Macmillan, 1903.

STRAUSS, LEO. *Natural Right and History*. Chicago: University of Chicago Press, 1953.

UNESCO. *Human Rights: A Symposium*. New York: Columbia University Press, 1949.

WASSERSTROM, RICHARD. "Rights, Human Rights and Racial Discrimination," *Journal of Philosophy*, LXI (1964), 628–641.

POLITICAL
OBLIGATION

THE YOUNG man who believes that the draft law is unjust, the Negro who feels that society has denied him an equitable share of its rewards, and the doctor who considers performing an illegal abortion (to use Wasserstrom's example), must decide if a particular law ought to be obeyed. They must make a decision about the limits of their political obligation. It might well be true that political obligation has always been the central problem in political philosophy. However, the contemporary importance of this problem makes the articles in this section especially relevant. Contemporary political philosophers have come to doubt the possibility of developing a general theory of political obligation. There are few who try to follow Hobbes, Locke, or Rousseau in attempting to find a single criterion or explanation for political obligation. Political philosophers do focus on certain criteria and arguments which they think relevant, although the criteria and arguments may not be relevant in all cases. In this section, the reader will not find instructions for determining the nature or limits of his obligations. But he can find arguments and principles which may aid him in understanding his situation, deciding what to do, and evaluating the decisions of others.

Richard Wasserstrom's article attempts to demonstrate the falsity of those arguments which claim that because one has an obligation to the state or an obligation to obey the law, it is therefore always immoral to disobey the law. Michael Walzer shares Wasserstrom's belief that such a claim is false, but goes much further in arguing that an individual not only may be morally justified in disobeying a law but may even be under a moral obligation to disobey.

Both articles assume that there is a distinction between civil disobedience and other types of illegal behavior. Civil disobedience is "morally serious," whereas criminal behavior is not. The thief does not question or disapprove of the laws he breaks; he seeks only to evade them. Walzer suggests that "morally serious" disobedience must be public, and justifiable by appeal to moral principles. As distinguished from revolutionary action, it must not endanger the personal security of the public or undermine the legal system. The nature of the distinctions between "civil disobedience" and other types of disobedience is an interesting problem, but it is not the central focus of these articles.

Wasserstrom's article proceeds by dissecting and examining several arguments which claim that illegal action must be immoral. Each argument is examined on various levels or is interpreted in different ways. For example, he interprets the claim that men have a prima facie duty to obey the law in three different ways. By showing each claim to

265

be inadequate, Wasserstrom seeks to avoid the charge that he is attacking a straw man. He first attacks the thesis that there is a conceptual or logical connection between legal and moral action. He argues that the statement "This act is illegal but morally justifiable" is not a contradiction in terms and does not necessarily commit a logical error. He then shifts to more substantive arguments. A common reply to the statement above is "What if everyone did that?" Wasserstrom shows that when this question is properly understood, the universalization of such disobedience does not preclude its morality. In discussing the universalization principle, he claims that the effects of one person's actions on others are relevant. If it is probable that when A disobeys a law, B will be disposed to disobey all laws, A must take that into consideration. But if it is clear that A's actions will not have that effect, the theoretical possibility that they might can be disregarded. "Disobeying the law is often — even usually — wrong, but this is so largely because the illegal is usually restricted to the immoral and because morally right conduct is still less often illegal."

The excerpt from the last paragraph of Wasserstrom's article (although not only this statement) suggests that he believes there is no necessary relationship between legal and moral behavior. This is a much stronger claim than asserting that an illegal action can be moral. Yet, is it not possible that our legal obligations do create some moral obligations? Is it not possible that a man may have a moral obligation to subordinate his own moral scruples to the requirements of law? Wasserstrom seems to answer "no" to these questions, but they may merit further consideration.

Whereas Wasserstrom's article is almost entirely philosophical, Walzer's article is, in his own terms, a "sociology of disobedience." Whereas Wasserstrom shows how one might be able to claim that an illegal action is morally justifiable, Walzer goes on to show a possible justification. Walzer begins with the assertion that men acquire actual and felt obligations as members of groups. Note that Walzer makes a crucial distinction between a "felt" obligation or a "sense of" obligation and an "actual" or "real" obligation. The obligations incurred in a group can be owed to the group as a whole, to the other members, or to the ideals of the group, although these are often mixed. Walzer claims that "real" obligations are acquired only through "willful membership" in groups. Where membership is inherited and/or compulsory one may acquire a "sense of obligation," but the obligation may not be real. It would seem, then, that Walzer's thesis would exclude any obligation of a child toward his parents, for example.

Voluntary or willful membership is not equally characteristic of all groups. Rather, it is usually indicative of small, unorthodox groups, i.e., "secondary associations with claims to primacy." Because such groups often go to great lengths to insure that membership is voluntary, the obligations incurred are often stronger than those incurred in large groups where membership is often compulsory or inherited. It seems inevitable that the obligations owed to various groups will conflict. If the obligations owed to a small, voluntary group conflict with the obligations owed to a larger, involuntary group (especially the state), one may have an obligation to disobey the laws of the state. In such cases, it is obedience to the laws of the state which demands justification. Walzer admits that men may have a prima facie obligation to obey the laws of the state. But he asserts that this means only that disobedience of those laws requires justification, and a stronger obligation to a small group is always a possible justification. The crucial element in the "obligatory calculus" Walzer has developed is the size and voluntary character of the group, although the relation between smallness and voluntary membership is by no means perfect.

Walzer's article has focused on the fact that obligations may conflict, necessitating that an individual decide between them. He has suggested one important criterion for making those decisions, although the importance of other criteria has not been precluded. The articles in this section raise a number of philosophical and practical questions which all morally conscious citizens ought to consider.

13

The Obligation
to Obey the Law

Richard A. Wasserstrom

I

THE question of what is the nature and extent of one's obligation to obey the law is one of those relatively rare philosophic questions which can never produce doubts about the importance of theory for practice. To ask under what circumstances, if any, one is justified in disobeying the law is to direct attention to problems which all would acknowledge to be substantial. Concrete, truly problematic situations are as old as civil society.

The general question was posed — though surely not for the first time — well over two thousand years ago in Athens when Crito revealed to Socrates that Socrates' escape from prison could be easily and successfully accomplished. The issue was made a compelling one — though once again surely not for the first time — by Crito's insistence that escape was not only possible but also *desirable*, and that disobedience to law was in *this* case at least, surely justified. And the problem received at the hand of Socrates — here perhaps for the first time — a sustained theoretical analysis and resolution.

Just as the question of what is the nature and extent of one's obligation to obey the law demanded attention then — as it has throughout man's life in the body politic — it is no less with us today in equally vexing and perplexing forms. Freedom rides and sit-ins have raised the question of whether the immorality of segregation may justify disobey-

From *UCLA Law Review*, X (1963), 780–807. Copyright 1963 by the Regents of the University of California.

ing the law. The all-too-awesome horrors of a nuclear war have seemed to some to require responsive action, including, if need be, deliberate but peaceful trespasses upon government-owned atomic testing grounds. And the rightness of disobedience to law in the face of court-ordered school integration has been insisted upon by the citizens of several states and acted upon by the governor of at least one.[1]

The problem is one of present concern and the questions it necessarily raises are real. But even if the exigencies of contemporary life were not such as to make this topic a compelling one, it is one which would still be peculiarly ripe for critical inquiry. In part this is so because despite their significance many of the central issues have been relatively neglected by legal or political philosophers and critics. Many of the important questions which bear upon the nature and extent of one's obligation to obey the law have been dealt with summarily and un-critically; distinguishable issues have been indiscriminately blurred and debatable conclusions gratuitously assumed.

More important is the fact that historically the topic has generally been examined from only one very special aspect of the problem. Those philosophers who have seriously considered questions relating to one's obligation to obey the law have considered them only in the context of revolution. They have identified the conditions under which one would, if ever, be justified in disobeying the law with the conditions under which revolution would, if ever, be justified, and they have, perhaps not surprisingly, tended thereby to conclude that one would be justified in disobeying the law if, and only if, revolution itself would in that case be justified.[2]

To view the problem in a setting of obedience or revolution is surely to misconstrue it. It is to neglect, among other things, something that is obviously true — that most people who disobey the law are not revolutionaries and that most acts of disobedience of the law are not acts of revolution. Many who disobey the law are, of course, ordinary criminals: burglars, kidnappers, embezzlers, and the like. But even of those who disobey the law under a claim of justification, most are neither advocates nor practitioners of revolution.[3]

If the traditional, philosophical treatment of this subject is unduly simplistic and restrictive, contemporary legal thought is seldom more instructive. It is distressing, for one thing, that those whose daily intellectual concern is the legal system have said so little on this subject. And it is disturbing that many of those who have said anything at all appear so readily to embrace the view that justified disobedience of the law is a rare, if not impossible, occurrence. What is so disturbing is not the fact that this view is held — although I think it a mistaken one — but rather that such a conclusion is so summarily reached or assumed.[4]

I must make it clear at the outset that it is not my purpose to devote the remainder of this article to a documentation of the claims just made concerning either historical or contemporary thought. I do not wish to demonstrate that people in fact do believe what they appear to believe about the possibility of justified disobedience to law. Nor do I wish to show why it is that people have come to believe what they appear to believe. Rather, in very general terms I am concerned here with *arguments* — with those arguments which have been or which might be given in support of the claim that because one does have an obligation to obey the law, one ought not ever disobey the law.

To describe the focus of the article in this manner is, however, to leave several crucial matters highly ambiguous. And thus, before the arguments can be considered properly, the following matters must be clarified.

There are several different views which could be held concerning the nature of the stringency of one's obligation to obey the law. One such view, and the one which I shall be most concerned to show to be false, can be characterized as holding that one has an *absolute* obligation to obey the law. I take this to mean that a person is never justified in disobeying the law; to know that a proposed action is illegal is to know all one needs to know in order to conclude that the action ought not to be done;[5] to cite the illegality of an action is to give a sufficient reason for not having done it. A view such as this is far from uncommon. President Kennedy expressed the thoughts of many quite reflective people when he said not too long ago:

> [o]ur nation is founded on the principle that observance of the law is the eternal safeguard of liberty and defiance of the law is the surest road to tyranny.
> The law which we obey includes the final rulings of the courts as well as the enactments of our legislative bodies. Even among law-abiding men few laws are universally loved.
> But they are universally respected and not resisted.
> Americans are free, in short, to disagree with the law, but not to disobey it. For in a government of laws and not of men, no man, however prominent or powerful, and no mob, however unruly or boisterous, is entitled to defy a court of law.
> If this country should ever reach the point where any man or group of men, by force or threat of force, could long deny the commands of our court and our Constitution, then no law would stand free from doubt, no judge would be sure of his writ and no citizen would be safe from his neighbors.[6]

A more moderate or weaker view would be that which holds that, while one does have an obligation to obey the law, the obligation is a prima facie rather than absolute one. If one knows that a proposed course of conduct is illegal then one has a good — but not necessarily a sufficient — reason for refraining from engaging in that course of conduct. Under this view, a person may be justified in disobeying the law, but an act which is in disobedience of the law does have to be justified, whereas an act in obedience of the law does not have to be justified.

It is important to observe that there is an ambiguity in this notion of a prima facie obligation. For the claim that one has a prima facie obligation to obey the law can come to one of two different things. On the one hand, the claim can be this: the fact that an action is an act of disobedience is something which always does count against the performance of the action. If one has a prima facie obligation to obey the law, one always has that obligation — although, of course, it may be overridden by other obligations in any particular case. Thus the fact that an action is illegal is a relevant consideration in every case and it is a consideration which must be outweighed by other considerations before the performance of an illegal action can be justified.

On the other hand, the claim can be weaker still. The assertion of a prima facie obligation to obey the law can be nothing more than the claim that as a matter of fact it is *generally* right or obligatory to obey the law. As a rule the fact that an action is illegal is a relevant circumstance. But in any particular case, after deliberation, it might very well turn out that the illegality of the action was not truly relevant. For in any particular case the circumstances might be such that there simply was nothing in the fact of illegality which required overriding — e.g., there were no bad consequences at all which would flow from disobeying the law in this case.

The distinction can be made more vivid in the following fashion. One person, A, might hold the view that any action in disobedience of the law is intrinsically bad. Some other person, B, might hold the view that no action is intrinsically bad unless it has the property, P, and that not all actions in disobedience of the law have that property. Now for A, the fact of disobedience is *always* a relevant consideration,[7] for B, the fact of disobedience may always be initially relevant because of the existence of some well-established hypothesis which asserts that the occurrence of any action of disobedience is correlated highly with the occurrence of P. But if in any particular case disobedience does not turn out to have the property, P, then, upon reflection, it can be concluded by B that the fact that disobedience is involved is not a reason which weighs against the performance of the act in question.

To understand *B*'s position it is necessary to distinguish the relevance of *considering* the fact of disobedience from the relevance of the fact of disobedience. The former must always be relevant, the latter is not.

Thus there are at least three different positions which might be taken concerning the character of the obligation to obey the law or the rightness of disobedience to the law. They are: (1) One has an absolute obligation to obey the law; disobedience is never justified. (2) One has an obligation to obey the law but this obligation can be overridden by conflicting obligations; disobedience can be justified, but only by the presence of outweighing circumstances. (3) One does not have a special obligation to obey the law, but it is in fact usually obligatory, on other grounds, to do so; disobedience to law often does turn out to be unjustified.

It must also be made clear that when I talk about the obligation to obey the law or the possibility of actions which are both illegal and justified, I am concerned solely with *moral obligations* and *morally justified* actions. I shall be concerned solely with arguments which seek to demonstrate that there is some sort of a connection between the legality or illegality of an action and its morality or immorality. Concentration on this general topic necessarily renders a number of interesting problems irrelevant. Thus, I am not at all concerned with the question of why, in fact, so many people do obey the law. Nor, concomitantly, am I concerned with the nonmoral reasons which might and do justify obedience to law — of these, the most pertinent, is the fact that highly unpleasant consequences of one form or another are typically inflicted upon those who disobey the law. Finally there are many actions which are immoral irrespective of whether they also happen to be illegal. And I am not, except in one very special sense, concerned with this fact either. I am not concerned with the fact that the immorality of the action itself may be a sufficient reason for condemning it regardless of its possible illegality.

My last preliminary clarification relates to the fact that there is a variety of kinds of legal rules or laws and that there is a variety of ways in which actions can be related to these rules. This is an important point because many moral philosophers, in particular, have tended to assimilate all legal rules to the model of a typical law or legal order which is enforced through the direct threat of the infliction by the government of severe sanctions, and have thereby tended to assume that all laws and all legal obligations can be broken or disobeyed only in the manner in which penal laws can be broken or disobeyed. That this assimilation is a mistake can be demonstrated quite readily. There are many laws that, unlike the typical penal law, do not require or prohibit the performance of any acts at all. They cannot, therefore, be disobeyed. There are laws, for example, that make testamentary dispositions of property ineffective, unenforceable, or invalid if the written instrument was not witnessed by the requisite number of disinterested witnesses. Yet a law of this kind obviously does not impose an obligation upon anyone to make a will. Nor, more significantly, could a person who executed a will without the requisite number of witnesses be said to have disobeyed the law. Such a person has simply failed to execute a valid will.[8]

The foregoing observations are relevant largely because it is important to realize that to talk about disobeying the law or about one's obligation to obey the law is usually to refer to a rather special kind of activity, namely, that which is exemplified by, among other things, actions in violation or disobedience of a penal law. It is this special type of activity which alone is the concern of this article.

II

One kind of argument in support of the proposition that one cannot be justified in disobeying the law is that which asserts the existence of some sort of *logical* or conceptual relationship between disobeying the law and acting immorally.[9] If the notion of illegality entails that of immorality then one is never justified in acting illegally just because part of the meaning of *illegal* is *immoral*; just because describing an action as illegal is — among other things — to describe it as unjustified.[10]

A claim such as this is extremely difficult to evaluate. For one has great difficulty in knowing what is to count as truly relevant — let alone decisive — evidence of its correctness. There is, nevertheless, a supporting argument of sorts which can be made. It might go something like this:

It is a fact which is surely worth noticing that people generally justify action that *seems to be* illegal by claiming that the action *is not really* illegal. Typically an actor who is accused of having done something illegal will not defend himself by pointing out that, while illegal, his conduct was nevertheless morally justified. Instead, he will endeavor to show in one way or another that it is really inaccurate to call his conduct illegal at all. Now it looks as though this phenomenon can be readily accounted for. People try to resist the accusation of illegality, it might be argued, for the simple reason that they wish to avoid being punished. But what is interesting and persuasive is the fact that people try just as hard to evade a charge of illegality even in those situations where the threat of punishment is simply not an important or even relevant consideration.

The cases of the recent sit-ins or freedom rides are apt. To be sure, the claim was that the preservation of segregated lunch-counters, waiting rooms, and the like was morally indefensible. But an important justification for the rightness of the actions employed in integrating these facilities in the fashion selected rested upon the insistence that the perpetuation of segregation in these circumstances was itself illegal. One primary claim for the rightness of freedom rides was that these were not instances of disobeying the law. They were instead attempts to invoke judicial and executive protection of legal, indeed constitutional, rights. While there were some, no doubt, who might have insisted upon the rightness of sit-ins even if they were clearly illegal, most people were confident of the blamelessness of the participants just because it was plain that their actions were not, in the last analysis, illegal. Were it evident that sit-ins were truly illegal many might hold a different view about the rightness of sitting-in as a means to bring about integrated facilities.

Language commonly invoked in the course of disputes between nations furnishes another equally graphic illustration of the same point. In the continuing controversy over the status of Berlin, for instance, both the United States and Russia have relied upon claims of legality and have been sensitive to charges of illegality to an appreciably greater extent than one would otherwise have supposed. And much the same can be said of the more recent dispute between India and China. Now if nations which have little to fear in the way of the imposition of sanctions for acting illegally are nevertheless extraordinarily sensitive to charges of illegal conduct, this also may be taken as evidence of the fact that *illegality* implies *immorality*.

Wholly apt, too, was the controversy over the Eichmann trial. To some, the fact that the seizure and trial of Eichmann by Israel was illegal was sufficient to cast grave doubts upon the justifiability of the proceedings. To others, the charge of illegality made it necessary to demonstrate that nothing really illegal had occurred. What is significant about all this is the fact that all of the disputants implicitly acknowledged that illegality was something which did have to be worried about.

Such in brief is the argument which might be advanced and the "evidence" which might be adduced to support it. I think that such an argument is not persuasive, and I can best show this to be so in the following fashion.

Consider the case of a law that makes it a felony to perform an abortion upon a woman unless the abortion is necessary to preserve *her* life. Suppose a teenager, the daughter of a local minister, has been raped on her way home from school by an escapee from a state institution for mental defectives. Suppose further that the girl has become pregnant and has been brought to a reputable doctor who is asked to perform an abortion. And suppose, finally, that the doctor concludes after examining the girl that her life will not be endangered by giving birth to the child.[11] An abortion under these circumstances is, it seems fair to say, illegal.[12] Yet, we would surely find both intelligible and appealing the doctor's claim that he was nonetheless justified in disobeying the law by performing an abortion on the girl. I at least can see nothing logically odd or inconsistent about recognizing both that there is a law prohibiting this conduct and that further questions concerning the rightness of obedience would be relevant and, perhaps, decisive. Thus I can see nothing logically odd about describing this as a case in which the performance of the abortion could be both illegal and morally justified.[13]

There is, no doubt, a heroic defense which can be made to the above. It would consist of the insistence that the activity just described simply cannot be both illegal and justified. Two alternatives are possible. First, one might argue that the commission of the abortion would indeed have been justified if it were not proscribed by the law. But since it is so prohibited, the abortion is wrong. Now if this is a point about the appropriateness of kinds of reasons, I can only note that referring the action to a valid law does not seem to preclude asking meaningful questions about the obligatoriness of the action. If this is a point about language or concepts it does seem to be perfectly intelligible to say that the conduct is both illegal and morally justified. And if this is, instead, an *argument* for the immorality of ever disobeying a valid law, then it surely requires appreciable substantiation and not mere assertion.

Second, one might take a different line and agree that other questions can be asked about the conduct, but that is because the commission of the abortion under these circumstances simply cannot be illegal. The difficulty here, however, is that it is hard to understand what is now meant by *illegal*. Of course, I am not claiming that in the case as I have described it, it is clear that the performance of the abortion must be illegal. It might not be. But it might be. Were we to satisfy all the usual tests that we do invoke when we determine that a given course of conduct is illegal, and were someone still to maintain that because the performance of the abortion is here morally justified it cannot be illegal, then the burden is on the proponent of this view to make clear how we are to decide when conduct is illegal. And it would further be incumbent upon him to demonstrate what seems to be highly dubious, namely, that greater clarity and insight could somehow be attained through a radical change in our present terminology. It appears to be a virtually conclusive refutation to observe that there has never been a legal system whose criteria of validity — no matter how sophisticated, how rational, and how well defined — themselves guaranteed that morally justified action would never be illegal.

Thus an argument as strong as any of the above must fail. There is, of course, a weaker version which may be more appealing. If it is true that there is something disturbing about justifying actions that are conceded to be illegal, then one way to account for this is to insist that there is a logical connection between the concepts involved, but it is something less than the kind of implication already discussed. Perhaps it is correct that *illegal* does not entail *immoral*; *illegal* might nevertheless entail *prima facie immoral*. The evidence adduced tends to show that among one's moral obligations is the prima facie duty to obey the law.[14]

Once again, it is somewhat difficult to know precisely what to make of such a claim. It is hard to see how one would decide what was to count as evidence or whether the evidence was persuasive. At a minimum, it is not difficult to imagine several equally plausible alternative explanations of the disturbing character of accusations of illegal activity. In addition, to know only that one has a prima facie duty to obey the law is not to know a great deal. In particular, one does not know how or when that obligation can be overridden. And, of course, even if it is correct that acting illegally logically implies acting prima facie immorally, this in no way shows that people may not often be morally justified in acting illegally. At most, it demands that they have some good reason for acting illegally; at best, it requires what has already been hypothesized, namely, that the action in question, while illegal, be morally justified.

Thus, it is clear that if the case against ever acting illegally is to be made out, conceptual analysis alone cannot do it. Indeed, arguments of quite another sort must be forthcoming. And it is to these that I now turn.

III

One such argument, and the most common argument advanced, goes something like this: The reason why one ought never to disobey the law is simply that the consequences would be disastrous if everybody disobeyed the law. The reason why disobedience is never right becomes apparent once we ask the question "But what if everyone did that?"

Consider again the case of the doctor who has to decide whether he is justified in performing an illegal abortion. If he only has a prima facie duty to obey the law it looks as though he might justifiably decide that in this case his prima facie obligation is overridden by more stringent conflicting obligations. Or, if he is simply a utilitarian, it appears that he might rightly conclude that the consequences of disobeying the abortion law would be on the whole and in the long run less deleterious than those of obeying. But this is simply a mistake. The doctor would inevitably be neglecting the most crucial factor of all, namely, that in performing the abortion he was disobeying the law. And imagine what would happen if everyone went around disobeying the law. The alternatives are obeying the law and general disobedience. The choice is between any social order and chaos. As President Kennedy correctly observed, if any law is disobeyed, then no law can be free from doubt, no citizen safe from his neighbor.

Such an argument, while perhaps overdrawn, is by no means uncommon.[15] Yet, as it stands, it is an essentially confused one. Its respective claims, if they are to be fairly evaluated, must be delineated with some care.

At a minimum, the foregoing attack upon the possibility of justified disobedience might be either one or both of two radically different kinds of objection. The first, which relates to the consequences of an act of disobedience, is essentially a *causal* argument. The second questions the *principle* that any proponent of justified disobedience invokes. As to the causal argument, it is always relevant to point out that any act of disobedience may have certain consequences simply because it is an act of disobedience. Once the occurrence of the act is known, for example, expenditure of the state's resources may become necessary. The time and energy of the police will probably be turned to the task of discovering who it was who did the illegal act and of gathering evidence relevant to the offense. And other resources might be expended in the prosecution and adjudication of the case against the perpetrator of the illegal act. Illustrations of this sort could be multiplied, no doubt, but I do not think either that considerations of this sort are very persuasive or that they have been uppermost in the minds of those who make the argument now under examination. Indeed, if the argument is a causal one at all, it consists largely of the claim that any act of disobedience will itself cause, to some degree or other, general disobedience of all laws; it will cause or help to cause the overthrow or dissolution of the state. And while it is possible to assert that any act of disobedience will tend to further social disintegration or revolution, it is much more difficult to see why this must be so.

The most plausible argument would locate this causal efficacy in the kind of example set by any act of disobedience. But how plausible is this argument? It is undeniable, of course, that the kind of example that will be set is surely a relevant factor. Yet, there is nothing that precludes any proponent of justified disobedience from taking this into account. If, for example, others will somehow infer from the doctor's disobedience of the abortion law that they are justified in disobeying *any* law under *any* circumstances, then the doctor ought to consider this fact. This is a consequence — albeit a lamentable one — of his act of disobedience. Similarly, if others will extract the proper criterion from the act of disobedience, but will be apt to misapply it in practice, then this too ought to give the doctor pause. It, too, is a consequence of acting.[16] But if the argument is that disobedience would be wrong even if no bad example were set and no other deleterious consequences likely, then the argument must be directed against the principle the doctor appeals to in disobeying the law, and not against the consequences of his disobedience at all.

As to the attack upon a principle of justified disobedience as a principle, the response "But what if everyone disobeyed the law?" does appear to be a good way to point up both the inherent inconsistency of almost any principle of justified disobedience and the manifest undesirability of adopting such a principle. Even if one need not worry about what others will be led to do by one's disobedience, there is surely something amiss if one cannot consistently defend his right to do what one is claiming he is right in doing.

In large measure, such an objection is unreal. The appeal to "But what if everyone did that?" loses much, if not all, of its persuasiveness once we become clearer about what precisely the "did that" refers to. If the question "But what if everyone did that?" is simply another way of asking "But what if everybody disobeyed the law?" or "But what if people generally disobeyed the laws?" then the question is surely quasi-rhetorical. To urge general or indiscriminate disobedience to laws is to invoke a principle that, if coherent, is manifestly indefensible. It is equally plain, however, that with few exceptions such a principle has never been seriously espoused. Anyone who claims that there are actions that are both illegal and justified surely need not be thereby asserting that it is right generally to disobey all laws or even any particular law. It is surely not inconsistent to assert both that indiscriminate disobedience is indefensible and that discriminate disobedience is morally right and proper conduct. Nor, analogously, is it at all evident that a person who claims to be justified in performing an illegal action is thereby committed to or giving endorsement to the principle that the entire legal system ought to be overthrown or renounced. At a minimum, therefore, the appeal to "But what if everyone did that?" cannot by itself support the claim that one has an absolute obligation to obey the law — that disobeying the law can never be truly justified.

There is, however, a distinguishable but related claim which merits very careful attention — if for no other reason than the fact that it is so widely invoked today by moral philosophers. The claim is simply this: While it may very well be true that there are situations in which a person will be justified in disobeying the law, it is surely not true that disobedience can ever be justified solely on the grounds that the consequences of disobeying the particular law were in that case on the whole less deleterious than those of obedience.[17]

This claim is particularly relevant at this juncture because one of the arguments most often given to substantiate it consists of the purported demonstration of the fact that any principle which contained a proviso permitting a general appeal to consequences must itself be incoherent. One of the most complete statements of the argument is found in Marcus Singer's provocative book *Generalization in Ethics:*

Suppose,... that I am contemplating evading the payment of income taxes. I might reason that I need the money more than the government does, that the amount I have to pay is so small in comparison with the total amount to be collected that the government will never miss it. Now I surely know perfectly well that if I evade the payment of taxes this will not cause others to do so as well. For one thing, I am certainly not so foolish as to publicize my action. But even if I were, and the fact became known, this would still not cause others to do the same, unless it also became known that I was being allowed to get away with it. In the latter case the practice might tend to become widespread, but this would be a consequence, not of my action, but of the failure of the government to take action against me. Thus there is no question of my act being wrong because it would set a bad example. It would set no such example, and to suppose that it must, because it would be wrong, is simply a confusion.... Given all this, then if the reasons mentioned would justify me in evading the payment of taxes, they would justify everyone whatsoever in doing the same thing. For everyone can argue in the same way — everyone can argue that if he breaks the law this will not cause others to do the same. The supposition that this is a justification, therefore, leads to a contradiction.

I conclude from this that, just as the reply "Not everyone will do it" is irrelevant to the generalization argument, so is the fact that one knows or believes that not everyone will do the same; and that, in particular, the characteristic of knowing or believing that one's act will remain exceptional cannot be used to define a class of exceptions to the rule. One's knowledge or belief that not everyone will act in the same way in similar circumstances cannot therefore be regarded as part of the circumstances of one's action. One's belief that not everyone will do the same does not make one's circumstances relevantly different from the circumstances of others, or relevantly different from those in which the act is wrong. Indeed, on the supposition that it does, one's circumstances could never be specified, for the specification would involve an infinite regress.[18]

Singer's argument is open to at least two different interpretations. One quite weak interpretation is this: A person cannot be morally justified in acting as he does unless he is prepared to acknowledge that everyone else in the identical circumstances would also be right in acting the same way. If the person insists that he is justified in performing a certain action because the consequences of acting in that way are more desirable than those of acting in any alternative fashion, then he must be prepared to acknowledge that anyone else would also be justified in doing that action whenever the consequences of doing that action were more desirable than those of acting in any alternative fashion. To take Singer's own example: A person, A, could not be morally justified in evading the payment of his taxes on the grounds that the consequences of nonpayment were *in his case* more beneficial, all things considered, than those of payment, unless A were prepared to acknowledge that any other person, X, would also be justified in evading his, i.e., X's taxes, if it is the case that the consequences of X's nonpayment would in X's case be more beneficial, all things considered, than those of payment. If this is Singer's point, it is, for reasons already elaborated, unobjectionable.[19]

But Singer seems to want to make a stronger point as well. He seems to believe that even a willingness to generalize in this fashion could not justify acting in this way. In part his argument appears to be that this somehow will permit everyone to justify nonpayment of taxes, and in part his argument appears to be that there is a logical absurdity involved in attempting to make the likelihood of other people's behavior part of the specification of the relevant consequences of a particular act. Both of these points are wrong. To begin with, on a common sense level it is surely true that the effect which one's action will have on other people's behavior is a relevant consideration. For as was pointed out earlier, if A determines that other people will be, or may be, led to evade *their* taxes even when the consequences of nonpayment will in their cases be less beneficial than those of payment, then this is a consequence of A's action which he must take into account and attempt to balance against the benefits which would accrue to society from his nonpayment. Conversely, if for one reason or another A can determine that his act of nonpayment will not have this consequence, this, too, must be relevant. In this sense, at least, other people's prospective behavior is a relevant consideration.

More importantly, perhaps, it is surely a mistake — although a very prevalent one in recent moral philosophy — to suppose that permitting a general appeal to consequences would enable everyone to argue convincingly that he is justified in evading his taxes. Even if I adopt the principle that everyone is justified in evading his taxes whenever the consequences of evasion are on the whole less deleterious than those of payment, this in no way entails that I or anyone else will always, or ever, be justified in evading my taxes. It surely need not turn out to be the case — even if no one else will evade his taxes — that the consequences will on the whole be beneficial if I succeed in evading mine. It might surely be the case that I will spend the money saved improvidently or foolishly; it might very well be true that the government will make much better use of the money. Indeed, the crucial condition which must not be ignored and which Singer does ignore is the condition which stipulates that the avoidance of one's taxes in fact be optimific, that is, more desirable than any other course of conduct.

The general point is simply that it is an empirical question — at least in theory — what the consequences of any action will be. And it would surely be a mistake for me or anyone else to suppose that that action whose consequences are most pleasing to me — in either the short or long run — will in fact be identical with that action whose consequences are on the whole most beneficial to society. Where the demands of self-interest are strong, as in the case of the performance of an unpleasant task like paying taxes, there are particular reasons for being skeptical of one's conclusion that the consequences of nonpayment would in one's own case truly be beneficial. But once again there is no reason why there might not be cases in which evasion of taxes would be truly justified, nor is there any reason why someone could not consistently and defensibly endorse nonpayment whenever these circumstances were in fact present.

There is one final point which Singer's discussion suggests and which does appear to create something of a puzzle. Suppose that I believe that I am justified in deliberately trespassing on an atomic test site, and thereby disobeying the law, because I conclude that this is the best way to call attention to the possible consequences of continued atmospheric testing or nuclear war. I conclude that the consequences of trespassing will on the whole be more beneficial than any alternative action I can take. But suppose I also concede — what very well may be the case — that if everyone were to trespass, even for this same reason and in the same way, the consequences would be extremely deleterious. Does it follow that there is something logically incoherent about my principle of action? It looks as though there is, for it appears that I am here denying others the right to do precisely what I claim I am right in doing. I seem to be claiming, in effect, that it is right for me to trespass on government property in order to protest atomic testing only if it is the case that others, even under identical circumstances, will not trespass. Thus, it might be argued, I appear to be unwilling or unable to generalize my principle of conduct.

This argument is unsound, for there is a perfectly good sense in which I am acting on a principle which is coherent and which is open to any-one to adopt. It is simply the principle that one is justified in trespassing on government property whenever — among other things — it happens to be the case that one can say accurately that others will not in fact act on that same principle. Whether anyone else will at any given time act on any particular principle is an empirical question. It is, to repeat what has already been said, one of the possible circumstances which can be part of the description of a class of situations. There is, in short, nothing logically self-contradictory or absurd about making the likelihood of even identical action one of the relevant justifying considerations. And there is, therefore, no reason why the justifiability of any particular act of disobedience cannot depend, among other things, upon the probable conduct of others.

IV

It would not be at all surprising if at this stage one were to feel considerable dissatisfaction with the entire cast of the discussion so far. In particular, one might well believe that the proverbial dead horse has received still another flaying for the simple reason that no one has ever seriously argued that people are never justified in disobeying the law. One might insist, for instance, that neither Socrates nor President Kennedy were talking about all law in all legal systems everywhere. And one might urge, instead, that their claims concerning the un-justifiability of any act of disobedience rest covertly, if not overtly, on the assumption that the disobedience in question was to take place in a society in which the lawmaking procedures and other political institu-tions were those which are characteristic of an essentially democratic, or free, society. This is, of course, an important and plausible restriction upon the original claim, and the arguments which might support it must now be considered.

While there are several things about a liberal, democratic, or free society which might be thought to preclude the possibility of justified disobedience, it is evident that the presence of all the important constitu-tive institutions *cannot* guarantee that unjust or immoral laws will not be enacted. For the strictest adherence to principles of representative government, majority rule, frequent and open elections, and, indeed, the realization of all of the other characteristics of such a society, in no way can insure that laws of manifest immorality will not be passed and enforced. And if even the ideal democratic society might enact unjust laws, no existing society can plausibly claim as much. Thus, if the case against the possibility of justified disobedience is to depend upon the democratic nature of the society in question, the case cannot rest simply on the claim that the only actions which will be made illegal are those which are already immoral.

What then are the arguments which might plausibly be advanced? One very common argument goes like this: It is, of course, true that even democratically selected and democratically constituted legislatures can and do make mistakes. Nevertheless, a person is never justified in disobeying the law as long as there exist alternative, "peaceful" procedures by which to bring about the amendment or repeal of undesirable or oppressive laws. The genuine possibility that rational persuasion and argument can bring a majority to favor any one of a variety of competing views both requires that disapproval always be permitted and forbids that disobedience ever be allowed. This is so for several reasons.

First, it is clearly unfair and obviously inequitable to accept the results of any social decision-procedure only in those cases in which the decision reached was one of which one approves and to refuse to accept those decisions which are not personally satisfying. If there is one thing which participation, and especially voluntary participation, in a decision-procedure entails, it is that all of the participants must abide by the decision regardless of what it happens to be. If the decision-procedure is that of majority rule, then this means that any person must abide by those decisions in which he was in a minority just as much as it means that he can insist that members of the minority abide when he is a member of the majority.

As familiar as the argument is, its plausibility is far from assured. On one reading, at least, it appears to be one version of the universalization argument. As such, it goes like this. Imagine any person, A, who has voted with the majority to pass a law making a particular kind of conduct illegal. A surely would not and could not acknowledge the right of any person voting with the minority justifiably to disobey that law. But, if A will not and cannot recognize a right of justified disobedience here, then A certainly cannot consistently or fairly claim any right of justified disobedience on his part in those cases in which he, A, happened to end up being in a minority. Thus, justified disobedience can never be defensible.

This argument is fallacious. For a person who would insist that justified disobedience was possible even after majoritarian decision-making could very plausibly and consistently acknowledge the right of any person to disobey the law under appropriate circumstances regardless of how that person had voted on any particular law. Consider, once again, the case already put of the doctor and the pregnant girl. The doctor can surely be consistent in claiming both that circumstances make the performance of the illegal abortion justified and that any comparable action would also be right irrespective of how the actor, or the doctor, or anyone else, happened to have voted on the abortion law, or any other law. The point is simply that there is no reason why any person cannot consistently: (1) hold the view that majority decision-making is the best of all forms of decision-making; (2) participate voluntarily in the decision-making process; and (3) believe that it is right for *anyone* to disobey majority decisions whenever the relevant moral circumstances obtain, e.g., whenever the consequence of obedience to that law at that time would on the whole be more deleterious than those of obedience.

But this may be deemed too facile an answer; it also may be thought to miss the point. For it might be argued that there is a serious logical inconsistency of a different sort which must arise whenever a voluntary participant in a social decision-procedure claims that not all the decisions reached in accordance with that procedure need be obeyed. Take the case of majority rule. It is inconsistent for anyone voluntarily to participate in the decision-process and yet at the same time to reserve the right to refuse to abide by the decision reached in any particular case. The problem is not an inability to universalize a principle of action. The problem is rather that of making any sense at all out of the notion of having a majority decide anything — of having a procedure by which to make group decisions. The problem is, in addition, that of making any sense at all out of the fact of voluntary participation in the decision-procedure — in knowing what this participation can come to if it does not mean that every participant is bound by all of the decisions which are reached. What can their participation mean if it is not an implicit promise to abide by all decisions reached? And even if the point is not a logical one, it is surely a practical one. What good could there possibly be to a scheme, an institutional means for making social decisions, which did not bind even the participants to anything?

The answer to this argument — or set of arguments — is wholly analogous to that which has been given earlier. But because of the importance and prevalence of the argument some repetition is in order.

One can simply assert that the notion of any social decision-making procedure is intelligible only if it entails that all participants always abide by all of the decisions which are made, no matter what those decisions are. Concomitantly, one can simply insist that any voluntary participant in the decision-process must be consenting or promising to abide by all decisions which are reached. But one cannot give as a plausible reason for this assertion the fact that the notion of group decision-making becomes incoherent if anything less in the way of adherence is required of all participants. And one cannot cite as a plausible reason for this assertion the fact that the notion of voluntary participation loses all meaning if anything less than a promise of absolute obedience is inferred.

It is true that the notion of a group decision-making procedure would be a meaningless notion if there were no respects in which a group decision was in any way binding upon each of the participants. Decisions which in no way bind anyone to do anything are simply not decisions. And it is also true that voluntary participation is an idle, if not a vicious, act if it does not commit each participant to something. If any voluntary participant properly can wholly ignore the decisions which are reached, then something is surely amiss.

But to say all this is not to say very much. Group decision-making can have a point just because it does preclude any participant from taking some actions which in the absence of the decision he might have been justified in performing. And voluntary participation can still constitute a promise of sorts that one will not perform actions which, in the absence of voluntary participation, might have been justifiable. If the fact of participation in a set of liberal political institutions does constitute a promise of sorts, it can surely be a promise that the participant will not disobey a law just because obedience would be inconvenient or deleterious to him. And if this is the scope of the promise, then the fact of voluntary participation does make a difference. For in the absence of the participation in the decision to make this conduct illegal, inconvenience to the actor might well have been a good reason for acting in a certain way. Thus, participation can create new obligations to behave in certain ways without constituting a promise not to disobey the law under any circumstances. And if this is the case, adherence to a principle of justified disobedience is not inconsistent with voluntary participation in the decision-making process.

Indeed, a strong point can be made. The notion of making laws through voluntary participation in democratic institutions is not even inconsistent with the insistence that disobedience is justified whenever the consequences of disobedience are on the whole more beneficial than those of obedience. This is so because a promise can be a meaningful promise even if an appeal to the consequences of performing the promise can count as a sufficient reason for not performing the promise.[20] And if this is the case for promises generally, it can be no less the case for the supposed promise to obey the law.

Finally, even if it were correct that voluntary participation implied a promise to obey, and even if it were the case that the promise must be a promise not to disobey on consequential grounds, all of this would still not justify the conclusion that one ought never to disobey the law. It would, instead, only demonstrate that disobeying the law must be prima facie wrong, that everyone has a prima facie obligation to obey the law. This is so just because it is sometimes right even to break one's own promises. And if this, too, is a characteristic of promises generally, it is, again, no less a characteristic of the promise to obey the law.

The notions of promise, consent, or voluntary participation do not, however, exhaust the possible sources of the obligation to obey the laws of a democracy. In particular, there is another set of arguments which remains to be considered. It is that which locates the rightness of obedience in the way in which any act of disobedience improperly distributes certain burdens and benefits among the citizenry. Professor Wechsler, for example, sees any act of disobedience to the laws of the United States as "the ultimate negation of all neutral principles, to take the benefits accorded by the constitutional system, including the national market and common defense, while denying it allegiance when a special burden is imposed. That certainly is the antithesis of law."[21]

On the surface, at least, Professor Wechsler's claim seems overly simple; it appears to be the blanket assertion that the receipt by any citizen through continued, voluntary presence of benefits of this character necessarily implies that no act of disobedience could be justified. To disobey any law after having voluntarily received these benefits would be, he seems to suggest, so unjust that there could never be overriding considerations. This surely is both to claim too much for the benefits of personal and commercial security and to say too little for the character of all types of disobedience. For even if the receipt of benefits such as these did simply impose an obligation to obey the law, it is implausible to suppose that the obligation thereby imposed would be one that stringent.

But there is a more involved aspect of Professor Wechsler's thesis — particularly in his insistence that disobedience of the law, where benefits of this kind have been received, is the negation of all neutral principles. I am not at all certain that I understand precisely what this means, but there are at least two possible interpretations: (1) Unless everyone always obeyed the law no one would receive these obviously valuable benefits. (2) Since the benefits one receives depend upon the prevalence of conditions of uniform obedience, it follows that no one who willingly receives these benefits can justly claim them without himself obeying. The first has already been sufficiently considered.[22] The second, while not unfamiliar, merits some further attention.

In somewhat expanded form, the argument is simply this. What makes it possible for any particular person to receive and enjoy the benefits of general, personal, and economic security is the fact that everyone else obeys the law. Now, if injustice is to be avoided, it is surely the case that any other person is equally entitled to these same benefits. But he will have this security only if everyone else obeys the law. Hence the receipt of benefits at others' expense requires repayment in kind. And this means universal obedience to the law.[23]

There are two features of this argument which are puzzling. First, it is far from clear that the benefits of security received by anyone necessarily depend upon absolute obedience on the part of everyone else. It just might be the case that an even greater quantum of security would have accrued from something less than total obedience. But even if I am wrong here, there is a more important point at issue. For reasons already discussed, it is undeniable that even in a democracy a price would be paid for universal obedience — the price that might have to be paid, for instance, were the doctor to refuse to perform the abortion because it was illegal. If this is so, then the fact that a person received benefits from everyone else's obedience does not necessarily entail that it is unjust for him to fail to reciprocate in kind. The benefit of general security might not have been worth the cost. A greater degree of flexibility on the part of others, a general course of obedience except where disobedience was justified, might have yielded a greater benefit. People may, in short, have done more or less than they should have. And if they did, the fact that anyone or everyone benefited to some degree in no way requires that injustice can only be avoided through like and reciprocal conduct. If it is better, in at least some circumstances, to disobey a law than to obey it, there is surely nothing unjust about increasing the beneficial consequences to all through acts of *discriminate* disobedience.

If the argument based upon the effect of receipt of certain benefits is therefore not very persuasive, neither in most cases is the argument which is derived from the way in which any act of disobedience is thought to distribute burdens unfairly among the citizenry. The argument can be put very briefly: If there is one thing which any act of disobedience inevitably does, it is to increase the burdens which fall on all the law-abiding citizens. If someone disobeys the law even for what seems to be the best of reasons, he inevitably makes it harder — in some quite concrete sense — on everyone else. Hence, at a minimum this is a good reason not to disobey the law, and perhaps a sufficient reason as well.

This argument is appealing because there is at least one kind of case it fits very well. It is the case of taxation. For suppose the following, only somewhat unreal, conditions: that the government is determined to raise a specified sum of money through taxation, and that, in the long, if not the short, run it will do so by adjusting the tax rate to whatever percentage is necessary to produce the desired governmental income. Under such circumstances it could plausibly be argued that one of the truly inevitable results of a successfully executed decision to evade the payment of one's taxes — a decision made, moreover, on ostensibly justifiable grounds — is that every other member of society will thereby be required to pay a greater tax than would otherwise have been the case. Thus in some reasonably direct and obvious fashion any act of disobedience — particularly if undetected — does add to the burdens of everyone else. And surely this is to make out at least a strong case of prima facie injustice.

Now, for reasons already elaborated, it would be improper to conclude that evasion of one's taxes could never be justified. But the argument is persuasive in its insistence that it does provide a very good reason why evasion always must be justified and why it will seldom be justifiable. But even this feature of disobedience is not present in many cases. Tax evasion, as opposed to other kinds of potentially justified disobedience, is a special, far from typical case. And what is peculiar to it is precisely the fact that any act of disobedience to the tax laws arguably shifts or increases the burden upon others. Such is simply not true of most types of acts of disobedience because most laws do not prohibit or require actions which affect the distribution of resources in any very direct fashion.

Thus, if we take once again the case of the doctor who has decided that he is justified in performing an illegal abortion on the pregnant girl, it is extremely difficult, if not impossible, to locate the analogue of the shifting of burdens involved in tax evasion. How does the performance of the abortion thereby increase the "costs" to anyone else? The only suggestion which seems at all plausible is that which was noted earlier in a somewhat different context. Someone might argue that it is the occurrence of illegal actions which increase the cost of maintaining a police force, a judiciary, and suitable correctional institutions. This cost is a burden which is borne by the citizenry as a whole. And hence, the doctor's illegal acts increase their burdens — albeit very slightly. The difficulty here is threefold. First, if the doctor's act is performed in secret and if it remains undetected, then it is hard to see how there is any shift of economic burden at all. Second, given the fact that police forces, courts, and prisons will always be necessary as long as unjustified acts of disobedience are a feature of social existence, it is by no means apparent that the additional cost is anything but truly de minimus.[24] And third, the added costs, if any, are in the doctor's case assumed by the doctor *qua* member of the citizenry. He is not avoiding a burden; at most he adds something to everyone's — including his own — existing financial obligations. Thus, in cases such as these, it is not at all evident that disobedience need even be prima facie unjust and hence unjustified.

V

There is one final argument which requires brief elucidation and analysis. It is in certain respects a peculiarly instructive one both in its own right and in respect to the thesis of this article.

It may be true that on some particular occasions the consequences of disobeying a law will in fact be less deleterious on the whole than those of obeying it — even in a democracy. It may even be true that on some particular occasions disobeying a law will be just whereas obeying it would be unjust. Nevertheless, the reason why a person is never justified in disobeying a law — in a democracy — is simply this: The chances are so slight that he will disobey only those laws in only those cases in which he is in fact justified in doing so that the consequences will on the whole be less deleterious if he never disobeys any law. Furthermore, since anyone must concede the right to everyone to disobey the law when the circumstances so demand it, the situation is made still worse. For once we entrust this right to everyone we can be sure that many laws will be disobeyed in a multitude of cases in which there was no real justification for disobedience. Thus, given what we know of the possibilities of human error and the actualities of human frailty, and given the tendency of democratic societies to make illegal only those actions which would, even in the absence of a law, be unjustified, we can confidently conclude that the consequences will on the whole and in the long run be best if no one ever takes it upon himself to "second guess" the laws and to conclude that in his case his disobedience is justified.[25]

The argument is, in part, not very different from those previously considered. And thus, what is to be said about it is not very different either. Nonetheless, upon pain of being overly repetitive, I would insist that there is a weak sense in which the argument is quite persuasive and a strong sense in which it is not. For the argument makes, on one reading, too strong an empirical claim — the claim that the consequences will in the long run always in fact be better if no one in a democracy ever tries to decide when he is justified in disobeying the law. As it stands, there is no reason to believe that the claim is or must be true, that the consequences will always be better. Indeed, it is very hard to see why, despite the hypothesis, someone might still not be justified in some particular case in disobeying a law. Yet, viewed as a weaker claim, as a summary rule, it does embody a good deal that is worth remembering. It can, on this level, be understood to be a persuasive reminder of much that is relevant to disobedience: that in a democracy the chances of having to live under bad laws are reduced; that in a democracy there are typically less costly means available by which to bring about changes in the law; that in a democracy — as in life in general — a justified action may always be both inaptly and ineptly emulated; and that in a democracy — as in life in general — people often do make mistakes as to which of their own actions are truly justified. These are some of the lessons of human experience which are easy to forget and painful to relearn.

But there are other lessons, and they are worth remembering too. What is especially troubling about the claim that disobedience of the law is never justified, what is even disturbing about the claim that disobedience of the law is never justified in a democratic or liberal society, is the facility with which its acceptance can lead to the neglect of important moral issues. If no one is justified in disobeying the Supreme Court's decision in *Brown* v. *Board of Education*[26] this is so because, among other things, there is much that is wrong with segregation. If there was much that was peculiarly wrong in Mississippi this fall, this was due to the fact, among other facts, that a mob howled and a governor raged when a court held that a person whose skin was black could go to a white university. Disobeying the law is often — even usually — wrong, but this is so largely because the illegal is usually restricted to the immoral and because morally right conduct is still less often illegal. But we must always be sensitive to the fact that this has not always been the case, is not now always the case, and need not always be the case in the future. And undue concentration upon what is wrong with disobeying the law rather than upon the wrong which the law seeks to prevent can seriously weaken and misdirect that awareness.

Notes

1. This is to say nothing of the stronger claim, involved in many of the war crimes prosecutions, that one does have a duty to disobey the law and, therefore, that one can be properly punished for having obeyed the law.

2. See, e.g., Austin, *The Province of Jurisprudence Determined* (1954), pp. 53–55; Hume, *A Treatise of Human Nature*, bk. III, secs. 9, 10; Locke, *The Second Treatise of Government*, chaps. 18, 19.

3. A subject which has surely not received the philosophical attention it deserves is that of the nature of revolution. What, for instance, are the characteristics of a revolution? Must the procedures by which laws are made or the criteria of validity be altered? Or is it sufficient that the people who occupy certain crucial offices be removed in a manner inconsistent with existing rules? Must force or resistance accompany whatever changes or alterations are made? Whatever the answers may be to questions such as these, it is, I think, plain that particular laws may be disobeyed under a claim of justification without any of these features being present. One can *argue* that for one reason or another, any act of disobedience must necessarily lead to revolution or the overthrow of the government. But then this is an argument which must be demonstrated.

4. Professor Hart, for example, in his extremely stimulating analysis of the aims of the criminal law seems to hold such a view. Professor Hart believes that the criminal law ought only be concerned with that conduct which is morally blameworthy. From this he infers that no real problem can ever be presented by laws which make knowledge of the illegality of an action one of the elements of the offense. And this is so because the "knowing or reckless disregard of legal obligation affords an independent basis of blame-worthiness *justifying the actor's condemnation as a criminal*, even when his conduct was not intrinsically antisocial." Hart, "The Aims of the Criminal Law," *Law and Contemporary Problems*, 23 (1958), 401, 418. (Emphasis added.) Some such view can also be plausibly attributed to, among others, Professor Lon Fuller, see text at section II, and Professor Herbert Wechsler, see text at section IV. Of course, all of these scholars, or any other person holding such a view, might well insist that the position is tenable only if an important qualification is made, namely, that the legal system in question be that of an essentially democratic society. For a discussion of this more restricted claim, see text at section IV.

5. Because I am concerned with the question of whether one is ever *morally justified* in acting illegally, I purposely make the actor's knowledge of the illegality of the action part of the description of the act. I am not concerned

with the question of whether ignorance of the illegality of the action ought to excuse one from moral blame.

6. *New York Times*, October 1, 1962, p. 22, col. 6. The same qualification must be made here as was made in note 4 *supra* — President Kennedy may well have meant his remarks to be applicable only to the legal system which is a part of the set of political institutions of the United States.

7. To repeat, though, it surely is not necessarily conclusive, or sufficient, since an action in obedience to the law may under some other description be worse, or less justifiable, than disobedience.

8. See Hart, *The Concept of Law* (1961), pp. 27–48, particularly for the clearest and fullest extant philosophical analysis of the important distinguishing characteristics of different kinds of legal rules.

In this connection a stronger point than the one made above can be made. It is that there are many laws which, if they can be disobeyed at all, cannot be disobeyed in the way in which the typical criminal law can be disobeyed. For there are many laws that either impose or permit one to impose upon oneself any number of different legal obligations. And with many of these legal obligations, regardless of how created, it seems correct to say that one can breach or fail to perform them without thereby acting illegally of in disobedience of the law. One's obligation to obey the law may not, therefore, be coextensive with one's legal obligations. In the typical case of a breach of contract, for example, the failure to perform one's contractual obligations is clearly a breach of a legal obligation. Yet one can breach a contract and, hence, a legal obligation without necessarily acting illegally. This last assertion is open to question. And arguments for its correctness would not here be germane. It is sufficient to recognize only that failing to honor or perform some types of legal obligations may be a quite different kind of activity from violating or disobeying a law or order which is backed up, in some very direct fashion, by a governmentally threatened severe sanction.

9. It is worth emphasizing that I am not at all interested in the claim — which in many ways is an odd one to belabor — that there is a logical relationship between disobeying the law and acting illegally. See, e.g., Carnes, "Why Should I Obey the Law?" *Ethics*, 71 (1960), 14.

10. Professor Fuller may hold to some version of this view in his article "Positivism and Fidelity to Law — A Reply to Professor Hart," *Harvard Law Review*, 71 (1958), 630, 656, where, after characterizing the position of legal positivism as one which says that "On the one hand, we have an amoral datum called law, which has the peculiar quality of creating a moral duty to obey it. On the other hand, we have a moral duty to do what we think is right and decent." Professor Fuller goes on to criticize this bifurcation of law and morality on the grounds that "The 'dilemma' it states has the verbal formulation of a problem, but the problem it states makes no sense. It is like saying I have to choose between giving food to a starving man and being mimsey with the borogroves. I do not think it unfair to the positivistic

philosophy to say that it never gives any coherent meaning to the moral obligation of fidelity to law."

Others who at least suggest adherence to such a position are: Baier, *The Moral Point of View* (1958), p. 134; Nowell-Smith, *Ethics* (1959), 236–237; and Weldon, *The Vocabulary of Politics* (1953), pp. 57, 62, 66–67. And there are surely passages in Hobbes that could also be read in this way. See, e.g., Hobbes, *Leviathan*, chaps. XIII, XVIII. The claim that *illegal* entails *immoral* is closely related to, but surely distinguishable from, the position that Professor Fuller, among many others, may also hold, namely, that there are certain minimum "moral" requirements that must be met before any rule can be a law.

11. These facts are taken from Packer and Gampell, "Therapeutic Abortion: A Problem in Law and Medicine," *Stanford Law Review*, 11 (1959), 417, where they are introduced in a different context.

12. Such would seem to be the case in California, for example, where the *California Penal Code*, sec. 274, makes the performance of an abortion a felony unless the abortion is necessary to preserve the life of the pregnant woman.

13. I am supposing, of course, that one would regard the performance of the abortion — in the absence of the relevant penal law — as clearly morally justified. If one disagrees with this assessment of the morality of the case, then some other example ought to be substituted. One likely candidate, drawn from our own history, is that of the inherent rightness in refusing to return an escaped Negro slave to his "owner." If one believes that refusing to do so would be clearly justifiable, then consider whether the existence of the fugitive slave laws necessarily rendered a continued refusal unjustified.

14. Sir W. David Ross, for example, suggests that the obligation to obey the law is a prima facie obligation which is a compound of three more simple prima facie duties. Ross, *The Right and the Good* (1930), pp. 27–28.

15. Socrates, for instance, supposes that were he to escape he might properly be asked: "[W]hat are you about? Are you going by an act of yours to overturn us — the laws and the whole state, as far as in you lies? Do you imagine that a state can subsist and not be overthrown, in which the decisions of law have no power, but are set aside and overthrown by individuals?" (Plato, *Crito*). Analogous arguments can be found in, for example: Austin, *The Province of Jurisprudence Determined* (1954), pp. 52–53; Hobbes, *Leviathan*, chap. XV; Hume, *A Treatise of Human Nature*, bk. III, pt. II, pp. 3, 6, 8, 9; Toulmin, *An Examination of the Place of Reason in Ethics* (1950), p. 151.

16. For a very special and related version of this argument, see text at section V.

17. This is a particular illustration of the more general claim that for one reason or another utilitarianism cannot be a defensible or intelligible moral theory when construed as permitting one's moral obligation to do any particular action to be overridden by a direct appeal to the consequences of performing

that particular action. For recent statements of the claim see, e.g., Nowell-Smith, *Ethics*; Rawls, "Two Concepts of Rules," *Philosophical Review*, 64 (1955), 3; Singer, *Generalization in Ethics* (1961), pp. 61–138, 178–216; Toulmin, *Examination of the Place of Reason*, pp. 144–165; Harrison, "Utilitarianism, Universalisation, and Our Duty to Be Just," *Proceedings of the Aristotelian Society*, 53 (1952–1953), 105.

For some criticisms of this restriction on utilitarianism see, e.g., Wasserstrom, *The Judicial Decision* (1961), pp. 118–137. But see Hart, "Book Review," *Stanford Law Review*, 14 (1962), 919, 924–926.

18. Singer, *Generalization in Ethics*, pp. 149–150.

19. Neither Singer nor I have adequately refuted the confirmed ethical egoist who insists that he is prepared to generalize but only in the sense that X's nonpayment is justified if, and only if, the consequences of X's nonpayment would in X's case be more beneficial *to A* than those of payment. This is a problem which surely requires more careful attention than it typically receives. It will not do simply to insist that the egoist does not understand ordinary moral discourse. Instead, what must be demonstrated are the respects in which the egoist's position is an inherently unjust one. But to make this showing is beyond the scope of this article.

20. The point here is analogous to that made in the discussion of Singer's argument. Moral philosophers have often argued that one cannot appeal simply to the consequences of performing or not performing a particular promise as a reason for not performing that promise. And the reason why this is so is that the notion of having promised to do something would be unintelligible if the promisor could always, when the time came for performance, be excused if it were the case that the consequences of nonperformance were more beneficial than those of performance. This would make promising unintelligible, so the argument goes, because promising entails or means obligating oneself to do something. But if the appeal to consequences is what is to be determinative of one's obligations, then the promise becomes a wholly superfluous, meaningless act. Rawls, for instance, puts the point this way: "Various defenses for not keeping one's promise are allowed, but among them there isn't the one that, on general utilitarian grounds, the promisor (truly) thought his action best on the whole, even though there may be the defense that the consequences of keeping one's promise would have been *extremely* severe. While there are too many complexities here to consider all the necessary details, one can see that the general defense isn't allowed if one asks the following question: what would one say of someone who, when asked why he broke his promise, replied simply that breaking it was best on the whole? Assuming that his reply is sincere, and that his belief was reasonable (i.e., one need not consider the possibility that he was mistaken), I think that one would question whether or not he knows what it means to say 'I promise' (in the appropriate circumstances). It would be said of someone who used this excuse without further explanation

that he didn't understand what defenses the practice, which defines a promise, allows to him. If a child were to use this excuse one would correct him; for it is part of the way one is taught the concept of a promise to be corrected if one uses this excuse. The point of having the practice would be lost if the practice did allow this excuse." Rawls, "Two Concepts of Rules," p. 17.

Now I am not concerned to dispute Rawls' remark if taken as descriptive of our institution of promising. For what I am here concerned with is the claim, implicit throughout, that promising would be a meaningless or pointless activity if the excuse were permitted. I should say though that the passage quoted from Rawls is not, I think, central to his main argument. I think I can show this to be a mistake through the following two examples.

(1) *A* has promised *B* that he will mow *B*'s lawn for *B* on Sunday. On Sunday, *A* is feeling lazy and so he refuses to mow the lawn.

(2) *A* is sitting home on Sunday, feeling lazy, when *B* calls him up and asks him to come over and mow *B*'s lawn. *A* refuses to mow the lawn.

Ceteris paribus, it would be the case that *A* is wrong in refusing to mow *B*'s lawn in example (1) but not blamable for refusing to mow *B*'s lawn in example (2). Why is this so? Because *A*'s promise to mow *B*'s lawn creates an obligation which in the absence of such a promise is nonexistent. If this is so, then permitting the general utilitarian defense does not make a promise a meaningless gesture. This is so because there are many situations in which, in the absence of having promised to do so, we are not, for example, obligated to inconvenience ourselves simply for another's convenience. Personal inconvenience then might be one excuse which must be inconsistent with the practice of promising, even if the general appeal to consequences is not. Thus, promising would and could have a real point even if the general appeal to consequences were a good defense.

21. Wechsler, "Toward Neutral Principles of Constitutional Law," *Harvard Law Review*, 73 (1959), 1, 35.

22. See text at section III.

23. For a somewhat related characterization of the source of the obligation to obey the law, see Hart, "Are There Any Natural Rights?" *Philosophical Review*, 64 (1955), 175, 185: "A third very important source of special rights and obligations which we recognize in many spheres of life is what may be termed mutuality of restrictions.... In its bare schematic outline it is this: when a number of persons conduct any joint enterprise according to rules and thus restrict their liberty, those who have submitted to these restrictions when required have a right to a similar submission from those who have benefited by their submission. The rules may provide that officials should have authority to enforce obedience and make further rules, and this will create a structure of legal rights and duties, but the moral obligation to obey the rules in such circumstances is *due to* the co-operating members of the society, and they have the correlative moral right to obedience. In social situations of this sort (of which political society is the most complex example)

the obligation to obey the rules is something distinct from whatever other moral obligations there may be for obedience in terms of good consequences (e.g., the prevention of suffering); the obligation is due to the co-operating members of the society as such and not because they are human beings on whom it would be wrong to inflict suffering."

I would point out only two things. First, as Professor Hart himself asserts—in a passage not quoted—the existence of this right in no way implies that one is never justified in disobeying the law. The right which any participating member has in others' obedience can justifiably be infringed in appropriate circumstances. Second, and here perhaps Professor Hart disagrees for reasons already elaborated, there is no reason that I can see why an appeal to the consequences of disobeying a particular law cannot be a sufficient justification for infringing upon that right. It is surely conceivable, at least, that this is all the submission to rules which anyone ought to have given, and hence all the submission which anyone is entitled to expect from others.

24. Curiously, perhaps, given a legal system in which laws are in general good and hence in which the possibility of justified disobedience is rare, the special or added cost of an occasional act of justified disobedience is diminished still further.

25. For fuller analyses and assessments of this argument in different contexts see, e.g., Rawls, "Two Concepts of Rules"; Wasserstrom, *Judicial Decision*, pp. 118–171.

26. 347 U.S. 483 (1954).

14

The Obligation
to Disobey

Michael Walzer

ACCORDING to liberal political theory, as first formulated by John Locke, any individual citizen oppressed by the rulers of the state has a right to disobey their commands, break their laws, even rebel and seek to replace the rulers and change the laws. In fact, however, this is not a right often claimed or acted upon by individuals. Throughout history, when men have disobeyed or rebelled, they have done so, by and large, as members or representatives of groups, and they have claimed not merely that they are free to disobey but that they are obligated to do so. Locke says nothing about such obligations, and, despite the fact that Thomas Jefferson claimed on behalf of the American colonists that "it is their right, it is their duty, to throw off [despotism]," the idea that men can be obligated to disobey has not played much part in liberal political theory.

"Here I stand; I can do no other" — Martin Luther's bold defiance — is hardly an assertion of freedom or a claim to rights. It is the acknowledgment of a new but undeniable obligation. Nor is this obligation often asserted, as it was by Luther, in the first-person singular. In a recent article on civil disobedience, Hugo Bedau has denied the validity of such an assertion unless it is supplemented by arguments which reach beyond the moral feelings of the individual. "The force of saying, 'I ought to disobey this law' cannot be derived from 'Obeying this law is inconsistent with my moral convictions.'"[1] Perhaps it cannot, and

From *Ethics*, LXXVII (1967), 163–175. Copyright © 1967 by the University of Chicago.

then we must wait upon Luther's further defense before we judge his defiance. But the first sentence is, in practice, rarely derived from the second. Generally it follows from an assertion of a very different sort: "Obeying this law is inconsistent with *our* moral convictions (on behalf of which we have made significant commitments, organized, worked together for so many months or years, etc.)." And it can be argued that, having said this, one can then go on, without offering additional reasons, to say, "Therefore I ought to disobey." This, at any rate, is the form that disobedience most often takes in history, even though additional reasons are usually offered. Men rarely break the law by themselves, or if they do they rarely talk about it. Disobedience, when it is not criminally but morally, religiously, or politically motivated, is almost always a collective act, and it is justified by the values of the collectivity and the mutual engagements of its members. In this paper I want first to describe the social processes by which men incur, or come to believe that they have incurred, the obligation to commit such acts. And then I want, very tentatively, to say something about the status of the obligations thus incurred.

I

The process by which obligations are incurred and the process by which they come to be felt are obviously not the same, or not necessarily the same. They are similar, however, in at least one respect: they are both social processes.[2] They occur in groups, and they can both occur simultaneously in different groups of different shapes and sizes. The duty to disobey arises when such processes are more successful (have greater moral and emotional impact) in parties, congregations, sects, movements, unions, or clubs than in states or churches. This happens often in human history, but precisely what is involved when it does needs to be carefully stated.

Obligations can arise in groups of two, between friends, partners, or lovers. But I am chiefly concerned with those which arise in groups of three or more, groups of a more general social, political, or religious nature. These can be obligations to the group as a whole (including oneself), or to the other members, or to the ideal the group stands for or claims to embody. In practice, none of these occur in pure form; obligations are generally, perhaps necessarily, admixtures of the three. But they are often described exclusively in terms of the last. Thus men announce that they are bound by God or the higher law, and bound "in conscience," which commonly means as morally sensitive individuals rather than as members. In fact, however, the very word "conscience" implies a shared moral knowledge, and it is probably fair to argue not only that the individual's understanding of God or the higher law is always acquired within a group but also that his obligation to either is at the same time an obligation to the group and to its members. "To be 'true to one's principles,'" Robert Paul Wolff has written, "is either a metaphor or else an elliptical way of describing loyalty to other men who share those principles and are relying upon you to observe them."[3] Perhaps this is exaggerated; clearly people feel that their principles embody what is right, and there is nothing odd or metaphorical about saying that one ought to do what is right (though it is not clear whether this "ought" implies an obligation).[4] All I want to suggest is that commitments to principles are simultaneously commitments to other men, from whom or with whom the principles have been learned and by whom they are enforced.

This becomes clear, I think, if one examines cases in which ideals are renounced or "sold out." For in all such cases it is individuals or groups of individuals who feel, and can plausibly be said to have been, betrayed. To "sell out" is to renounce heretical ideals for the sake of orthodox ones (but actually, it is generally suggested, for the sake of material gain) or to desert a small nonconformist group and join or rejoin society at large. Most likely, as the common descriptions of this common phenomenon suggest, it is to do both. "An affront to God and an injury to His congregation"—this is the way one's former colleagues describe a conversion to religious orthodoxy. And if God alone can judge the affront, they can rightly weigh the injury, taking into account the kind of commitment which had been made, the expectations which had been aroused, the ridicule to which they are (or are not) subjected, the possible weakening of their community, and so on.[5] Similarly, but more loosely, an artist who "sells out" by "going commercial" is not merely giving up an ideal; he is giving up an ideal to which others still adhere, and those others are his former colleagues. His offense, in their eyes, is not only his betrayal of Art but also his betrayal of them. He injures the cause of Art, they would claim, both in its ideal form and in its concrete social manifestation.

The individual involved, of course, may be doing or think he is doing no such thing. He may have changed his mind for good reasons. And he may believe (rightly, I think) that there is or ought to be some due process whereby he can announce this change of mind, explain its reasons, and so escape the charge of betraying his former colleagues. But however far his obligations extend, insofar as he is obligated at all it is to other men as well as to ideals. Indeed, to think of the effect of his actions upon the ideal he once espoused, which is surely a necessary part of any due process of renunciation or withdrawal, is also to think of its effect upon those who still hold fast to that ideal.

Obligation, then, begins with membership, but membership in the broadest sense, for there are a great variety of formal and informal ways of living within a particular circle of action and commitment. Membership itself can begin with birth. Then the sense of obligation is acquired simply through socialization; it is the product and most often the intended product of religious or political education, of incessant and unrelenting communal pressure, of elaborate rites of passage, periodic ceremonial communions, and so on. One does not acquire any real obligations, however, simply by being born or by submitting to socialization within a particular group. These come only when to the fact of membership there is added the fact of willful membership. Different groups, of course, define willfulness in different ways, some in such minimal ways that willful membership becomes nothing more than continued membership after a certain age, some in such maximal ways that even formal adherence by an adult is inadequate without a public profession of the faith or a period of intensive participation in specified group activities. Sixteenth- and seventeenth-century protests against infant baptism depended upon a maximum definition of individual willfulness, as did Lenin's attack upon the Menshevik view of party membership. And willfulness can be carried even further. Elaborate tests of would-be members, frightening initiation ceremonies, solemn oaths: these mechanisms of the secret society and the revolutionary brotherhood raise to the highest level the individual's sense of having made a choice of enormous personal significance and thereby assumed the most profound obligations.[6]

In general, well-established groups, especially those like the state, which claim to be coterminous with society as a whole, are likely to defend the minimum definition, assume the commitment of their members, and punish those who disobey. Radical or nonconformist groups, precisely because they cannot make the assumption or guarantee the punishment, are likely to require that commitments take the form of explicit and public professions or acts. Through such professions and acts men can and do take on obligations to disobey the rules of the more inclusive group and also accept in advance the risks of their disobedience.

There is also a third sort of group, not sufficiently organized to make any precise determinations as to the character of membership. Disobedient citizens sometimes say that they are obligated by their membership in the "human community" or by their "solidarity with the oppressed." These obligations, if they exist at all, must be said to be universal (and men have indeed been punished for "crimes against humanity"). But they are generally cultivated in relatively small groups, often themselves loosely constituted, whose members can plausibly accuse one another, but not everyone else, of selling out when they fail to live up to their commitments. Since the community which is presumably being sold out is not the smaller but the larger group, which does not have any concrete existence and is only an aspiration, it is difficult to see how or whether anyone else can have made a commitment or what his betrayal would involve.[7] It must be said that efforts to enforce such obligations by individuals against their own states, or by groups of states against individuals, are really efforts to create them. Insofar as these efforts win general support, insofar as an entity like "humanity" acquires some "collective conscience" and some legal and institutional structure, real obligations are in fact incurred by membership. Obviously in such an absolutely inclusive community the willfulness of individuals will play an absolutely minimal part. Humanity can indeed be renounced, but only by becoming a criminal of the very worst sort, by turning oneself into what Locke called a "monster." At the present time, since no group exists which can satisfactorily define crimes against humanity, such "monsters" are necessarily punished ex post facto, not for betraying humanity but in the hope of creating a humanity whose members are capable of recognizing treason.

The state itself can sometimes be imagined as an ideal or potential community, obligating its members to oppose those authorities who act legally but (it is thought) immorally in its name. Thus those men who disobey the commands of a collaborationist government after military defeat, or of a satellite government after some less formal capitulation, often claim that their state has been betrayed and that they are obligated by their previous membership and driven by their patriotism to resistance. But they cannot claim that all their fellow citizens are similarly obligated. In the aftermath of such struggles, if the resistance is successful, active collaborators may be punished (the legal basis for such punishment is unclear enough), but nothing can be done to those who merely declined to join the fight.[8] They had never incurred any duty to do so. On the other hand, those who did join and subsequently deserted can rightly be said to have broken tangible and morally significant commitments.[9]

To insist that obligations can only derive from willful undertakings is to restate the theory of the social contract. This has very interesting consequences given the rough typology of groups and kinds of membership just outlined. For contract theory clearly applies best to those sects, congregations, parties, movements, unions, and clubs in which individual choices are made explicit, acted out in some public fashion. It is most useful in discussing what are commonly called secondary associations, less useful (though by no means of no use at all) in discussing larger groups like states and established churches or vague and inclusive entities like humanity. Indeed, if the contract is taken at all seriously, it is difficult to avoid the conclusion that groups in which willfulness is heightened and maximized can rightfully impose greater obligations upon their members than can those catholic religious and political associations where membership is, for all practical purposes, inherited. Of course, inherited membership is often seconded by voluntary participation; in such cases the sense of obligation, as well as the obligation itself, is probably strongest of all. But even participation is likely to be more active and willful and so a more satisfactory token of continuing consent in nonconformist than in established and socially orthodox groups. Day-to-day procedures will be less conventionalized, the modes of participation and communion less habitual. In short, it is possible to conclude from contract theory, as Jean Jacques Rousseau did, that small societies are (generally) morally superior to large ones. For is it not the case that obligations incurred within some Protestant sect, derived from an explicit covenant and sustained by a continual round of activity, ought to take precedence over obligations incurred in society at large, derived from a largely mythical "tacit" consent and sustained by mere residence or occasional, largely passive, participation? I do not want to attempt an answer to that question immediately; perhaps there are good reasons for the negative answer conventionally given. But I do want to make two points: first, that obligations are in fact incurred within groups of these different sorts; second, that the conventionally assigned relative weights of these different obligations are not obviously accurate.

The duty to disobey (as well as the possibility of selling out) arises when obligations incurred in some small group come into conflict with obligations incurred in a larger, more inclusive group, generally the state. When the small group is called a secondary association, it is being suggested that there is no point at issue here. Secondary associations ought to yield without argument, conflict, or moral tension to primary ones.[10] This is true only of associations clearly secondary, that is, with purposes or ideals which do not bring them into conflict with the larger society. Rotarians cannot sell out.[11] But there exist in every society groups which may be called "secondary associations with claims to primacy." Serious conflict begins when groups of this sort are formed and their claims announced. But here a crucial distinction must be made: these claims can be of two very different kinds. Some groups announce what are in effect total claims. Their members are obligated, whenever commanded, to challenge the whole established legal system, to overthrow and replace one government with another, to attack the very existence of the larger society. These are revolutionary groups. There are others, however, which make only partial claims. They demand that the larger society recognize their primacy in some particular area of social or political life and so limit its own. They require of their members disobedience at certain moments, not at every moment, the refusal of particular legal commands, not of every legal command.

It is worth insisting upon the great difference between such groups and between the assertions they make, for defenders of state sovereignty often confuse them, arguing that any challenge to constituted authority is implicitly revolutionary and any group which claims to authorize such challenges necessarily subversive. They thus assign the labels "rebel" and "subversive" to all sorts of people who explicitly reject them. When this is done by officials of the state, the labels often turn out to be accurate, since the men who originally chose not to revolt are eventually forced to do so in self-defense. But there is considerable evidence to suggest that the state can live with, even if it chooses not to accommodate, groups with partial claims against itself. The disobedience of the members of such groups will be intermittent and limited; it is unlikely to be conspiratorial in any sense; it does not involve any overt resistance to whatever acts of law enforcement the public authorities feel to be necessary (unless these are radically disproportionate to the "offense"). Such disobedience does not, in fact, challenge the existence of the larger society, only its authority in this or that case or type of case or over persons of this or that sort. It does not seek to replace one sovereign power with another, only to call into question the precise range and incidence of sovereignty. This is not revolution but civil disobedience, which can best be understood, I think, as the acting out of a partial claim.

Limited claims against larger societies can themselves be of two kinds. They can involve assertions that the larger society cannot make demands of a certain sort against *anyone*, or they can involve claims for exemptions for the members (and the future members) of the smaller society. When a man refuses to register for military service without challenging state authority in any other sphere, he may be saying that the state cannot require anyone to fight on its behalf or to fight this or that particular sort of war, or he may be saying that people like himself cannot be so required. The second statement generally accompanies acts of conscientious objection, which represent only one kind of civil disobedience.

The larger society can always recognize the claims of smaller groups and so relieve their members from the burdens and risks of disobedience. Indeed, the historical basis of liberalism is in large part simply a series of such recognitions. Thus the limited disobedience of religious sectarians was transformed into mere nonconformity when the state decided to tolerate the sects. Tolerance required a limit on the power of the state, a recognition that with regard to religious worship any church or sect could rightfully claim primacy. Contemporary conscientious objectors are also tolerated nonconformists, but here the tolerance is of a different sort. It is a recognition of the claims of a particular type of person (or of particular groups of people) rather than of the claims of any person (or group) in a particular area. There is no necessary logical restriction on either type of toleration: the state could withdraw all its claims from an infinite number of areas, or it could add to every one of its laws a provision specifying that conscientious disobedience cannot be punished.[12] But few states seem likely to move very far in either of these logically possible directions, doubtless for good reasons.

What is the situation of men who join groups with limited claims to primacy in states where such claims are not recognized? It is a situation which political philosophers have never adequately described — though Rousseau surely understood the possibility of divided allegiance and divided men and bent all his efforts to avoid both. Locke provides a convenient outline of the possibilities more generally thought to be available: (1) A man can be a *citizen*; this involves a full recognition of the primacy of his society and its government. Certain areas are set beyond the reach of the government, but in such a way as to bar any possible obligations against it. There are only rights and ultimately, so far as action goes, only one right, the right of rebellion. Hence, (2) a man can be a *rebel*, seeking to overthrow and replace a particular government and its laws. These are the only two possibilities available to members of the larger society. But Locke suggests two further options for those persons who do not wish to be members: (3) A man can be an *emigrant*, willfully withdrawing from the larger society and physically leaving its territory. Emigration is the only due process through which social obligations can be renounced, for the rebel is still bound, if not to his government, then to society itself. Finally, (4) a man can be an *alien* who, having left the society of his fathers, fails to commit himself to any other and lives here or there at the discretion of the public authorities. An alien, for Locke, has obligations, for he is afforded protection within some particular society and tacitly consents in return to obey its laws. He presumably has rights, at least in theory, since rights are natural. But he does not possess, as citizens do, the practical right to rebel. It is a curious feature of Locke's thought that this appears to be the single most important difference between aliens and citizens.

Now the member of a group with partial claims to primacy falls into none of these categories. His loyalties are divided, so he is not in any simple sense a citizen. He refuses to call himself a rebel, and with good reason, for he seeks no total change in the government, no transformation of state or society (though he would surely claim the right to rebel, in Locke's sense, given the conditions under which Locke permits rebellion). He is not an emigrant, since he does not leave, though joining such a group may well constitute a kind of internal emigration. He is not an alien, for while an alien can always leave, he cannot demand to stay on conditions of his own choosing.

Yet the situation of such a man — obligated to obey because of his membership in a larger society, obligated to disobey (sometimes) because of his membership in a smaller one — is, for all its tensions, very common in history and has often been fairly stable over long periods of time. It is the situation of any person who, like Sophocles' Antigone, retains strong tribal or clan loyalties while becoming a member of some (almost any) political order.[13] It is virtually institutionalized in feudal systems.[14] It was lived through with extraordinary intensity by early modern Protestants and has been lived through since with greater or lesser intensity by a considerable variety of religious groups (including Roman Catholics, for Rousseau the visible embodiments of double obligation and moral division) — even in liberal societies, which have recognized some but not all the claims of pious brethren of this or that persuasion. It was the situation of European socialists during the period when their parties and movements had ceased to be revolutionary but had not yet accepted the status of secondary associations. (Otto Kircheimer describes German Social-Democracy as a "loyalty-absorbing counterorganization."[15]) It is often the situation of trade unionists, especially when their country is at war. It is the situation today of all those persons who object to military service on other than the permitted religious grounds. It is, despite considerable confusion, increasingly the situation of many members of the American civil-rights movement.

What all these oddly assorted people have in common is this: none of them admits without qualification the political sovereignty or moral supremacy of the larger society of which they are members. None of them absolutely denies that sovereignty or supremacy. They are, then, partial members; they are simultaneously partial emigrants, partial aliens, partial rebels. The very existence of such people — even more, their obvious moral seriousness — ought to call into question the conventional definition of citizenship as involving an absolute commitment (it is sometimes said, "under God") to obey the laws. Surely such a commitment will never be found among every one of those persons who consider themselves, with reason, citizens of the state. For the processes through which men incur obligations are unavoidably pluralistic. Even in a liberal society, which allows considerable room for divergent groups and recognizes many of their claims, what might be called the incidence of obligation is bound to be uneven, the obligations themselves at least sometimes contradictory. Unless the state deliberately inhibits the normal processes of group formation, and does so with greater success than has ever yet been achieved, it will always be confronted by citizens who believe themselves to be, and may actually be, obligated to disobey. As J. N. Figgis wrote: "The theory of sovereignty . . . is in reality no more than a venerable superstition. . . . As a fact it is as a series of groups that our social life presents itself, all having some of the qualities of public law and most of them showing clear signs of a life of their own."[16]

II

Many political philosophers have insisted that there exists a prima facie obligation to obey the laws of the most inclusive organized society of which one is a member, that is, for most men, the state.[17] This is not unreasonable, so long as the state provides equally to all its members certain essential services. It is not unreasonable even though the state maintains a monopoly of such services and tolerates no competition, for it may be that the monopoly is itself essential to the provision of the services. But the existence of a prima facie obligation to obey means no more than that disobedience must always be justified. First explanations are owed to those of one's fellow citizens who do not join in, who remain obedient. I think it can be argued that membership (i.e., morally serious membership) in groups with partial claims to primacy is always a possible explanation.

But I want to attempt a stronger argument than this, loosely derived from the preceding discussion of the uneven incidence of obligation in any larger society. I want to suggest that men have a prima facie obligation to honor the engagements they have explicitly made, to defend the groups and uphold the ideals to which they have committed themselves, even against the state, so long as their disobedience of laws or legally authorized commands does not threaten the very existence of the large society or endanger the lives of its citizens. It is obedience to the state, when one has a duty to disobey, that must be justified. First explanations are owed to one's brethren, colleagues, or comrades. Their usual form is an argument that personal security or public health or some other such necessity of the common life — which the smaller groups cannot supply, which is actually supplied by the state — is being threatened or is likely to be threatened by particular acts of disobedience, however limited their scope. This, of course, is precisely what is asserted (usually by an official of the state) in every case of disobedience, but it is not necessarily asserted rightly. Indeed, there is very little evidence which suggests that carefully limited, morally serious civil disobedience undermines the legal system or endangers personal security.[18] One can imagine situations in which the acting out of partial claims might encourage or inspire the acting out of total claims. But the two sorts of action remain distinct. It may be necessary for a man contemplating civil disobedience to worry about the possibilities of revolutionary violence, but only if such possibilities actually exist. It is by no means necessary for him to reflect upon the purely theoretical possibility that his action might break the laws or claim exemptions from them. For his action implies nothing more than that those men ought to do so who have acquired obligations to do so. And the acquiring of such obligations is a serious, long-term business which if undertaken by everybody would simply obviate the necessity for disobedience: if all men joined the sect, it would become the church; if all men joined the movement, there would be no state to resist; if all men joined different sects and movements, tolerance would not be the claim of this or that group but a common necessity.

The state can thus be described as a purely external limit on group action, but it must be added that the precise point at which the limit becomes effective cannot be left for state officials to decide. For them, the law must be the limit. At the same time, it must be the claim of the disobedient members that the law is overextended, that its sphere ought to be restricted in some fashion, that this activity or this type of person should be exempted, at this particular moment or for all time. There can be no possible judge of this disagreement. All that can be said is that the moral seriousness of the disobedient members is evidenced in part by their respect for those genuine goods the state provides not only to themselves but to everyone. To argue that the state does not provide such goods at all, or that it denies them entirely to particular sections of the population, is to justify unlimited and uncivil disobedience. Revolution always requires (and generally gets) some such special justification.

There are two other ways of describing the state which appear to argue against the claim that disobedience can ever be a prima facie obligation. The first is to insist that the state is itself a group, that its members too are willful members who have incurred obligations of the most serious kind. It was the original purpose of social-contract theory to uphold just this conception of the state. But there are serious problems here. Since for most men there is no real alternative to state membership, the willfulness of that membership does not seem to have even the most minimal moral significance.[19] A theory like Locke's requires the argument that one can always leave the state; therefore, mere residence can meaningfully be described as a choice. Whatever the value of that description in Locke's time, it has very little today. But there is, I think, another way of describing the willfulness of state membership: this is to take very seriously the possibility of joining secondary associations with limited claims to primacy. Such engagements represent, as has already been suggested, a kind of internal emigration or partial alienation, and as long as the processes of group formation are not controlled or repressed, they offer real alternatives to full state membership. Thus, the possibility of becoming a conscientious objector establishes the possibility of incurring an obligation to military service. One incurs such an obligation by *not* becoming an objector (though perhaps the alternative must bulk somewhat larger in our common life than conscientious objection presently does if it is to have this effect). The obligation is real even if it is incurred for no other reason than that conscientious objection involves penalties, though this is not so if the penalties are unlimited or without proportion or if the state interferes in any way with the groups within which the duty to object is both learned and incurred. The state can only be regarded as a choice, then, if the possible legitimacy of countergroups of a limited sort is admitted.

But the obligations of citizens to the state can be derived in yet another way: not from their willfulness but from its value. "If all communities aim at some good," wrote Aristotle, "the state or political community, which is the highest of all, and which embraces all the rest aims, and in a greater degree than any other, at the highest good."[20] Obviously, groups which aim at the highest good take priority over groups which seek lower or partial goods. There are two major difficulties, however, with Aristotle's description. First of all, it is not the case that the state necessarily embraces all other communities. A state with an established church and no legal provision for religious toleration obviously excluded a dissenting sect. Groups with universalist or international pretensions, like the Catholic church or any early twentieth-century socialist party, necessarily exclude themselves. Political or religious communities which oppose war are in no simple sense "embraced" by states which fight wars. It is precisely the nature of secondary associations with claims to primacy that they cannot and do not exist wholly within the established political or legal frame. Second, while the state may well provide or seek to provide goods for all its members, it is not clear that these add up to or include the highest good. Perhaps they are goods of the lowest common denominator and only for this reason available to all, for it may be that the highest good can be pursued only in small groups — in pietist sects or utopian settlements, for example, or, as Aristotle himself suggested, in philosophic dialogue. In any case, men do not agree as to the nature of the highest good, and this fact is enormously significant for the processes of group formation. Groups are formed for a great variety of reasons, but one of the chief reasons is to advocate or act out ("without tarrying for the magistrate," as a late sixteenth-century Puritan minister wrote) a new conception of the highest good, a conception at which the state does not aim, and perhaps cannot. To form such a group or to join one is to reject Aristotle's argument and renounce whatever obligation is implied by it. I fail to see any reason why this is not an option available to any morally serious man.

In the argument thus far, a great deal of weight has been attached to the phrase "morally serious." Obviously, the term is not easy to define, nor the quality easy to measure. Yet frivolous or criminal disobedience cannot be justified by membership in a group. There are obligations among thieves, but not prima facie obligations against the state. This is true, first of all, because the activities of thieves endanger the security of us all. But it is also true because a robbers' gang does not make claims to primacy. Thieves do not seek to limit the authority of the sovereign state; they seek to evade it. But there is nothing evasive about civil disobedience: a public claim against the state is publicly acted out. This willingness to act in public and to offer explanations to other people suggests also a willingness to reflect upon and worry about the possible consequences of the action for the public as a whole. Neither of these by themselves legitimate the action; but they do signal the moral seriousness of the group commitment which legitimates it.[21]

Frivolous disobedience can also never be a duty, and so groups that do not encourage an awareness in their members of the purposes and actions to which they may become committed cannot commit them. Awareness of this sort would appear to be required by social-contract theory; even the notion of tacit consent implies that there exists some knowledge of the duties being incurred. Nor, it seems to me, are the requirements of the theory entirely satisfied if such knowledge is but glimpsed at one brief moment in time. Continued awareness, a kind of shared self-consciousness, is necessary before the consent and participation of individuals carry sufficient moral weight to establish obligations — or, at any rate, to establish such obligations as I am trying to defend. A morally serious member of a group with partial claims may, then, be described as follows: he joins the group voluntarily, knowing what membership involves; he devotes time and energy to its inner life, sharing in the making of decisions; he acts publicly in its name or in the name of its ideals. Such a person — not any person — is obligated to act as he does, unless he is given good reasons why he ought not to do so.

III

The problem of civil disobedience needs to be placed squarely in the context of group formation, growth, tension, and conflict. There is a sociology of disobedience which has greater relevance for philosophy than has generally been thought; it helps establish the proper units of analysis. Now these units doubtless have their limits, for it is true that there come moments when individuals must make choices or sustain actions alone — or rather, and this is not at all the same thing, when they must endure the anguish of loneliness. The state always seeks to isolate its disobedient citizens because it is far more likely to bend their wills to its own if it can break the cohesion of the group which initially planned the disobedience and convince its members that they are members no longer. But this only suggests that the men who run prisons are always very much aware of the sociology of disobedience. Surely philosophers should be no less so.

The heroic encounter between sovereign individual and sovereign state, if it ever took place, would be terrifyingly unequal. If disobedience depended upon a conscience really private, it might always be justified and yet never occur. Locke understood this very well, for even while he proclaimed the right of individuals to rebel, he recognized that "the right to do so will not easily engage them in a contest, wherein they are sure to perish."[22] Rebellion, he thought, is only possible when it engages "the whole body" of the people. But clearly, rebellion and, even more, civil disobedience are most often the work of groups of much more limited extent. Clearly, too, it is not the mere individual right to rebel, unchanged in groups large or small, which sustains the enterprise but, rather, the mutual undertakings of the participants. Without this mutuality, very few men would ever join the "contest" — not because of the fear of being killed but because of the greater fear of being alone. "This is what is most difficult," wrote Jean Le Meur, the young French army officer who was imprisoned for refusing to fight in Algeria, "being cut off from the fraternity, being locked up in a monologue, being incomprehensible." And then: "Do tell the others that this is not a time to let me down."[23]

All this is not to suggest that there is anything unreal about individual responsibility. But this is always responsibility *to someone else* and it is always learned *with someone else*. An individual whose moral experiences never reached beyond "monologue" would know nothing at all about responsibility and would have none. Such a man might well have rights, including the right to rebel, but his possession of the right to rebel would be purely theoretical; he would never become a rebel. No political theory which does not move beyond rights to duties, beyond monologue to fraternal discussion, debate, and resolution, can ever explain what men actually do when they disobey or rebel, or why they do so. Nor can it help us very much to weigh the rightness or wrongness of what they do.

Notes

1. Hugo Bedau, "On Civil Disobedience," *Journal of Philosophy*, LVII (October 1961), 663.
2. The best description of these processes is probably still Emile Durkheim's *L'Education morale* (Paris, 1925).
3. R. P. Wolff, "An Analysis of the Concept of Political Loyalty," in Wolff, ed., *Political Man and Social Man* (New York, 1966), p. 224.
4. See Alexander Sesonske, *Value and Obligation* (New York, 1964), pp. 20 ff. and *passim*.
5. Where such judgments cannot be made at all, there is no obligation. And this means that obligations are always shared among men, who must judge one another. "The only obligation which I have a right to assume," wrote Thoreau, "is to do at any time what I think right." But when, in jail, he greeted the visiting Emerson with the famous question, "What are you doing out there?" he clearly implied the existence of a common obligation. Common to whom? Common at least to New England philosophers, one of whom was failing to meet it. Emerson believed the same thing when he spoke in his lecture on the Fugitive Slave Law of the "disastrous defection of the men of letters" from the cause of freedom (*The Complete Essays and Other Writings of Ralph Waldo Emerson* [New York, 1940], p. 867).
6. Eric Hobsbawm, *Primitive Rebels* (New York, 1963), chap. ix; for some examples of secret oaths, see Appendix 13.

7. Sesonske, *Value and Obligation*, p. 107.

8. Henry L. Mason, *The Purge of Dutch Quislings* (The Hague, 1952), chap.ii.

9. See Guillain de Benouville's defense of capital punishment in the French Resistance: "in the Maquis each man had chosen his own lot, fashioned his destiny with his own hands, picked his own name. Everyone had accepted in advance and without question all possible risks" (*The Unknown Warriors* [New York, 1949], p. 220).

10. S. I. Benn and R. S. Peters, *The Principles of Political Thought* (New York, 1965), chap. xii.

11. People who accuse trade-union leaders of selling out are, in effect, accusing them of acting like leaders of secondary associations, the implication of their accusation being that the union (or the labor movement generally) is something more than secondary.

12. Bedau, "On Civil Disobedience," p. 655.

13. The conflict in Sophocles' play is, of course, between primary groups. In general, conflicts between groups of relatives or friends and the state take forms similar to those described above, especially in modern times when such alliances tend increasingly to be voluntary. E. M. Forster's statement that "if I had to choose between betraying my country and betraying my friend, I hope I should have the guts to betray my country" is roughly analogous to the sorts of assertions sometimes made on behalf of groups. But it is an extreme statement and has reference to exceptional cases. Most often, the choice is between betraying one's friend (or colleagues) and *disobeying the laws* of one's country. Antigone's act is not treason, on any usual interpretation of that tricky term (Forster, *Two Cheers for Democracy* [New York, 1951], p. 78).

14. See Marc Bloch, *Feudal Society* (Chicago, 1961), chap. ix–xvii.

15. Kircheimer, *Political Justice* (Princeton, N.J., 1961), p. 9.

16. Figgis, *Churches in the Modern State* (London, 1914), p. 224. See also G. D. H. Cole, "Conflicting Social Obligations" and "Loyalties," *Proceedings of the Aristotelian Society*, N.S., XV (1915), XXVI (1926).

17. See, e.g., W. D. Ross, *The Right and the Good* (Oxford, 1930), pp. 27–28; and discussion in Richard Wasserstrom, "Disobeying the Law," *Journal of Philosophy*, LVII (October 1961), 647.

18. It is often enough said that disobedience even of bad laws undermines the habit of law abidance and so endangers that fundamental order upon which civilized life depends. But I have never seen this argued with careful attention to some particular body of evidence. In the absence of such an argument, I would be inclined to agree with David Spitz that there are clearly *some* laws obedience to which is not required for the maintenance of social order. Even more important, perhaps, there are many laws which can be disobeyed by *some men*, without prejudice to social order (Spitz, "Democracy and the Problem of Civil Disobedience," *Essays in the Liberal Idea of Freedom* [Tucson, Ariz., 1964], pp. 74–75).

19. Wolff, "Analysis of the Concept of Political Loyalty," pp. 227–228.
20. Aristotle, *Politics* I. 1; see discussion in Benn and Peters, *Principles of Political Thought*, pp. 315 ff.
21. Secret societies, if they are not criminal, are implicitly revolutionary; the moral seriousness of their members must be signaled differently.
22. Locke, *The Second Treatise of Government*, par. 208.
23. Jean Le Meur, "The Story of a Responsible Act," in R. P. Wolff, ed., *Political Man and Social Man*, pp. 204, 205.

Select Bibliography

BEDAU, HUGO. "On Civil Disobedience," *Journal of Philosophy*, LVII (1961), 653–665.

BEDAU, HUGO A., ed. *Civil Disobedience*. New York: Pegasus, 1969.

BENN, S. I., and PETERS, R. S. *The Principles of Political Thought*. New York: Macmillan, 1964. Chapter 14.

CARNES, JOHN R. "Why Should I Obey the Law?" *Ethics*, LXXI (1960), 14–26.

CARRITT, E. F. *Ethical and Political Thinking*. Oxford: Clarendon Press, 1947.

GREEN, T. H. *Lectures on the Principles of Political Obligation*. London: Longmans, Green, 1965.

HOOK, SIDNEY, ed. *Law and Philosophy*. New York: New York University Press, 1964.

MACDONALD, MARGARET. "The Language of Political Theory," in A. G. Flew, ed., *Logic and Language*, First Series. Oxford: Blackwell, 1952.

PITKIN, HANNA. "Obligation and Consent," *American Political Science Review*, LIX (1965), 990–999; LX (1966), 39–52.

PLAMENATZ, J. P. *Consent, Freedom, and Political Obligation*. Oxford: Oxford University Press, Second Edition, 1968.

PRITCHARD, H. *Moral Obligation*. Oxford: Clarendon Press, 1949.

REES, J. C. "The Limitations of Political Theory," *Political Studies*, II (1954), 242–257.

SPITZ, DAVID. "Democracy and the Problem of Civil Disobedience," *American Political Science Review*, XLVIII (1954), 386–403.

TUSSMAN, JOSEPH. *Obligation and the Body Politic*. New York: Oxford University Press, 1960.

WASSERSTROM, RICHARD. "Disobeying the Law," *Journal of Philosophy*, LVII (1961), 641–653.

Index